6/17/75

Exploitation from 9 to 5

Exploitation from 9 to 5

Report of the Twentieth Century Fund Task Force on Women and Employment

Background Paper by

Adele Simmons
Ann Freedman
Margaret Dunkle
Francine Blau

The Twentieth Century Fund ● New York ● 1975

Lexington Books
D.C. Heath and Company
Lexington, Massachusetts
Toronto   London

Library of Congress Cataloging in Publication Data

Task Force on Working Women.
   Exploitation from 9 to 5, report of the Twentieth Century Fund Task
Force on Women and Employment.

   Bibliography: p.
   1. Women—Employment—United States. 2. Discrimination in employment—United States. 3. Women's rights—United States. I. Simmons, Adele.
II. Twentieth Century Fund. III. Title.
HD6093.T37 1974   31.4'0973   74-14614

ISBN 0-669-96099-3

Contents

List of Figures

ix

List of Tables

Foreword

In the spring of 1970, the board of trustees of the Twentieth Century Fund responded to the new wave of feminism in the United States by creating an independent Task Force of distinguished and knowledgeable citizens to consider the status of working women. The Fund's board was familiar with the ample evidence of sex discrimination in the labor market. In 1963, for example, a Presidential Commission on the Status of Women had issued a report that dealt in detail with the problems of working women. The commission had made many valuable recommendations, but it had failed to suggest the means for implementing and enforcing them. Thus, although the commission recommended that each state enact laws requiring equal pay for equal work, only twenty-five states had in fact adopted such laws, and these were, in general, not enforced. The commission also recognized the need for day care centers, but did not adequately consider ways of financing them or whether more elaborate multipurpose centers should be created.

The mandate given the Task Force was to consider not only the need for legislation but also the means of enforcing it through affirmative action. In addition to dealing with the role of employers, the Task Force considered many other aspects of the problem, including the responsibilities of labor unions; the importance of equal employment opportunity legislation; the position of the government as employer and as provider of welfare, job training, social security, and tax regulations; and such controversial areas as child care, the educational system, and the media.

Summoned from the fields of law, business, economics, government, education, and labor, members of the Task Force brought to bear a diversity of perspectives. They quickly realized that they were working in an area in which opinions were strong and prejudices rampant and difficult to dislodge. But all of them believed that bringing sex discrimination to an end would have positive consequences for both men and women, broadening the options available to all. After lengthy deliberation and arduous effort, they arrived at a unanimous set of recommendations that were beneficial, just, and practicable. The Fund is grateful to them.

The Task Force was assisted by Adele Simmons, Dean of Student Affairs at Princeton University, who was asked to provide a factual background on the many problems of working women. With her co-authors, Ann Freedman, Margaret Dunkle, and Francine Blau, she not only prepared and updated the voluminous materials researched but also wrote the final background paper that accompanies the report of the Task Force.

M.J. Rossant
November 1974

xiii

Task Force on Working Women (1971)

William Asher
Manager, Industrial Relations, U.S. Operations,
Xerox Corporation, Rochester, New York

David Bazelon
Judge, U.S. Court of Appeals,
Washington, D.C.

Antonia Chayes
Lecturer in Law, Boston University Law School,
Boston, Massachusetts

Anthony Downs
Senior Vice President, Real Estate Research
Corporation, Chicago, Illinois

Jo Freeman
Associate Professor, Program in American Studies,
State University College at Old Westbury,
New York

Harold Gibbons
Vice President, International Brotherhood of
Teamsters, St. Louis, Missouri

Rita E. Hauser
Attorney, Stroock & Stroock & Lavan,
New York, New York

Aileen Hernandez
Project Director, National Committee Against
Discrimination in Housing, San Francisco, California

Eleanor Holmes Norton, chairperson
New York City Commissioner of
Human Rights, New York, New York

Esther Peterson
Consultant on Consumer Affairs, Giant Food Inc.,
Landover, Maryland

Sylvia Roberts
Attorney, Baton Rouge, Louisiana

Thomas Winship
Editor, *Boston Globe*, Boston, Massachusetts

Harris Wofford
President, Bryn Mawr College,
Bryn Mawr, Pennsylvania

Rapporteur:
Adele S. Simmons
Dean of Student Affairs, Princeton University,
Princeton, New Jersey

Part I
Report of the Task Force

I. Introduction

Men and women in the labor force are not treated equally. Employers, unions, and women themselves often cooperate in channeling women into low-status, low-paying jobs. Despite this, over 34 million women, or about 48 percent of the women between sixteen and sixty-four, work.

Several generalizations about working women can be made:

1. Working women earn, on the average, only 58 percent of what working men earn: Black women earn even less.

2. Women who want to work are much more likely than men to be unemployed.

3. Most women work in "female occupations" (such as stenographer, teacher, waitress, household worker), which are often neither unionized nor protected by strong federal legislation.

4. Over a third of the families headed by women live in poverty, compared to only about 12 percent of all families.

5. Women's chances for top management jobs are slim, regardless of their abilities.

In sum, a woman knows that no matter what her qualifications, there is comparatively more room for her in the lower levels of an occupation than in the upper levels.

What then of the fundamental American values of equal rights and equal opportunity? Although traditionally men and women in this country have had different work roles and received different treatment, women are now asking if this has not led to a denial of their potentialities. The Twentieth Century Fund Task Force has found their arguments compelling. Yet, few groups outside the women's movement have been actively concerned with ending discrimination based on sex. Further, the rhetoric of some women's groups has often distracted public attention from the validity of their arguments.

This Task Force Report provides guidelines for those in a position to assume leadership in ending sex discrimination in the labor force. This report is addressed to legislators, employers, unions, educators, women's organizations, and working women themselves. We believe that action by just one of these groups is not enough; thus, our recommendations are interrelated. The implementation of some without the implementation of others cannot be effective. The Task Force, therefore, urges action by all parts of American society to ensure that women are accorded equal rights and equal opportunity.

3

Stereotypes about women have helped keep them from employment or promotion and channeled them into certain "feminine" jobs. Over a third of all employed women in 1972 were in clerical jobs, and nearly all private household workers are women. Yet, women can perform most of today's "male" jobs. Furthermore, although studies have shown that there is little difference in productivity, turnover, or absenteeism between men and women, the traditional stereotypes persist. Corporations and trade unions who maintain these misconceptions contribute to discrimination and keep women from participating in the work force according to their abilities.

Discriminatory practices of employers and unions are not the only cause of the secondary place of women in the labor force. Women have been conditioned from childhood not to expect or demand equal treatment. Until recently most have accepted their secondary status. Now women are challenging this attitude. Women workers, by and large, are no longer content to earn less than their male counterparts. Welfare mothers are objecting to being trained for nonexistent or low-paying jobs. Women are finally demanding that the nation demonstrate its commitment to equal rights.

Discrimination is not only an abstract injustice; it is a cause of severe economic hardship. Almost 60 percent of the women provide sole or vital support for themselves or others. While only one out of ten households in the United States is headed by a woman, below the poverty line this figure is one out of three. Even women who work full time, year round are often unable to lift their family income above the poverty line.

The psychological impact of not being able to provide for oneself and one's family can be profound. Even women who have economic security so long as they stay married often seek the sense of identity and security and self-esteem that comes from holding a job and earning an independent income.

The Task Force recognizes that sex discrimination pervades American society. We are focusing on working women because of the overwhelming numbers of women who work and because the end of sex discrimination in the labor market will have an impact extending outside the labor force.

Some of the Task Force recommendations seek to guarantee equal rights by law, but the Task Force feels that legal rights are not enough. Legislation alone will not end discrimination and assure women an equal opportunity to compete for jobs. The Task Force has, therefore, also proposed recommendations for changes in the work environment and for changes that extend beyond the work environment. Many of these changes require new attitudes toward working men and women.

Employment practices must be adapted to enable employees who are parents to fulfill parental as well as work responsibilities. Child care centers, increased opportunities for both men and women to work part time, leaves for childbearing, and parental leaves for child rearing are prerequisites for equal opportunity for women and men in employment. Employment practices, then, need to be adapted to human life cycles that permit both men and women time to care for home and family responsibilities, and no longer require one partner to sacrifice either family or career.

Changes in employment practices must be accompanied by changes in traditional sex roles. Even if discriminatory employment practices are abolished, many women will still have two jobs, but be paid for only one. The double burden of work and home responsibilities explains, at least in part, why there are so few women in politics, trade union leadership, and business management. Presently, few men or women can choose among working, staying home, or combining a job with home responsibilities. The Task Force feels that it is essential for both men and women to be able to choose from a broader spectrum of work opportunities and family arrangements.

Justice requires that individuals have equal opportunity. Furthermore, there are advantages to the economy in encouraging both men and women to participate equally in the labor force. We believe that denying equal opportunity to women harms both sexes, as well as society as a whole. We therefore urge the immediate implementation of our recommendations.

II. Employer Practices and Affirmative Action

Tradition and continuing social norms have encouraged employers to treat men and women differently. Sometimes this differential treatment reflects an explicit policy; more often it reflects the conditioned attitudes of employers toward women who work. Even where legislation forbidding discrimination against women exists, these traditions make both implementation and enforcement difficult. In many cases, women themselves are not fully aware of this differential treatment and its effects.

Sex discrimination can appear in many forms—in hiring, in job assignment, in promotion, in organizational structure, in pay scales, and in benefit programs. In many cases, these practices are contrary to the law. In every case, they deny women equal opportunity and are, therefore, unjust. While justice alone is sufficient reason for modifying employment practices to ensure equal opportunity, a policy of equal opportunity will, in many cases, enlarge the pool of applicants from which employers can select the most qualified workers.

Some of the recommendations below can be implemented immediately with little cost to the employer. Others are more far-reaching and require changes which some employers and employees may view as too progressive or costly. Many of the recommendations, although already legally required of some employers, should be enforced more strongly and extended to all employers. All of the recommendations require an increased awareness on the part of employers about the role of women in our society.

The primary recommendation of the Task Force to employers is that they use their resources to act immediately to end sex discrimination. Federal law presently requires each employer who has a federal contract to develop an affirmative action program that establishes specific goals and timetables for correcting imbalances in the number of men and women in all job categories at all levels. The Task Force recognizes that a number of companies have established affirmative action programs. However, more time is required before we know whether they will meet their goals and to what extent the federal government will require them to implement their programs. *The Task Force recommends that all employers develop and implement an affirmative action program.*

We do not recommend adopting rigid quota systems, but we do believe that specific objectives are required to make employers choose workers on the basis of their skills, rather than their sex. While the specific nature of an affirmative action plan may vary according to conditions in different institutions, in every case affirmative action programs involve a number of steps.

Personnel Inventory

Before developing an affirmative action program, employers must examine the occupational structure of their organization and the distribution by salary of female and male employees. Although there may be much variation, the distribution of employees by sex and wage typically reveals disproportionately more women at the lower levels and fewer at the upper levels of the organizational hierarchy. *The Task Force recommends that employers use personnel inventories to determine if women are distributed throughout the salary and occupational structure.*

Job Analysis

Another aspect of an affirmative action program is job analysis, or identifying the skills necessary to perform a given job. This analysis is important, because people who perform essentially the same tasks often have different job titles. For example, the responsibilities of female "secretaries" are often identical to and sometimes more demanding than those of male "administrative assistants," "managers," or "executives." But the salary, status, and opportunity for promotion are usually lower for "secretaries." The principle of equal pay for equal work means that people who do the same quantity and quality of work should be paid at the same rate and should have the same opportunity for advancement. By defining the skills necessary to perform each job, job analysis reveals obvious discrepancies by sex. Consequently, it can be an important tool for identifying and eliminating discrimination based on sex. We therefore urge employers to use job analysis to describe jobs in terms of skills and to identify and rectify inequities in titles, salaries, and opportunities for advancement under established personnel policies.

Employee Qualifications

Job analysis goes hand-in-hand with examining the qualifications of employees. Employers should look at the qualifications of individual employees to determine if equally qualified men and women hold similar positions, receive the same salaries, and have the same opportunities for promotion. Often there are great discrepancies, discrepancies that began at the moment of employment. For example, recent studies suggest that many employers offer women lower-paying and less responsible jobs than they offer men with similar experience and qualifications. Studies also indicate that some qualifications set by employers are discriminatory in nature. *As a part of an affirmative action plan, employers should work toward placing equally qualified men and women in jobs that are comparable in terms of salary and opportunities for advancement.*

Many women currently hold jobs that have traditionally offered little hope of advancement. Because opportunities for training and advancement have been denied to women in the past, many women may need special orientation or training. *We recommend that employers actively promote such training programs.*

Hiring Practices and Promotion

Affirmative action includes review and, when necessary, revision of hiring procedures and policies. This review should first compare the number of male and female applicants with the number of men and women actually hired. Any imbalances that emerge from this comparison may reflect discrimination at some stage in the recruitment and hiring process.

Newspaper advertisements are an important source for job applicants. A few employers can still legally advertise job openings in sex-labeled want ads; others continue to do so even though it is illegal. Until the practice of listing job opportunities in this discriminatory manner is abolished, we recommend that employers advertise job openings in the "help wanted—male-female" columns rather than in either the "help wanted—male" or "help wanted—female" columns. *We recommend that employers insist on this form of nondiscriminatory job advertising, which may discourage newspapers from maintaining sex-segregated want ads which continue to allow other employers to discriminate. Indeed, we strongly recommend that all sex-segregated job advertising be abolished.*

Employment agencies are accustomed to channeling male and female jobseekers into different job categories. *We urge employers to instruct employment agencies, school and college placement offices, and other preliminary screening services to refer qualified job applicants of both sexes for all job openings.*

The procedures of company recruiters also contribute to discrimination in the hiring process. Recruiters often communicate either directly or indirectly the assumption that women should be interested in, and are eligible for, only the usual "women's jobs." *We encourage employers to hire both men and women as recruiters, to send them to male and female as well as coeducational institutions, and to eliminate both explicit and implicit biases from hiring procedures. Recruitment brochures should clearly indicate, in both text and illustrations, that jobs are open to qualified applicants without regard to sex.*

Some employers have anti-nepotism rules which specify that they will not employ two members of the same household, including a husband and wife. Although these rules were originally intended to prevent the development of father-son blocs and avoid the complications of personal relationships among employees, they can serve to limit the job opportunities of women. For example, in universities, policies that prevent a husband and wife from both serving on the faculty or receiving research funds interfere with the careers of many women academics. *The Task Force therefore recommends that employers review anti-nepotism policies and eliminate them if they are found to restrict unfairly a person's job opportunities.*

The reluctance of employers to hire women who have been outside the labor force for several years is another obstacle to equal employment. The law prohibits employers from discriminating against men who have been absent from the labor force because of the military service. In fact, many employers regard a service record as a positive job credential. But women who temporarily leave the labor force to start a family do not have any comparable legal protection upon their return to the work force. Further, effective techniques for assessing the skills that women acquire while they are housewives are not available. There is no way now for employers to evaluate the practical problem-solving and managerial skills that many women develop while running a household, raising children and, in many cases, doing volunteer work. Presently, the largest group of unemployed women is composed of these potential reentrants. *Employers should develop techniques and procedures both for evaluating experience outside the paid labor force and for making use of the reentrant's skills and aptitudes.*

Some employers have developed policies that kept them from hiring or promoting women, but not men, on the basis of marital or parental status. For example, such employers were often particularly reluctant to employ or promote women, but not men, who were married or who had children, regardless of their job qualifications. Unwed mothers, in particular, have had difficulty finding jobs. Happily, the policies that encouraged these practices are now illegal. *We urge employers to eliminate hiring and promotion policies based on marital or parental status.*

Many companies have maintained separate seniority lists for men and women. This practice, which is illegal, often meant that a woman was less likely to be promoted and more likely to be "laid off" than a man. *The Task Force urges employers to maintain one seniority list and to eliminate discriminatory promotional patterns.*

Training

A number of jobs require prior training that has traditionally been available to men but not to women. Federal law requires that all training and apprenticeship programs be open to both sexes. But the tradition of excluding women is so firmly established in both unskilled and skilled jobs that often the workers themselves, without deliberately practicing discrimination, follow the custom of recruiting only their male friends and relatives. They actively discourage women from applying to such programs. Understandably, these attitudes work to keep women from seeking training for occupations that have traditionally been exclusively male. *Therefore, the Task Force urges employers to recruit members of previously excluded groups into training and apprenticeship programs.*

Flexible Work Schedules

The Task Force considers flexibility in work schedules a critical step toward equal opportunity. Many employers have begun to realize that the five-day, forty-hour work week does not necessarily make the most effective use of an employee's skill and energy. Alternative, more flexible schedules are being successfully tried; by 1971 over 370 employers had already adopted a four-day, forty-hour work week. Others had divided one job between two people, one of whom works in the morning and the other in the afternoon. Other jobs need not be done during the usual working hours and can be scheduled at times more convenient for the worker. In some cases, an employer could allow an employee to shift between part-time and full-time work, an arrangement that may be more satisfactory for both employer and employee than termination of the employment. Such an arrangement would also permit professional employees to remain in touch with developments in their fields. Similarly, if an employee dropped out of the work force temporarily, it might be a good investment for employers to develop ways of keeping him or her in touch with developments in the field, so that when the employee returns he or she will find reentry easier and be useful sooner.

Flexible work schedules have definite advantages for workers, particularly parents, as well as for employers. Parents, especially those of young children, often cannot work a regular nine-to-five day. Flexible working hours can be equally valuable to men and women who wish to spend more time with their families or who simply wish more leisure time.

Child Care

Child care should be a service to children. But quality, low-cost group care facilities are scarce; working parents often have no choice but to leave their children in unsatisfactory situations. Other potential workers stay out of the labor force longer than they wish because of the lack of adequate child care facilities. *The Task Force urges employers to consult with their employees and to assist in making quality care available to the children of both male and female employees.*

Employee Benefits

We urge employers to provide comparable fringe benefits to both male and female employees. Most benefit programs provide only token coverage for obstetrical costs, yet they cover the total cost of such predominantly male medical problems as ulcers. Studies have shown that adding obstetrical care to group medical plans would not significantly increase the cost of the health policy. *The Task Force proposes that employers provide all individuals covered by their health programs the same benefits for obstetrical care that are available for the diagnosis, treatment, and hospitalization of other conditions that require medical attention.*

The practices of many employers that require female employees to cease working either when they become pregnant or several months before the baby is due are being challenged in the courts. Normally healthy women are fully capable of working throughout pregnancy. In fact, many women need these earnings to cover the costs of childbirth and to support a larger family. Most employers lack the medical competence to determine whether or when the physical well-being of an employee or her unborn child is endangered by her continuing to work. We therefore urge employers to refer this question to the individual employee and her doctor. *If the employee is unable to work because of complications of pregnancy or childbirth, she should receive the same temporary disability allowance she would receive if she could not work for other medical reasons.*

Medically justified maternity leave must be distinguished from the leave of absence that either parent of a small child might wish to take, particularly if alternative facilities for infant care are not available. While we realize that some work environments lend themselves to greater flexibility than others, we recommend that employers work to develop policies that permit workers of either sex to take no more than two leaves of absence (of up to one year duration each) without loss of seniority for child care purposes. In addition, we urge employers to make provision analogous to ordinary sick leave for a maximum number of days that parents may take to care for their sick children.

We recommend that employers establish policies that allow parents to care for their children under special circumstances.

Benefit programs are usually designed to meet the needs of fathers with unemployed wives. For example, many benefit programs have provided coverage for the wives of male employees, but have not covered, or have covered less fully, the husbands of female employees. These policies are contrary to the Equal Employment Opportunity Commission's guidelines under Title VII of the 1964 Civil Rights Act. *We recommend that employers provide equivalent benefits to the spouses of male and female employees.*

If more flexible work schedules come into common use, benefit programs will have to be adapted to a variety of work contracts. Today, although part-time adult workers (about three-quarters of whom are women) receive Social Security benefits, they are usually excluded from employer-sponsored benefit programs. *The Task Force believes that employees who work more than twenty hours a week are entitled to a pro rata share of the benefits enjoyed by full-time workers.*

Discrimination against women is deeply ingrained in the social, economic, and political structures of this country. It will not end until employers set definite goals and timetables to eliminate discriminatory practices. Much legislation has been passed to encourage employers to do this. More legislation is needed. The final responsibility, however, lies with employers and employees: it is they who must provide opportunities to women equal to those presently available to men and create an environment in which a woman's right to work is respected.

III. Equal Employment Opportunity Legislation and Enforcement

In recent years, Congress has passed legislation to prohibit employers and unions from discriminating on the basis of sex. Still, working women are not protected effectively against all discriminatory practices. Legislative change is necessary to eliminate the areas in which sex discrimination is still legal. Although present laws and executive orders provide protection against discrimination in many areas, they are not sufficiently effective. The federal government lacks the funds to enforce the laws, and as a result, the legislation is often ignored. *The Task Force, therefore, urges Congress to appropriate funds so that agencies charged with enforcing civil rights and fair employment legislation can become more effective.*

The Civil Rights Act of 1964

The Civil Rights Act of 1964 bars discrimination on the basis of race, creed, color, and national origin in public accommodations, federally assisted programs, and employment. But sex discrimination is prohibited only in the area of employment and, to a limited extent, the practices of educational institutions. *The Task Force recommends that the Civil Rights Act of 1964 be amended to prohibit sex discrimination in all the same areas as it prohibits other forms of discrimination.*

Three sections of the act, Title II, Title VI, and Title VII, are of special importance to women. By not clearly prohibiting sex discrimination, these sections of the act perpetuate present practices. Title II prohibits discrimination in public accommodations based on race, creed, color, and national origin, but not sex. Restaurants and hotels often provide facilities for business and professional meetings. Excluding women from these facilities limits their opportunities to develop beneficial business and professional relationships. *The Task Force recommends that Title II be amended to prohibit sex discrimination in public accommodations.*

Title VI of the Civil Rights Act bars discrimination in federally assisted programs, including job-training programs whose primary purpose is to provide employment or employment training. *The Task Force urges that Title VI be amended to prohibit sex discrimination in all federally assisted programs, including employment and employment training programs.*

Title VII has been interpreted to allow discrimination based on sex if sex is a *"bona fide* occupational qualification" for a position. Since 1969, the Equal Employment Opportunity Commission has interpreted this exception very narrowly: according to the EEOC, sex is a *bona fide* occupational qualification only if "it is necessary for the purpose of authenticity or genuineness," such as in the casting of a play. *The Task Force endorses the EEOC's narrow definition of a bona fide occupational qualification.*

Though its coverage is broad and detailed, the sanctions available to the EEOC have been weak. In 1972, Title VII was amended to give the EEOC greater enforcement powers. Earlier, the commission was limited to investigation, conciliation, and the issuance of guidelines. Now, however, the commission can go to court to enforce Title VII against private employers. In addition, the act now covers sex discrimination by federal, state, and local governments. Depending on the level of government involved, these provisions are enforceable by a variety of government agencies and, after exhaustion of remedies, through civil suits by aggrieved individuals. Unfortunately, the enforcement efforts of the commission are plagued by an enormous and growing backlog of complaints. *The Task Force urges Congress to increase its appropriation to the EEOC so that it can enforce the law on a current and comprehensive basis.*

Coverage under the National Labor Relations Act (NLRA) is limited to businesses engaged in interstate commerce or the production of goods for interstate commerce whose total annual volume of business is above $250,000. The act does not cover hospital workers, agricultural workers, domestic workers, and government workers. Although some of these exclusions are justified by the limits on federal jurisdiction, their net effect is to deprive more than a fourth of all female workers of protection under the NLRA. *The Task Force recommends that the NLRA be amended to extend its coverage as far as federal jurisdiction permits to secure the rights and protection that the act guarantees for as many workers as possible.*

The National Labor Relations Act establishes the rights of employees to organize and bargain collectively with their employers through representatives of their own choosing. The act outlines procedures for employees to choose their representatives freely in a secret ballot election conducted by the National Labor Relations Board (NLRB), the principal enforcement agency for the act. The NLRA prohibits both employees and employers from engaging in certain unfair labor practices.

Workers covered by the NLRA can organize by forming a bargaining unit. A bargaining unit can select a bargaining agent to negotiate with the employer for contract terms that will be binding on all the employees in the unit. Although bargaining agents are required to represent all employees fairly, they sometimes perpetuate discrimination based on sex. Some local unions, with the cooperation of employers, have even set up sex-segregated bargaining units, even though production lines were sexually integrated. Dividing men and women into separate units typically limits the opportunities of women workers. Although the NLRB outlaws such divisions, the practice of assigning different job titles to male and female employees doing essentially the same work has often effectively concealed the sex segregation of bargaining units. *The Task Force recommends that the NLRB screen out and bar bargaining units that have been established primarily on the basis of sex.*

The Task Force urges the NLRB to take action against employers who engage in discriminatory practices *based on sex.* The courts have found that racial discrimination violates the NLRA, causing unjustified clashes of interest between groups of employees and undercutting their ability to work together and achieve their rights under the act. Sex-discriminatory employer policies and practices have similar harmful effects. *We urge the NLRB to apply to sex discrimination the same principles and remedies used for racial discrimination.*

The Task Force recommends that, whenever possible, employees file charges of discrimination with the NLRB. An employee can seek redress both through the EEOC and the NLRB, at least until the court stage. Presently the NLRB has some power to take remedial action against both unions and employers.

The Equal Pay Act

The Fair Labor Standards Act (FLSA) of 1938 established minimum wages, maximum hours, and overtime rates for about half of the employers in the United States. The Equal Pay Act of 1963 amended the FLSA by prohibiting sex discrimination in the payment of wages to all employees covered by the Fair Labor Standards Act. Executive, administrative, and professional positions exempted from the original legislation are now also covered. *The Task Force recommends that the FLSA be extended to the maximum extent possible.*

Executive Orders 11246 and 11375

As amended by Executive Order 11375, Executive Order 11246 prohibits discrimination based on race, color, religion, sex, or national origin in government employment, employment by federal contractors and subcontractors, and employment under federally assisted construction contracts. The wording of the actual orders provides no justification for the assignment of higher priority for enforcement purposes to some forms of discrimination than to others. Yet, the enforcement agencies have only begun to make sex discrimination a serious priority concern. *We urge the Office of Federal Contract Compliance (OFCC) and the compliance agencies to combat all forms of discrimination outlined in the order equally.*

The Department of Labor's Office of Federal Contract Compliance, together with other agencies within the federal government, has been responsible for enforcing the executive order. It has strong sanctions available. Not only can it issue rules and regulations to implement the order, investigate individual complaints, conduct compliance reviews and hearings, but it also can publicize the names of defaulting contractors, suspend or terminate contracts, and debar contractors from future bidding on government contracts.

The OFCC has assigned compliance responsibilities to fifteen different agencies. The Department of Health, Education and Welfare, for example, is responsible for assuring that all educational institutions under government contract comply with the order, and any proposed contract between the federal government and an educational institution must be approved by HEW. Earlier, OFCC regulations and guidelines distinguished between women and minority groups, and the lower priority accorded sex-based discrimination was reflected in the more generally phrased, less stringent guidelines concerning women. New regulations, however, treat women and minority groups together, making allowance for specifically differentiating problem areas. While they are not as far-reaching as the numerical hiring goals and timetables required of construction contractors under the Philadelphia Plan, these regulations do require detailed market analysis and elaborate procedural steps essential to creation of an effective affirmative action program.

As standard enforcement procedure, the order requires periodic compliance reviews, which involve visits from federal government investigators to evaluate efforts of federal contractors to comply with the order. Each compliance agency is responsible for reviewing at least half of the contractor facilities assigned to it each year. Employers who are to receive amounts of one million dollars or more through federal contracts or subcontracts must also undergo preaward compliance reviews. Although compliance reviews are essential to enforcement of the order, many compliance agencies fail to complete them. The OFCC often has neither the staff nor the funds to conduct adequate reviews. *The Task Force recommends that the agencies conduct all required reviews (including the preaward reviews) and develop effective follow-up procedures to ensure that the OFCC regulations are followed meticulously. To this end, we urge that Congress provide additional funds to permit adequate staff to analyze employment practices of complex organizations and to help them make satisfactory changes.*

The compliance agencies and the OFCC have made relatively little use of the major sanctions that they can impose on noncomplying employers. These sanctions include:

1. publishing the names of employers and unions that have failed to comply

2. recommending suits by the Justice Department to compel compliance

3. recommending action by the Equal Employment Opportunity Commission or the Justice Department under Title VII of the 1964 Civil Rights Act

4. recommending criminal actions by the Justice Department against employers who have furnished false information

5. cancelling the contract of a noncomplying employer

6. making a noncomplying employer ineligible for future government contract work until he has demonstrated his willingness to comply with the order.

We urge the enforcement agencies to use all necessary sanctions, particularly contract termination and exclusion from bidding, against employers who do not make significant progress toward compliance with the executive order.

The executive order covers all those employees—a third of the labor force—who work in institutions under federal government contract, including educational institutions and hospitals. If enforced, it can go a long way toward eliminating discrimination in employment.

State Legislation

Although the Task Force has concerned itself primarily with federal legislation, we believe that states must share the responsibility of assuring women equal opportunity. Thirty-eight states, the District of Columbia, and Puerto Rico have fair employment practices laws, nearly all of which prohibit discrimination based on sex. But the legislation barring sex discrimination varies widely from state to state and in some instances provides only minimal protection.

All the states should have fair labor practices laws, and all of these laws should prohibit discrimination based on sex. *Specifically, the Task Force urges all states to enact laws that prohibit employers, labor unions, and employment agencies from practicing any form of discrimination in employment. We further urge states to set up adequately funded agencies to enforce this legislation.*

The states can play a particularly important role in providing much needed protection from discrimination to household and other low-paid workers who are not covered by federal legislation. Since most household and domestic workers are both female and unprotected by federal fair employment legislation, they are of special concern. *The Task Force urges states to broaden the coverage of their minimum wage, unemployment compensation, and workmen's compensation laws to cover workers not now covered, especially household workers.*

The enactment of fair labor practices laws that prohibit all forms of discrimination will necessitate changes in state "protective" legislation. These laws, which theoretically prevent the exploitation of women by regulating their working conditions, are often in practice barriers both to equal employment opportunity for women and to decent working conditions for men. State protective laws fall into three categories:

1. laws that confer *benefits*, such as minimum wages, meal breaks, or rest periods;

2. laws that *exclude* women from certain jobs, such as mining or bartending, or from employment in any job before or after childbirth;

3. laws that *restrict* women's employment under certain conditions, such as at night, or in jobs requiring lifting weights above a set limit.

Under Title VII, the courts are now reviewing state protective laws on a case by case basis. *The Task Force recommends that all state legislatures review the protective laws of their respective states, adapt them to contemporary standards for working conditions, and apply them equally to men and women.*

The Constitution of the United States promises all citizens equal protection of the laws and equal enjoyment of the privileges and immunities of citizenship. The Task Force regrets that the courts have been reluctant to apply these constitutional protections to women in many instances and have continued to affirm as lawful various legal distinctions and differences in treatment based purely on sex in matters such as employment and access to public education and public accommodations. The Task Force supports efforts to secure these rights. Full enjoyment by men and women of equality before the law is long overdue.

IV. Labor Unions

Unions are unique in the organizational, political, and economic resources that they can marshal to attack discrimination in the work environment. The primary concern of unions—because it is the primary concern of workers, both male and female—has been to improve wages and working conditions.

While some unions have a proud tradition of concern for their female members and were working to organize women and to obtain contracts and legislation to benefit them when few others cared, most are just beginning to give priority to issues important to women, such as child care and parental leave, and to make intensive efforts to develop leadership among their female members. *In view of their concern for workers' rights, unions can and should play a key role in the struggle to bring equal opportunity to women.*

Internal Union Education

Such issues as equal pay for work of comparable quantity and quality, promotion based on ability rather than on sex, the availability of quality child care, and nondiscriminatory medical and pension benefits have a profound significance for both men and women who work. They affect equality of opportunity and the adequacy of benefits for all workers; but women workers can be especially effective in bringing these issues to the attention of union leaders. *The Task Force recommends that unions conduct intensive educational campaigns to deal with issues that are of special concern to women and to encourage both male and female workers to participate in all aspects of union concern.*

We propose that unions establish policy-making committees to be responsible for internal affirmative action and reporting about affirmative action programs. These committees should sponsor leadership training programs at all levels and for all members. Special emphasis should be placed on recruiting female members to undertake leadership training, to run for union office, and to assume positions of responsibility in the various areas of union activity.

Efforts should be made to develop leadership in women and to involve them in making policy decisions. *Women's caucuses should be formed. Furthermore, these caucuses should be encouraged to contribute (as some already have) findings and recommendations toward the formulation of policy.*

Policies can be developed through cooperative and coordinated efforts to identify areas of special concern to women and to develop plans and programs to overcome discrimination against women. *We suggest that unions sponsor regional conferences for the exchange of information and the development of new programs to deal with issues concerning discrimination against women.*

Public Education and Political Action

We recommend that unions collect information about discrimination and exploitation by employers and use this information in legal and educational campaigns for equality of job opportunity. Unions are in a good position to observe and identify broad patterns of discrimination. The present laws against discrimination provide a basis for the development of research, education, and legislative programs. The enforcement agencies for the existing laws often lack the funding and enforcement power they need to be effective. The Task Force urges unions, in cooperation with other groups, to continue working to develop public support for:

1. strengthening the laws against discrimination in employment;

2. increasing the budgets and staffs of enforcement agencies;

3. enacting or extending labor standards so that they protect female and male workers equally.

The Task Force urges unions to select individuals for their bargaining committees who will take the initiative in working to eliminate discriminatory aspects of seniority systems, job security programs, and promotional ladders from their contracts. Unions should also negotiate for changes in line with our recommendations regarding employee benefits, supporting services, and child care. *The Task Force urges trade unions to negotiate actively with employers to eliminate employer policies and practices that discriminate against women.*

We further propose that unions extend their reciprocity agreements both internally and with other unions. Workers who must change jobs should not lose retirement and other benefits that they have earned. The ultimate objective of this effort is the development of industrywide benefit programs responsive to the fact that workers, male and female, may occasionally need to be absent temporarily from the work force. *We recommend the enactment of constructive legislation to promote this objective.*

Apprenticeship

Apprenticeship programs are essential for entry into most skilled crafts. Although by law these programs cannot discriminate, a few are still not open to both sexes. Although many others have become open to women in recent years, the changes taking place are not widely known. *The Task Force urges unions, in conjunction with employers, to publicize the fact that sex segregation in admission to apprenticeship programs is illegal. We further recommend that where applicants of the formerly excluded sex are scarce, apprenticeship committees conduct recruiting campaigns to ensure the participation of both sexes in these programs.*

Union Membership

We believe that all workers should be organized on a nondiscriminatory basis. Women workers as a group are less well organized than men workers. Lower-level workers, many of whom are women, are the most systematically exploited and are frequently difficult to organize because of the individual worker's isolation from other workers, relationship with the employer, and snobbishness on the part of some white-collar and professional workers. As a result, many women's occupations, household workers, and secretaries remain underpaid and unorganized. *We recommend that unions use new approaches to reach workers who have not yet been organized and help them formulate demands relevant to their concerns.*

Labor unions are in a position to do much to eliminate discrimination based on sex. As organizations with large memberships, their influence is great. More and more unions are recognizing the value for all workers of many of the expressed concerns of women. Unions should be made even more aware of their responsibility to work for equal opportunity for women.

V. Government Programs and Employment Opportunity

A government that preaches equality has a special responsibility to practice it. The federal government has pioneered in offering equal opportunity to workers, setting an example for state and local governments and for private employers. But inequities still persist in both the sex composition of the civil-service hierarchies and in government employee benefit programs. For example, in 1969 over three-quarters of the workers earning salaries at GS-4 or below were women. Further, many government programs still discriminate on the basis of sex. *The Task Force urges government at all levels to demonstrate its commitment to equality by guaranteeing equal opportunity for men and women in all aspects of government activity.*

Social Security

No employer should base personnel policies on the assumption that the spouse of one sex is always financially dependent on the spouse of the other sex. This assumption, however, is implicit in the federal government's nationwide Social Security system. The wife or widow of a retired or deceased working man receives Social Security benefits based on his earnings, whether or not she has been economically dependent on him. At the same time, the husband or widower of a retired or deceased working woman receives these benefits only if he can prove that his wife has contributed to at least half of his support. Clearly this is a discriminatory practice.

There are other inequitable practices. For example, if both husband and wife have worked, upon retirement she may choose to receive either benefits based on her earnings or benefits based on her husband's earnings, but not both. Even if she had never worked, she would automatically receive stipends based on her husband's earnings (presently 50 percent of her husband's benefits up to a maximum of $105). This policy means that in some instances a working wife could receive fewer benefits than a woman who has never worked. Since Social Security benefits increase with the individual worker's earnings (up to a maximum of $7800 per year in 1969), the benefits for a working couple whose total combined annual income was $7800 would be lower than the benefits received by a couple in which only the husband worked and earned $7800 per year. Similarly, even when both members of a working couple earn good salaries and pay Social Security taxes on these salaries, they ultimately receive proportionately fewer benefits than a couple in which only the husband worked. These arrangements discriminate against the poor as well as against working couples. *The Task Force recommends that the Social Security program provide equal benefits for men and women and their spouses.*

Income Taxes

Most spouses who do not work are engaged in caring for children or disabled dependents. Although these are necessary and valuable functions, they may deprive a person who wants to participate in the paid labor force of that opportunity. Working couples and single household heads who have children or disabled dependents often must pay a housekeeper, nurse, or institution to provide care.

The Task Force commends the recent legislation that allows working single parents and couples earning up to $18,000 a year to deduct up to $400 a month for care of children under fourteen and disabled dependents of any age. (For families with incomes above $18,000 the amount that may be deducted is decreased gradually so that persons or families with incomes of $27,600 or more may claim no deductions.) While these deductions will benefit many households, the Task Force regrets that they are considered personal deductions, rather than employment-related business expenses, making the deduction available only to taxpayers who itemize their personal deductions. *The Task Force recommends that the legislation be amended to allow parents to deduct child care costs from the gross income as employment-related business expenses.*

Welfare

An extimated 3.7 million families receive public assistance under the Aid to Families with Dependent Children program. Three-fifths of these families have three or more children, and more than four-fifths of these families are headed by women.

Welfare legislation and individual welfare departments have been ambivalent and inconsistent toward these women; some policies have encouraged women to join the world of work, while others have encouraged them to stay at home with their children. The result is that welfare programs have not offered women a realistic choice between working and caring for their children full time. On one hand, women are encouraged to participate in welfare department subsidized training programs; on the other, adequate child care arrangements are usually not available.

The welfare system fails to acknowledge that housekeeping and child rearing are as essential to the maintenance of a household as paid employment. In two-parent households the parents can share these two work loads. The single parent must maintain a house, care for children, and earn an income. Welfare programs are often neither sensitive nor responsive to these special problems. The Task Force proposes the enactment of welfare legislation that gives single parents on welfare a choice between receiving adequate financial assistance while staying home to care for their children, and placing their children in alternative child care centers while they are being trained, seeking employment, or working for pay. We also urge the Welfare Department to offer more adequate counseling services. *To summarize, the Task Force recommends that the welfare programs be more responsive to the special needs of single-parent families.*

Job Training

Government manpower training programs are usually just that—*man*power training. Women are often admitted to programs only if no men can be found. The training programs to which they are most often admitted prepare them for low-paying, traditionally feminine jobs. Programs often do not provide adequate services, such as child care (which is critical if a woman with children is expected to succeed). Furthermore, few programs make any special efforts to expose and eliminate job discrimination by employers against women. *We urge the government to eliminate those training and placement practices that discriminate against women.*

Government-sponsored job-training programs are generally as sex segregated as the job market itself. At present, the government virtually always gives preferential treatment to men in determining eligibility to receive both job training and training allowances or stipends, regardless of individual needs. *The Task Force recommends that training and stipends be given on the basis of a person's individual need, rather than his or her sex.*

In 1969, although 44.4 percent of the enrollees in federal manpower programs were women, only 40 percent of the total budget was spent on women. In 1972, 37 percent of the enrollees were women. The discrepancy between the amount spent on men and women is even greater than it appears. These gross figures include the cost of supportive services provided to women by the program, including child care. But the proper beneficiary of child care is the child, not the parent. When supportive services are not included, proportionately much more money is spent on training men than women. *We recommend that the government allocate comparable funds and other resources to train men and women.*

The very term *manpower development* suggests that women who wish to acquire job skills have come to the wrong place. For the sake of accuracy as well as equal opportunity, we propose that the Manpower Administration of the Department of Labor change its name to the Human Resources Administration and that the word *manpower* be replaced by the term *human resources* unless it specifically and exclusively applies to men.

Despite claims to the contrary, most government-funded training programs perpetuate sex labeling of jobs in a labor market stratified by sex. For example, the *Manpower Evaluation Report* noted that the Manpower Development and Training Act Institutional Program has trained more than half of the women (but less than 4 percent of the men) for relatively low-paying clerical work. At the same time, almost half of the men (but only 2 percent of the women) were trained for skilled and relatively high-paying work. Another training program, the Job Corps, has advertised training for women as stenographers, business machine operators, file clerks, and other business-oriented jobs, and training for men as bakers, auto body repairmen, and other, better-paying occupations. *We urge the government to recruit both men and women for all training programs and positions.*

The government is generally ahead of private industry in providing equal opportunities to women. Clearly, however, many inequities still exist. The government should continue and accelerate all of its efforts to eliminate discrimination against women.

VI. Education

Because of its critical role in forming attitudes of both men and women, and because many employers look toward educational institutions for leadership, the educational system should be a model for a society free from discrimination. Apart from its wider influence upon society, the educational system has a direct bearing upon both a woman's place in the work force and her salary. The more education a woman has, the more likely she is to be employed. Although the demand for educated and trained workers of both sexes is greater than the demand for unskilled workers, "women's jobs," in spite of their low pay scales, are more likely than "men's jobs" to require at least a high-school education.

Most educational institutions in the United States today continue to perpetuate sex discrimination and reinforce sex stereotypes. Although it is now almost always illegal, some schools continue to exclude women from educational and employment opportunities that are open to men. More often, schools reinforce stereotypes about women and encourage women to limit their vocational and career aspirations. Children learn skills and methods at school. But a school's curriculum, hiring practices, and policies toward students also convey values and ideas about sex roles. The Task Force urges educational institutions at all levels—primary, secondary, undergraduate, and graduate—to undertake comprehensive steps to eliminate sex bias and sex discrimination.

We make specific recommendations for change in four areas: governance, personnel policies and practices, student admissions and student services, and curriculum. These issues are relevant to all educational institutions, although both their importance and their impact may vary according to the level of the educational institution.

Governance

The policies of educational institutions at all levels are formulated and approved by either elected or appointed governing boards. Presently the percentage of women on these governing boards is small. Until women are elected or appointed as members, however, the Task Force recommends that governing boards make special efforts to include women in an advisory capacity.

Governing boards are in a position to ensure that each school has a committee composed of student, faculty, administrative, and other staff members to conduct systematic reviews of the status of women at the institution. *The Task Force believes that governing boards should take the responsibility for appraising the status of women in each institution and ensuring that the policies of their institutions convey to women students and faculty a sense that they are entitled to equal opportunity both within the institution and in society at large.*

Personnel Policies and Practices

All aspects of affirmative action described in section I apply to educational institutions as employers. But some employer practices have *special* significance for educational institutions, especially colleges and universities. For example, women in education are often held back by informal and closed methods of recruiting and hiring. Also, anti-nepotism rules, which prevent husband and wife from teaching in the same department or institution, are especially harmful to the careers of female academics. Promotion and tenure policies that discourage part-time work make it difficult for women with children to advance in their academic profession. These policies should be changed so that educational institutions have fair, comprehensive, and coherent policies toward women.

The Task Force feels that men and women should have an equal opportunity to participate in the administration and decision-making processes of educational institutions at all levels. Although most elementary and many high-school teachers are women, most principals and superintendents are men. Similarly, while most colleges have one female administrator to deal specifically with the problems of women students, few college presidents, provosts, or deans are women. *The Task Force urges educational institutions actively to seek to select and train qualified women to fill administrative positions. We support the present effort of the federal government to withhold federal funds from educational institutions with personnel policies and practices that are discriminatory and in violation of federal policy and legislation. We recommend even more strongly that schools and colleges assume the leadership in providing equal opportunities for women and seek qualified women to fill high-level posts.*

As serious as the lack of female administrators—and the less conspicuous thinning of the ranks of female teachers in the upper grades—is the shortage of male teachers in the primary grades. Even the smallest schoolchildren are aware that teaching young children is a "woman's job." Children see that although the principal might be male, their teacher is female. Further, because their mothers, rather than their fathers, stay home to care for them, children soon learn that interacting extensively with children is a "woman's job." More men should be encouraged to teach young children, just as many men teach in high schools. In public schools, primary and secondary public-school teachers are paid on the same salary scale; there are few male teachers in elementary schools for cultural and social, not economic, reasons. *The Task Force urges both school systems and universities to encourage men to teach in child care centers, kindergartens, and the primary grades.*

The problem in universities is the opposite of that in the elementary schools. The number of women teaching in the country's universities is small and does not reflect the number of women qualified for these jobs. *The Task Force recommends affirmative action to end imbalances and to increase the number of women faculty members.*

The Task Force commends the formation of women's groups and caucuses in professional organizations, and their activities in pointing out sex discrimination in educational institutions and in recommending ways to eliminate it. One of the most effective activities of women's caucuses has been helping university departments locate women qualified to fill job openings. Because qualified women have been excluded from academic positions, there is a need to look outside the traditional networks to locate them. We urge the professional associations to support the efforts of their women's caucuses to equalize opportunities for women and men in the academic profession. This support may include funding their activities, requesting detailed plans of affirmative action from the relevant academic departments, or, if necessary, applying sanctions against institutions that persist in discriminatory practices. *The Task Force feels that women's caucuses should be encouraged to identify patterns of sex discrimination and work to eliminate them at all levels.*

Student Admissions and Student Services

Public education must be available to everyone, regardless of sex. Even though it still exists, segregation in public high schools is unlawful. Throughout the country, in private schools and at the college level, fewer places are available for women students than for men students. As long as this situation prevails, the Task Force welcomes the present trend toward coeducation in institutions that were previously open to men only. However, the Task Force does not now recommend that all female schools be abolished; under some circumstances a female school can provide much needed support to women.

The Task Force notes with concern evidence that decisions regarding admissions and financial aid are often based on sex, particularly at the graduate level in medical, law, and business schools. *We urge colleges and universities to conform with the law and apply the same standards for both admission and financial aid to male and female applicants and to publicize these nondiscriminatory policies.*

Many would-be students, particularly older women, lack orthodox credentials and find most institutions too rigid to meet their educational needs. The student who has children and who wishes to attend classes on a part-time basis during the day encounters rules that require carrying full course loads for a fixed number of terms, completion of the course work within a fixed number of years, or on-campus residence rules based on a rigid and outdated notion of the typical student. *Flexible and part-time programs that lead to a degree should be designed to meet the scheduling needs of students who cannot enroll on a full-time basis.*

Part-time students should be eligible for scholarships and loans and should have access to the entire university curriculum and all university services. The Task Force urges universities to use their influence to remove those restrictions that prevent the federal government from making loans and scholarships available to part-time students. *The Task Force recommends that part-time students be eligible for all services and financial aid on a pro-rata basis.*

We are also concerned about the apparent reluctance of universities to admit as students adult women who have been away from school for several years. Many of these women have acquired valuable work experience. *We urge educational institutions to admit more adult women and to develop testing and evaluation techniques to determine the level of their competency in a variety of fields.* Students should then be permitted to begin work at an appropriate level, regardless of the number of years of formal education they have had.

Many educational institutions that enroll both women and men discriminate against women in the provision of services and facilities, such as athletics, health care, and access to libraries. For example, at almost all educational levels more money is spent for athletic activities for males than for females. The regulations governing the use of services or facilities, particularly housing, are often more restrictive for women than men. *We therefore recommend that all of the services and facilities of educational institutions be made available to male and female students on a nondiscriminatory basis.*

At all levels, counseling offices need to evaluate their present practices. Too often counselors encourage students to select a college, a field of study, or a job that seems appropriate to their sex, rather than to their interests and abilities. Generally, only the best female students receive the encouragement that average male students receive routinely. It is important that students, especially women students, be fully aware of all of the alternatives open to them so that they can plan wisely and realistically for the future. *The Task Force recommends that counselors at all levels develop programs that focus on counseling students according to their own capabilities and interests, rather than their sex.*

We also urge placement officers to give equal importance to the successful placement of male and female students in jobs for which their capabilities and interests qualify them regardless of sex. It is especially important that placement officers avoid placing women in positions for which they are overqualified. Placement officers should encourage qualified and interested female applicants to interview for jobs in traditionally sex-segregated institutions or fields, such as the physical sciences or mathematics. *We recommend that educational institutions close their campuses to recruiters who refuse either to interview or to hire qualified applicants of both sexes.*

As teachers who are pregnant should be allowed to teach for as long as they are able to continue to meet their responsibilities as a teacher, so should pregnant students be able to remain in the classroom. Pregnant women, whether married or single, are sometimes even expelled from secondary schools or colleges. Male students, whether married or not, do not face any similar consequence if they father a child. This discriminatory policy deprives young mothers of the education that they will need to support themselves and their children. *We feel that the schools have the duty to encourage students who are pregnant or have children to continue their studies and to provide a supportive environment in which they can do so.*

Curriculum

The Task Force recommends that educational institutions at every level review their curricula to insure that courses do not reflect sex bias.

Although the socialization of both girls and boys into rigid sex roles often begins before children enter school, this sex stereotyping often is reinforced in school. The toys children use in nursery school, the stories they hear, and the different activities boys and girls are encouraged to participate in, all help them shape limited and often unrealistic images of the roles of men and women. For example, although almost half of the women between the ages of sixteen and sixty work, almost none of the women described in current first-grade readers are in the labor force. However, some textbook publishing companies are now reviewing their material to eliminate sex bias. *The Task Force believes textbooks, especially children's textbooks, should be revised to reflect accurately the many different kinds of work that women do and to eliminate sex stereotypes.*

Sex-role conditioning continues through all education levels. Many junior high schools and high schools still require girls to take home economics courses and boys to take industrial or vocational courses. These courses can be useful to both men and women, although their content should be revised to appeal to students of both sexes. High schools especially should reevaluate their vocational and commercial tracks; all too often a girl is counseled to take secretarial courses which train her for a low-paying and dead-end job, while a boy is counseled to take vocational courses which prepare him for a higher-paying job with greater opportunities for promotion. It is clear that changes in curriculum must be accompanied by complementary changes in the counseling that students receive. *The Task Force recommends that schools eliminate differential course requirements for women and men and conform with the laws to end the exclusion of women or men from certain courses through formal regulations or informal practices.*

Courses on women are beginning to appear in curricula at all levels, especially in universities. These courses are analogous in some ways to black studies programs: both attempt to cover important topics not discussed in traditional textbooks or classes. *Until the content of these women's courses is incorporated into the regular curricula, we recommend that educational institutions at all levels offer courses that emphasize women—their history, their literature, their role in the economic and political life of the country, and their psychological and sociological characteristics.*

Universities, like educational institutions at all levels, should review their curricula to ensure that women and women's issues are given adequate and fair treatment. In addition, they are in a position to support research of the particular psychological, economic, and cultural factors that have affected women throughout history. The prospect of a society in which women and men enjoy equal opportunity raises a number of questions that the social sciences are not yet able to answer. Some of these critical issues are: the psychological and economic implications of equal employment opportunity, the effectiveness of part-time employees, and factors that are important for effective alternative child care. The importance of this research should not be underestimated; research provides a basis for policy decisions at many levels. Universities are in a good position to obtain government and other funding for this type of research. *The Task Force proposes that one university in each region of the United States establish a major research center to study issues of concern to women.*

Both male and female students learn about women's place in life in a number of ways. The attitudes and actions of teachers, counselors, and administrators help to shape students' images of themselves and their sex. The status and treatment of women in the institution also helps students develop views about women and men. Educational institutions, then, need to work toward evolving consistent policies which emphasize equal opportunity for women and demonstrate an awareness of the social and psychological implications of equal opportunity.

VII. Child Care

While the availability of quality child care facilities will benefit all children and parents, it will especially benefit one-parent families and families in which both parents work. Child care facilities are essential if women and men are to have an equal opportunity to participate in the labor force. The Task Force believes that child care is a universal need, and that the provision of high-quality child care should be recognized as a primary responsibility of society. For this reason, the Task Force condemns President Nixon's 1971 veto of the Comprehensive Child Development Bill. It further deplores the president's belief that a national child care program would necessarily diminish "both parental authority and parental involvement with children."

The need for child care is obvious. Nearly four million women who work have at least one child under the age of six, and one-third of these working mothers are heads of families. More mothers of young children are joining the labor force each year. Yet there are only one million spaces available for children in licensed child care centers. Nearly half of preschool children of working mothers are cared for in their homes by either a relative or a baby-sitter. Another third are cared for in the homes of relatives or neighbors who keep them for a fee. Thirty-eight thousand preschool children stay at home without any supervision at all, and many older children return from school to empty homes.

While many of the existing formal and informal child care arrangements provide merely custodial care, the Task Force believes that child care should and can be an educative experience for children. Thus, the recommendations of the

Task Force focus on the provision of high quality, reliable, inexpensive, and convenient child care. Nothing short of this will meet the needs of both children and parents. *Our most important recommendation is that high-quality, reasonably priced child care be made available as soon as possible to families of all income levels.*

Availability of Child Care

Since families have different needs and communities have different resources, no one approach to child care can be considered either the best or the most appropriate. Child care should be provided by a wide variety of sources in order to allow parents to choose from a range of locations, curricula, and methods of governance. The Child Development Bill of 1971 provided for such variety. Adequate child care will not be a reality until all levels of government, as well as business and community groups, clearly identify child care as a national priority. *The Task Force proposes that places of employment, community organizations, churches, unions, public and private schools, universities, and government agencies identify child care needs and work to establish good child care facilities.*

Because good child care facilities can benefit every child and parent in the country, government at all levels should take the lead in providing them. Congress has recognized the responsibility of the federal government to provide leadership. The Child Development Bill that President Nixon vetoed provided funds for child care, for construction, and for research and training.

The present federal policy of providing child care only to children whose mothers are on welfare tends to isolate poor children and maintain the present stereotype of the child care center as a place for children whose mothers cannot provide proper care. It does not recognize the right of all women to work.

The Task Force urges Congress to pass legislation comparable to the 1971 Child Development Bill in its next session and urges the president to approve such legislation. In addition to the federal government, and especially in the absence of federal leadership, the Task Force urges state and local governments to assume responsibility for making comprehensive alternative child care facilities available to families at all income levels. State and local governments can work actively to identify child care needs on a local level and to develop strategies to meet these needs. They should fund the training of child care staff and model or demonstration programs. They should encourage construction and renovation of buildings to house child care facilites through grants, loans, and subsidies. They could expand and experiment more extensively with the education voucher system of direct grants to parents. In addition, both the federal and state governments should permit parents to deduct child care costs as business expenses from their gross income, as explained in section V.

At the same time, the Task Force feels that private corporations should contribute toward child care in an appropriate manner. A few private corporations have already done so. Some have established centers for their employees' children. Others have contributed money and services, such as accounting and secretarial help, to community programs. Still others, through their benefit programs, reimburse their employees in part or in full for the cost of child care. A few provide tuition payments, time off, or both while employees receive training in child care.

Good infant care is especially important. Infant care is an intrinsic part of child care and should be routinely available to families who seek it. However, many states have legislation that prohibits or seriously hinders the establishment of infant care centers. There are, moreover, many unanswered questions about the necessary components of quality infant care. *The Task Force urges that different program models for infant care be explored and evaluated in depth. We further recommend that legislation replace unrealistic and restrictive regulations regarding infant care with standards that are responsive to the needs of children and parents.*

Inadequate after-school care can have as profound an effect on the development of children as inadequate pre-school care. In wealthy neighborhoods, clubs and piano lessons occupy children after school. The Task Force feels that all children should have a positive alternative to returning to an empty home. In addition, the lack of after-school child care facilities keeps many women who would prefer to work from joining the labor force. *The Task Force recommends that alternative child care programs recognize the need for good after-school care of older children.*

Facilities for the care of children of all ages must be coordinated and made convenient in order to meet the needs of families. Many women have two or more children of different ages, all of whom must be cared for while they work. *Therefore, we recommend that full day care facilities for infants and other preschool children be coordinated with after-school care for older children.*

It is important that different types of child care facilities be available so that parents can choose the care that is most appropriate. One increasingly popular alternative to formal, licensed child care centers is "family care," where a person in the community is paid to care for up to six children in her own home. Although this sort of care is fairly common, it is only now being recognized as a legitimate and even desirable alternative to formal child care centers, particularly for children under three years of age. This type of arrangement can provide families with convenient, inexpensive, community-centered, individualized child care and at the same time provide work for people in the community. Nevertheless, the Task Force recognizes that quality control and adequate training of the "home care mothers" are often difficult in such a decentralized system. Also, it is more difficult to provide valuable supportive services to the children and their families. Coordinating family care with comprehensive formal child care centers could help to overcome some of these disadvantages. *We recommend that alternatives to formal child care centers, such as family care, be explored.*

Most child care centers are geared to the schedule of the typical worker and are open only between 8:00 A.M. and 6:00 P.M. Few communities have evening facilities for children whose parents work at night. Still fewer provide board for children whose parents must be away overnight. *We recommend that some child care facilities be in operation twenty-four hours a day in every community.*

A child who becomes sick and must stay home requires care. Usually, if both parents work it is the mother who stays home to take care of the child, possibly jeopardizing her job or chances for promotion. One alternative is that parents share this responsibility equally. Another possibility is that homemaker services be available to provide good care for children who are too sick to leave their homes and to meet other emergencies that may arise. *We recommend that, for the benefit of both children and parents, all communities establish homemaker services.*

The lack of adequate transportation is often a big obstacle to wide use of child care facilities. Studies have shown that parents are much more likely to use child care facilities that are near either their homes or their places of work. Facilities that are geographically inconvenient are much less likely to be used. *The Task Force recommends that transportation be provided to and from child care centers. We urge local governments to explore the possibility of including transportation to day care centers in the present public school transportation system.*

Quality of Child Care

Quality child care requires that children receive services that contribute to their total development. Custodial child care does not constitute quality child care. The primary responsibility of a child care center is to children. Parents and teachers together should develop educational programs that encourage the personal and intellectual development of the child. Parents and teachers should continually evaluate each center's program to see if, in fact, the center meets these goals. *While programs will vary from center to center, the Task Force believes that the quality of child care must remain a primary concern of all people involved in child care.*

Good child care programs are concerned with the physical as well as the personal and cognitive development of individual children. Child care centers should provide such health services as regular physical examinations, dental checkups, routine innoculations, and sight and hearing tests. A qualified health professional should be available at the center. Also, all staff members should receive special training to help them identify and refer children with health problems. *The Task Force recommends that child care centers provide comprehensive health care.*

We share the federal government's view that parental participation in both the planning and governance of child care centers is essential to quality. *Therefore, we urge child care centers to encouarge parent participation and to develop significant and innovative methods of involving parents.*

The Task Force proposes the establishment of innovative model child care centers in every community. Model or demonstration centers can be a way of continuously investigating and improving the quality of child care. These centers should be a place of constant innovation and improvement, focusing their activity on providing high-quality day care for the lowest possible cost. Because of their special resources, universities are often good places to locate these model centers.

More research on the methods of teaching young children and the curricula that are most effective is needed. The National Center for Child Development, described in the Child Development Bill of 1971, is one model. But even if it comes into being, other federal agencies, state and local government, universities, and private sources are also in a position to contribute. *We recommend that child care centers, especially model centers, conduct extensive research in the area of curriculum development to develop effective methods of teaching small children.*

The inevitable expansion of knowledge in the field of child development should make for improvement and expansion of child care in the years to come. It is important that program staff be aware of and responsive to research findings, successful approaches in other programs, and the individual needs of the families they serve. *We urge everyone involved with planning and operating child care programs to be flexible and willing to change the programs in the face of the needs of the families they serve, the experiences of other programs, and research findings.*

More qualified people are needed to staff child care centers. While existing university training programs cannot meet the projected demands, universities can become centers for child care training. The expertise and resources available at universities also can be used to evaluate existing programs and experiment with new approaches. Both women and men should be encouraged to train for jobs as administrators, teachers, associate and assistant teachers, and aides in child care centers. These training programs should also encourage parents to participate in this training, either to qualify them for jobs in child care or to provide them with knowledge and skills that would enable them to understand the goals and limitations of child care centers. *Since the skills, capabilities, and motivations of the people who staff child care centers are vital to the quality of the care, we recommend that comprehensive training programs for those who staff child care centers be established in every community.*

While formal training is of value, the Task Force realizes that it is not necessarily proof of a person's ability to work well with children. Child care centers should select their staff only after observing them interacting with children. *We recommend that child care centers remain flexible enough to hire people who have the ability to relate effectively to children as teachers and aides, whether or not they have specific credentials or training.*

Many states have licensing requirements for centers. While both quality and safety are essential, some of the present regulations are so rigid that they prevent centers from ever being established. For example, the requirements for the physical plant are often prohibitively and unrealistically high. On the other hand, there are often no standards for the educational and recreational programs of the center. *We urge legislators to review licensing requirements for child care centers and to revise them realistically to encourage the formation of high-quality, reasonably priced child care centers.*

Attitudes and practices based on the assumption that a mother is the best person to care for her child all day need to be challenged. We join with the Joint Commission for Mental Health in urging people to publicize the clinical evidence that disputes the belief that working mothers exert a negative influence on their children.

Although our recommendations have centered on the impact that good child care facilities could have on families with working parents, especially working mothers, it is vital to realize that comprehensive child care facilities can benefit *all* families regardless of their social or economic level. Good alternative child care can provide children with rich experiences which help them to grow and develop. Good child care can give individual parents more time to develop and explore their own interests—which, in turn, often makes them more competent and satisfied parents.

Part II
Background Paper

Acknowledgments

In keeping with the spirit of the women's movement, this book is a collective and collaborative effort. The final draft was prepared by Adele Simmons, Ann Freedman, Margaret Dunkle, and Francine Blau. Gail Falk did the major research and wrote the first draft of the trade union chapter; and Margaret Dunkle edited and updated the entire manuscript in 1971-72. A number of other people contributed to this project. Portions of the chapter on child care are based on an unpublished article by Antonia Chayes and Adele Simmons; Erica Grubb provided sections on maternity benefits and leaves as well as on current efforts of unions to end discrimination; Lenore J. Weitzman prepared a paper on the sociology of working women for the Twentieth Century Fund, portions of which are included as indicated in Chapter 5; Barbara Rosenberg developed much of the initial material on employment law and welfare; Susan Meisel did research on government job training programs; Harriet Katz wrote a memorandum on the NLRB employers; Jane Weaver Cowan wrote from personal experience about employer practices and the occupation of secretary; Evelyn Silver explored the media and its practices; and Elinor Yalen assisted with background research in several areas. The notes and bibliography were checked and compiled by Andrea Olicker, who also assisted in the updating and review of the final draft. The draft of the manuscript was typed by Janet Putnam.

The members of the Twentieth Century Fund Task Force reviewed an earlier version of the background paper. Esther Peterson, Antonia Chayes, and Anthony Downes in particular commented extensively on portions of the manuscript.

Adele Simmons
Ann Freedman
Margaret Dunkle
Francine Blau

Cambridge 1972
Princeton 1974

Preface

Nearly all women work. However, this book is about women who work for pay, the 50 percent of the women between eighteen and sixty-four who are considered labor force participants. Women who work for pay have different jobs than men. In addition, they earn less, are less likely to be promoted, and are less likely to be members of a union.

In a society that links status with income, the position of working women has particular importance. It is no coincidence that secondary income earners are also considered second-class citizens. The pattern of excluding women from jobs that carry high status—medicine, law, business and architecture—and designating female jobs—elementary-school teaching and nursing—as low-pay, low-status jobs, in spite of the fact that they are essential to our society, reflects traditional views about women and their abilities. As long as women have limited access to high-paying jobs and as long as they receive less pay for the same work, their work will not command the respect that a man's work does, and they will remain second-class citizens.

For some women, equal pay for equal work is a psychological issue. It guarantees that women's work is as highly valued as men's. For more women, however, the link between participation in the labor force and income has significant economic importance. Many working women are poor women, working out of necessity, often to support families. As this book demonstrates, the present closed structure of the labor force ensures that these women will have little chance to lift themselves above the poverty level. Before women have access to all jobs for which they are qualified, the attitudes of most Americans will have to change. Even greater changes will be required so that women can succeed or fail in these jobs and be judged as individuals rather than as representatives of a class.

This book is not written for longtime participants in the women's movement, though it may serve as a useful resource for them. Rather, it is directed to those who are sympathetic to the concerns of working women but who are not yet familiar with the reasons for, and patterns of, discrimination. It brings together data already available from a variety of sources and attempts to present a coherent analysis of the status and problems of working women.

Since this book is based on available knowledge, its gaps reflect areas in which further research is required. It was written over a two-year period, between 1970 and 1972. More recent data have been included in each chapter, but it has not always been possible to include an analytic framework that reflects the situation women are confronting in 1974. In the past four years, Congress has approved legislation that greatly strengthens the legal position of working women, and women themselves are now shifting their focus from seeking legislation to ensuring that the legislation is implemented. In many areas, barriers have been broken, but it remains to be seen whether the few women who have entered formerly male preserves are "token" women or whether they represent a real shift in employment practices.

A profile of women in the labor force demonstrates more clearly than anything else the second-class status of working women. The first chapter, therefore, discusses the place of women in the labor force and analyzes some of the reasons women traditionally have been accorded second-class status. It is difficult to predict what effect the removal of traditional barriers to employment will have for working women in the future. A review of current trends and an examination of available statistics make possible some tentative projections. The impact of greater opportunity for women is only one factor, however, as women and men both will have to contend with growing unemployment and an increasingly tight job market.

In Chapter 2, some of the reasons for present discriminatory practices are discussed. The source of these feelings lies not so much in the behavior of individual women workers, but in the feeling of employers about the place of women as a class. To provide examples of how employers place women at a disadvantage, the practices of two employers, AT&T and the federal government, are described. In conclusion, the chapter reviews several areas in which fairly simple changes in policy could improve work opportunities for women.

In theory, once those responsible for inequities are aware that their actions violate widely held social values, as well as laws, they will introduce remedies. However, this is rarely the case. Change is usually resisted when it threatens an established order. It often costs money and can require the discriminating group to share some of its advantages with those who are discriminated against. Change is, therefore, more often a response to legal and economic pressures rather than an act of good will. The third chapter, then, outlines the laws presently available to working women and describes ways in which women have used these laws. It also points up the weakness of the existing legislation and enforcement policies. It is significant that while much of the impetus for the women's movement comes from middle-class and professional women, most of the employment discrimination cases have been brought by factory and working-class women.

Employers and co-workers are not the only sources of discrimination. While sociologists have much to learn about how women view themselves and other women, and how male and female employees feel about working with women, we do know that unions, which control access to many jobs in the country, have a history of discriminating against women. Unions have been in the forefront of a drive for the rights of employees, but only a few have focused on the problems of women employees. The ways in which most unions have traditionally excluded women from their ranks, as well as the programs for change some unions are adopting, are described in Chapter 4.

Ensuring that women and men have equal rights and are treated equally at work does not necessarily mean that women will have an equal opportunity to participate in the labor force. There are two areas of significant concern: child care and education. In spite of efforts to change traditional patterns, women are likely to continue to be primarily responsible for child rearing. They will not be able to participate equally in the work force, and employers will continue to be reluctant to employ them until quality child day care is readily available. Furthermore, women's attitudes about themselves, their abilities, and their opportunities will continue to be limited as long as the schools they attend perpetuate assumptions about male and female sex and work roles, and as long as they are not encouraged to develop their full talents and abilities. Child care and education, the issues discussed in Chapters 5 and 6, are deeply linked to equal opportunity in the work force. The nature and availability of both influence the extent to which women will take advantage of these opportunities.

While the women's movement has been associated with middle-class women, for whom the choice between working in the home and participating in the labor market is a real one, much of the recent legislation and some of the recent agreements between employers and employees will help working-class and poor women, many of whom are black and face both sex and race discrimination. For poor women also, ending discrimination within government training programs is especially important. The ways in which these federal manpower-training programs place women at a disadvantage are presently being explored on a nationwide basis by the Civil Rights Commission. Available data hint at patterns of discrimination; the forthcoming report is expected to provide strong evidence of discrimination and to identify areas in which the discrimination is most marked. Because of this study, we have chosen not to discuss the government training programs. It should not have to be said, however, that discriminatory employment training programs place women at a serious disadvantage when they enter the work force.

Equal opportunity will help break the economic barriers that ensured that women earn less than men, as well as help poor women develop viable alternatives to the self-defeating welfare cycle. In addition, equality, reflected in changes in the attitudes of both women and men in society, will bring a sense of self worth to many women who, though a statistical majority in our population, still perceive themselves as a minority. A society that permits all of its members to develop their abilities to the fullest can only be a richer society than the one in which we currently live.

Adele Simmons
Cambridge 1972
Princeton 1974

1 Women in the Labor Force

Women have always been indispensable to the American economy. During the colonial period, women produced many of the essentials for daily living. They spun and wove and made clothing, soap, shoes and candles. In addition, they cared for their households and families.[1] Spurred by the Puritan ethic, which condemned idleness as a sin, and the continual labor shortages of this early period, women also pursued a wide range of market activities. They were tavern keepers and store proprietors, traders and speculators, printers and publishers, as well as domestic servants and seamstresses.[2]

The involvement of women in industry in this country is as old as the industrial system itself. During the birth of the manufacturing industry in the textile mills of New England in the late eighteenth and early nineteenth centuries, women and young girls comprised the overwhelming majority of industrial workers.[3] But from the beginning, women factory workers held jobs that were quickly identified as "women's jobs." The results of this long tradition of sex segregation in the labor market are apparent today.

This chapter reviews the current status of women in the labor market, describes the distribution of women among different industries and occupations, and shows how this distribution limits women's access to prestigious and highly paid jobs. It examines the income differences between men and women, and explores some of the popular myths that perpetuate discrimination against working women. Finally, the future prospects for women in the labor market are investigated.

A Profile of Working Women

During the past fifty years, an increasing number of women have entered the labor market. In 1920, 22.7 percent of the female population was employed outside the home; by 1970, this figure had risen to 43.3 percent (Table 1-1). Between 1940 and 1945, the female labor force expanded by over 5.5 million as women went to work in order to meet the defense needs of the country. While considerable ground was lost immediately after the war, over the past thirty years the number of working women has more than doubled. In this period, the women's share in the total civilian labor force rose from 25 to nearly 40 percent; by 1970, nearly 50 percent of all women between the ages of sixteen and sixty-four were either working or seeking work.

Table 1-1
Women in the Civilian Labor Force: Selected Years, 1920-70 (Sixteen years of age and over)[a]

Year	Number (in thousands)		As Percent of All Workers	As Percent of Female Population
1920	8,229		20.4	22.7
1930	10,396		21.9	23.6
1940	13,783		25.4	28.9
1945		19,290	36.1	38.1
1947		16,664	27.9	30.8
1950	18,389		29.6	33.9
1955		20,548	31.6	35.7
1960	23,240		33.4	37.7
1965		26,200	35.2	39.2
1970	31,520		38.1	43.3

[a]Pre-1940 figures include all those fourteen years of age and over.
Source: U.S. Department of Labor, Women's Bureau, *1969 Handbook on Women Workers* (Washington, D.C.: U.S. Government Printing Office, 1969), p. 10 and U.S. Department of Labor, Manpower Administration, *Manpower Report of the President*, March 1972, pp. 129-30, 135.

As the female labor force has increased in size, its composition has also changed significantly. In 1940, the typical female worker was young and single; most older women were married and worked only in their own homes. Over the next ten years, this pattern began to change as older married women entered or reentered the labor force in increasing numbers. This trend continued, and by 1960 the contours of the "age profile" of the female labor force had undergone a major shift (Figure 1-1). The percentage of women over thirty-five years of age who were in the labor force rose dramatically, with the largest increase in the forty-five-to-fifty-five-year age group. During the last ten years, women have continued to enter the labor force in increasing numbers, with the most rapid increases in participation occurring among women in the twenty-to-thirty-four-year-old group, many of whom are mothers of preschool children.

As a result of these postwar changes, the profile of the female labor force now corresponds more closely to the profile of the total female population. That is, women in the labor market now closely resemble the total female population in terms of their racial composition, age, educational attainment, marital and family status, and other characteristics. For example, in 1969, the median age of working women was thirty-nine, only slightly below the median age of forty-two for the entire female population. Similarly, 21 percent of married working women and 28 percent of all married women had children under six, while 34 percent of married women workers and 28 percent of all married women had children between the ages of six and seventeen.[4] Thus, it is rapidly becoming

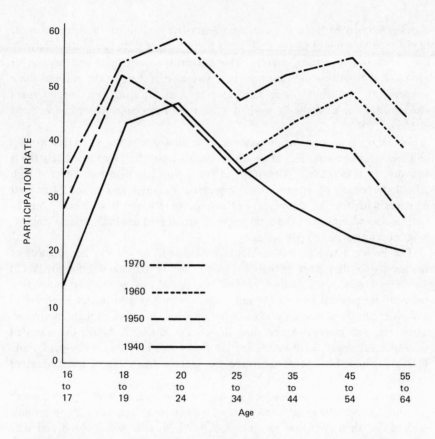

Figure 1-1. Labor Force Participation Rates of Women By Age, 1940-70. Source: U.S. Department of Labor, Manpower Administration, *Manpower Report of the President*, 1972, Washington, D.C.: U.S. Government Printing Office, p. 254 and U.S. Department of Labor, Women's Bureau, *1969 Handbook on Women Workers*, p. 18.

more difficult to consider working women as an unrepresentative or atypical group.

For obvious economic reasons, single, widowed, divorced, and separated women are more likely to work than married women. However, because married women are by far the largest group in the adult female population, the postwar increases in their labor market activity have meant that the majority of working women are now married. Married women living with their husbands comprised 30.3 percent of the female labor force in 1940 and 59 percent in 1970.[5]

One major factor in determining whether or not a married woman participates in the labor force is the presence of children. In March 1971, 29.6 percent of wives with preschool children were in the labor force as compared to 49.4 percent with children between the ages of six and seventeen years.[6] Since married women between the ages of twenty-five and thirty-four are the most likely to have young children, their labor force participation rate is still relatively low. However, it is rising rapidly. The difficulty of obtaining and paying for adequate alternative child care may be a serious deterrent to the entry of these women into the labor force. According to a recent study, mothers of small children are more likely to work if a relative is available to look after their children.[7]

Education is another major factor in determining whether a married woman will seek employment. The more education a woman has, the more likely she is to work. In March 1969, 33 percent of wives with less than four years of high school, 43 percent of wives who had graduated from high school, and 51 percent of wives with four or more years of college were in the labor force.[8] Among both male and female workers, educational attainment generally affects employment opportunities and pay scales.

The better a woman's educational credentials, the greater her chances of finding a job that pays enough to enable her to purchase those goods and services to ease the "double burden" of home and work. The correlation between educational attainment and employment may also reflect a process of self-selection; those women who earn diplomas may be more strongly motivated, ambitious, and career-oriented than those who do not. Although the educated woman often meets with discrimination that keeps her from better-paid, more prestigious jobs, her opportunities are still greater than those of a less educated woman.

Financial need, as measured by a husband's income, may also affect a wife's decision to enter the labor force. Married women most frequently give economic reasons for their decisions to seek work.[9] Whether or not husband and wife perceive the husband's income as adequate depends, among other things, on the size of the family, the standard of living to which they aspire, and their age. Thus, the same level of income may meet the needs of one family but not another. Moreover, the response of a married woman to insufficient family income may depend on the kind of employment opportunities available to her and whether her earnings will cover the cost of services such as child care.

Proportionately more black women than white participate in the labor force, although the differential has been declining in recent years. In 1948, 31 percent of all white women and 46 percent of all nonwhite women sixteen years of age and over were working. By 1971, 43 percent of white women and 49 percent of nonwhite women were working.[10] There are several reasons for these differences. A higher proportion of black women are widowed, divorced, or separated from their husbands. These women must rely heavily on their own earnings to support themselves and their families. Furthermore, the lower average earnings of black men increase the importance of a wife's contribution to family income.

But these factors do not explain all of the differences in labor force participation between black and white women. Even when marital status, age, children's ages, and husbands' incomes are held constant, black women are still more likely to work outside the home than white women. For example, in March 1969, among families in which the husband's income was $10,000 or more, half of the black wives, but only one-third of the white wives, were in the labor force. Forty-four percent of black wives with preschool children were in the labor force in March 1969, as compared to 28 percent of white wives.[11]

The labor force participation rates of women, particularly of married women and teenagers, are very sensitive to the general level of economic activity. The impact of economic conditions on female labor force participation can take either of two forms. In times of economic downturn, if the male family head becomes unemployed, the wife or other members of the household may enter the labor force to supplement the family income. These "additional workers" often leave the labor force once the major breadwinner is reemployed on a regular basis. At the same time, if a working woman loses her job and finds it impossible to locate a new one after prolonged search, she may become a "discouraged worker" and leave the labor force. Other women, especially wives and teenagers, who are not yet working but have been planning to look for jobs postpone their entry into the labor market until economic conditions improve.

Studies show that the group of discouraged workers predominates, so that the female labor force either declines or grows more slowly during periods of high unemployment.[12] Unemployment statistics then tend to underestimate the extent of female unemployment, particularly during periods of low economic activity.

Thus, the gap between women's and men's unemployment rates tends to decline during recessions as women leave the labor force and to widen when the economy is buoyant as women are drawn into the labor force by increased employment opportunities. However, regardless of the stage in the business cycle, the incidence of unemployment among women is considerably higher than among men. For example, in 1972, the unemployment rates were 5.7 percent for white women and 11.3 percent for nonwhite women; these figures may be compared with 4.5 percent for white men and 8.9 percent for nonwhite men.[13]

Industrial and Occupational
Distribution of Women

Once a woman decides to work, she finds only a limited number of jobs available. Despite the rapid growth of the female labor force in recent years, women are still primarily concentrated in certain industries and occupations. In 1968 more than 73 percent of all working women were employed in the service sector, broadly defined to include wholesale and retail trade, finance, insurance, real estate, and public administration, as well as professional, personal, entertainment, business, and repair services.[14] An additional 20 percent worked in the manufacturing sector, including public utilities. This distribution of women among industries is essentially the same as it was in 1940, when 71 percent of all working women were employed in the service sector and 25 percent in manufacturing.[15]

Within the service sector, women tend to be concentrated in specific industries that have traditionally employed them. For example, in 1973 women made up 46 percent of the employees in retail trade, but only 23 percent in wholesale trade; more than 80 percent of the workers in hospitals; and 61 percent of the employees in elementary and secondary schools, but only 42 percent in colleges and universities.[16]

In manufacturing also, certain industries are "women's industries." In January 1973, when women comprised 28 percent of all manufacturing workers, they were 46 percent of the work force in textile mill products, 81 percent in apparel and related products, 41 percent in electrical equipment and supplies, 60 percent in leather, and 42 percent in tobacco industries, but less than 10 percent in the petroleum refining, primary metal, and lumber industries.[17]

The industrial distribution of women workers shows that some industries rely more heavily on women workers and employ them more readily than others. But the representation of women in an industry gives an incomplete picture of the opportunities open to them. Within a given industry women may fill a broad or narrow range of jobs and have full or limited opportunities for career advancement. An industry in the service sector may have a high proportion of women in its work force simply because it employs large numbers of clerical workers, not because it provides opportunities for women in professional, technical, and managerial positions. Similarly, manufacturing firms may welcome women into their operative and clerical categories, but exclude them from their skilled craft and supervisory jobs. Thus, the occupational distribution of women workers reflects the differences in employment opportunities between male and female workers more accurately than does the industrial distribution (Table 1-2).

The distribution of female and male workers by major occupation reveals striking differences between the two groups. In 1971, over 60 percent of female white-collar workers (more than one-third of all employed women) worked in clerical jobs. Yet almost 70 percent of male white-collar workers (28 percent of the male work force) were in either the professional and technical or the managerial category. Since 1960 women have been entering the skilled trades at a faster rate than men. There were nearly twice as many women in these trades in 1970 as in 1960, but this total is less than 2 percent of the total female labor force.[18]

Men also have the highest-status, highest-paying blue-collar jobs. Only 8 percent of women blue-collar workers (1.3 percent of employed women) were craftsmen or foremen in 1971. Yet over 43 percent of the men in this group (20 percent of the male labor force) were categorized as craftsmen and foremen. Data collected by the Equal Employment Opportunity Commission indicate that

Table 1-2
Occupational Distribution of the Labor Force by Sex and Race

		Percent Distribution			
			Females		
Major Occupation Group	Males[b] 1971		Total[b] 1971		Nonwhite[c] 1968
Total employed	100.0[a]		100.0[a]		100.0[a]
White-collar workers	40.9		60.6		37.7
Professional and technical		13.7		14.5	10.6
Managers, officials and proprietors		14.6		5.0	2.4
Clerical		6.7		33.9	22.0
Sales		5.9		7.2	2.7
Blue-collar workers	45.9		15.4		16.7
Craftsmen and foremen		19.9		1.3	0.8
Operatives		18.3		13.3	15.4
Nonfarm laborers		7.7		0.8	0.5
Service workers	8.2		22.2		43.5
Private household		0.1		4.9	16.5
Other		8.1		17.4	27.0
Farm workers	5.1		1.7		2.1
Farmers and farm managers		3.2		0.3	0.2
Farm laborers and foremen		1.9		1.4	1.9

Sources:

[a]Figures may not add to totals because of rounding.

[b]U.S. Department of Labor, Manpower Administration, *Manpower Report of the President* March 1972, p. 172. Washington, D.C.: U.S. Government Printing Office.

[c]U.S. Department of Labor, Women's Bureau, *Facts on Women Workers of Minority Races*, p. 8 (undated). Washington, D.C.: U.S. Government Printing Office.

even in industries where women represent a large proportion of operatives, they may be excluded from craft jobs. For example, in the printing and publishing industry in Cleveland, over 60 percent of the operatives, but only 1 percent of the craftsmen, were women. Similarly, in the electronics industry of that city, 57 percent of the operatives, but just 3 percent of the craftsmen, were women.[19]

The employment distribution of nonwhite women is particularly skewed toward the lower rungs of the occupational ladder. Forty-four percent of nonwhite working women were employed in service jobs in 1971, compared to 22 percent of all women workers. Seventeen percent of nonwhite women workers were in the lowest-paying occupation of private household worker; they comprised 64 percent of all women in this occupation. Only 38 percent of nonwhite women held white-collar jobs, and 58 percent of this group were clerical workers.

Viewing the distribution of female employment by detailed occupations further highlights two aspects of the employment problems of women. First, women are heavily concentrated in an extremely small number of occupations. One indication of the limited job opportunities open to women is that half of all working women were employed in just twenty-one of the 250 occupations listed by the Bureau of the Census in 1969. Male workers were more widely distributed throughout the occupational structure, with half in sixty-five occupations. One-quarter of all employed women worked in only five jobs: secretary-stenographer, household worker, bookkeeper, elementary-school teacher, and waitress.[20]

Second, most women work in predominantly female jobs. Women's share of total employment increased from 18 percent in 1900 to 33 percent in 1960, but the proportion of women in predominantly female occupations, occupations in which 70 percent or more of the workers were women, declined only slightly from 55 percent to 52 percent. Such a small change can hardly be interpreted as a trend toward reduced segregation.[21]

Another way of approaching the issue of the concentration of women in sex-segregated occupational categories is to construct an "index of segregation" based on the percentage of women in the labor force who would have to change jobs in order for the occupational distribution of women workers to match that of men. This "index of segregation" has remained virtually the same since 1900; it was 66.9 in 1900 and 68.4 in 1960, showing that sex segregation has been virtually unaffected by the vast social and economic changes of the present century. It is interesting to note that the figure for racial segregation in 1960 was 46.8, less than three-fourths of the figure for sex segregation.[22]

Thus, it appears that the growing numbers of working women have been absorbed into the labor force not through an across-the-board expansion of employment opportunities, but rather through an expansion of traditionally female jobs, through the emergence of new occupations that were rapidly defined as female, and perhaps occasionally through shifts in the sex composition of some occupations from male to female.

A number of variations on the theme of sex segregation are worth noting. The sex composition of occupations is subject to regional variation. For example, in the Midwest, cornhuskers are traditionally women, while trimmers are almost always men. In the Far West, cornhuskers are men and trimmers are women.[23] In addition to complete reversals of sex labels, the concentration of women in a job category may also vary geographically. For example, in 1960, 64 percent of spinners in textile mills were female in the Northeast as compared with 83 percent in the South.[24]

Furthermore, since women are not evenly distributed among industries, an occupation that is predominantly female in one industry may be predominantly male in another. For example, in 1960 the census reported that 44 percent of all assemblers were women. This included assemblers in electrical machinery equipment and supplies, of whom 67 percent were women, as well as assemblers in motor vehicles and motor vehicle equipment, of whom only 16 percent were women.

Additional examples of regional and industrial differences may be drawn from data collected by the Equal Employment Opportunity Commission. For example, the occupation of salesworker in manufacturing exhibited a great deal of variation. In the textile industry in 1966, women comprised 31 percent of sales personnel in Cleveland, but less than 1 percent in Chicago. Moreover, the mere representation of women in an industry is frequently not a very good predictor of their access to higher-level jobs. In the Chicago apparel industry 68 percent of all workers and 30 percent of the sales workers were women, while in Atlanta, where over 80 percent of apparel workers were women, they held only 9 percent of sales positions.[25] It is doubtful that such large differences can be explained in terms of differences among the cities in industry composition or in the availability of qualified women.

The sex typing of a job often may also vary from one business establishment to another. One firm may hire only men as elevator operators, while another may hire only women; many restaurants employ either waiters or waitresses, but not both. A recent study of employment patterns of workers in office and factory jobs showed that the majority of men and women in nine of the eleven job categories studied worked for companies that hired only one sex in that occupation.[26]

U.S. census data tend to underestimate the extent of sex segregation in the labor market, because the tabulations are reported across regions, industries, and firms. Thus, predominantly male and predominantly female classifications may be combined to yield apparently integrated occupational categories. The variations in the sex composition of occupations also reveal the extremely arbitrary way in which jobs are sex typed. Efforts to justify the exclusion of one sex from a job on the basis of differences in training or ability will have to be reconciled with the evidence that in different locales, industries, or companies, a "man's job" may be a "woman's job."

Income Differences Between Men and Women

The pay differentials between men and women parallel the occupational differences. Statistics for full-time, year-round employees show that in 1971 the median annual income was $9399 for men and $5593 for women. Thus, women earned only 59.5 percent of the male median.[27] In 1970, the median income of white men was $9373; of nonwhite men, $6598 (70.4 percent of the white male median income); of white women, $5490 (58.6 percent); and of nonwhite women, $4674 (49.9 percent).[28]

Furthermore, the gap between women's and men's incomes increased between 1956 and 1969 and has narrowed only slightly since that time. In 1970,

12 percent of all year-round, full-time working women earned less than $3000 as compared to 5 percent of working men, while only 7 percent of the women, as compared to 40 percent of the men, earned $10,000 or more.[29]

Earnings differentials by sex persist even when we control for major occupation group. In 1971 the ratio of the median earnings of full-time, year-round men workers to those of full-time year-round women workers was 66.4 percent for professional and technical workers; 53 percent for managers, officials, and proprietors; 62.4 percent for clerical workers; 42.4 percent for sales workers; 56.4 percent for craftsmen and foremen; 60.5 percent for operatives; and 58.5 percent for service workers.[30] These pay differences are in large part due to sex segregation in employment, which means that even within broad occupational groups, men and women tend to be concentrated in different detailed occupational categories or to work in different industries.

The data on earnings of female and male workers suggest that the "separate but equal" doctrine has consequences for the sexes in employment not unlike those for the races in education. The artificial division of occupations into men's and women's jobs results in substantially higher earnings for men than for women. This is because the demand for women workers tends to be restricted to a small number of occupational categories that are segregated by sex. At the same time, the supply of women available for work is highly responsive to small changes in the wage rate as well as to employment opportunities in general. Moreover, employers can often attract more women into poorly paid jobs simply by increasing the flexibility of work schedules. Thus, in most predominantly female jobs there exists a reserve pool of qualified women outside the labor market who would be willing to enter if the price or job were right. The abundance of supply relative to demand, or what has been termed the "overcrowding" of female occupations, results in a lower determination of earnings for women's jobs.[31] This is not to say that men and women never receive different pay for the same work within an establishment. However, since men and women seldom work together in the same occupational classification, such instances of "unequal pay for equal work" account for a relatively small proportion of the aggregate earnings difference. Moreover, the limited job opportunities open to women give them little defense against such wage discrimination short of litigation. The problem is further complicated by the use of nominal differences in job titles to disguise existing inequalities.

One of the most popular explanations for the difference between men's and women's incomes is that women are merely secondary earners or, as one economist put it, "assistant breadwinners." Even if one ignores the principle of equal pay for equal work, this is not a valid reason for paying women less. Of the women in the labor force in March 1971, 23 percent were single, 19 percent were widowed, divorced, or separated from their husbands, and 23 percent had husbands whose incomes were below $7000.[32] Thus, a substantial proportion of the female labor force has little or no alternative means of support for themselves or their dependents. The economic plight of families headed by women is particularly serious. In 1971, 6 million American families, about 11.5 percent of all the families in the population, were headed by women. More than a third of these families, including over half of the families headed by nonwhite women, lived in poverty. Only 7 percent of the families headed by men had incomes below the low-income level.[33]

The financial contribution of the "assistant breadwinner," the working wife of a working husband, can frequently mean the difference between poverty and a decent standard of living for her family. In 1966, 11 percent of white families in which only the husband worked lived in poverty, but only 3 percent of the white families in which both spouses worked were below the poverty line. Among nonwhite families in which only the husband was in paid employment, 34 percent lived in poverty. In nonwhite families in which both spouses worked, 19 percent were below the poverty line.[34] That a fifth of the nonwhite families lived in poverty even with both spouses working testifies to the severity of the combined effects of racial and sexual segregation in employment.

Another frequently heard explanation of the difference between women's and men's incomes is that men are better trained. However, a study of the starting salaries of 1970 college graduates indicates that employers of professional and managerial workers intended to pay women less than men, even when these workers had the same college major. Employers planned to pay women accounting majors 90 percent of a man's salary, 92 percent in the case of liberal arts majors, 95 percent for chemistry majors, and 97 percent for majors in economics, engineering, and mathematics.[35] Since these plans preceded any actual hiring, this pay differential could in no way reflect differences in job performance.

Among professional and technical workers, women's median earnings are 66 percent of men's. The heavy concentration of women in the traditional women's jobs of teacher, nurse, librarian, and social worker undoubtedly contributes to this differential. Occupations in which women predominate are often dismissed as unskilled or unimportant, even for men. Although it is extremely difficult to compare skill levels across occupations, educational attainment does provide a crude index. A recent study compared the levels of educational attainment and earnings of men and women workers within a number of predominantly female job categories in which the educational attainment of both men and women was higher than the median for the total male experienced civilian labor force (11.1 years). According to the study, the median income of the male workers was slightly above the median for the male labor force in six of the eleven cases; it was less in five cases; and in none was it commensurate with their educational attainment. In no case did the median earnings of female workers approach either those of the total male experienced civilian work force or those of their own male counterparts in the same occupation. To put it another way, men were somewhat underpaid and women were severely underpaid, relative to their educational attainment, in these predominantly female occupations.[36]

A growing body of research into the question of male-female pay differences supports the view that discrimination accounts for a significant share of the differential. After controlling for education, experience, and other factors that might tend to cause productivity differences between men and women, the proportion of the differential attributable to pure discrimination has been estimated at between 29 and 43 percent.[37]

Turnover

Somewhat different issues are raised by the argument that discrimination against female employees can be justified on the grounds that women workers are less likely than men to stay on the job. Before considering the empirical evidence on this question, one point deserves special emphasis. Even if it were true that women are *on the average* more likely to quit their jobs than men, this does not justify treating *individual* women as if they all conform to the average. In the absence of discrimination against women as a group, each female applicant would be entitled to consideration on the basis of her own job history or work aspirations.

But are women workers less likely than men to stay on the job? Unfortunately, the evidence does not exist to definitely answer this question. According to the Bureau of Labor Statistics, in 1968 the average voluntary turnover rate for male factory workers was 2.2 per hundred compared to 2.6 for female factory workers.[38] Further, in 1966, men averaged 5.2 years of continuous employment at one job and women averaged only 2.8 years.[39] However, overall averages can be misleading. A number of factors influence turnover rates for both sexes. What appear to be sex differences may actually be due to the differential impact of these factors on men and women.

Age is an important determinant of voluntary labor turnover. Younger workers of both sexes change jobs more often than older workers. They are often able to experiment with occupations to a greater extent than older workers, because generally they have fewer financial responsibilities, and, having little seniority to lose, they risk less by changing jobs. In addition, their turnover rate imposes a lesser burden on the employer, because on the average they have not received as much training as older workers. Conversely, the longer a worker stays in a job, the more likely he or she is to remain. Length of service increases a worker's stake in his job in the form of nontransferable fringe benefits and seniority rights. Jobs that require substantial on-the-job training tend to have lower turnover rates, in part because the job skills acquired may not be transferable. Good prospects for promotion and high salary levels also diminish the worker's incentive to change jobs.

A U.S. Civil Service Commission study of the voluntary turnover rates of full-time employees in the federal government confirmed that, on average, women had a higher turnover rate than men.[40] However, the study also revealed that many more women than men were in the low-grade jobs that have the highest turnover rates for both men and women. Such things as age, grade level, type of job, and length of service were found to be more predictive of job success and retention than the single factor of sex. For example, women over thirty years of age had substantially lower turnover rates and were better employment risks than men between the ages of nineteen and twenty-four. The authors of the study conclude: "Much better predictions about the probability of loss can be made when age, grade level, etc., are taken into consideration than simply to assume that (1) probability of loss is the same for all women, and (2) probability of loss will be much greater for a woman than it would be for a man."[41]

The American public's view of the effect of sex differences on turnover rates evolved during the period when the typical woman worker was young, single, and apt to leave the work force permanently upon marriage. Today, the typical woman worker is forty years old, married, and a mother. Women with children under six are the least represented but fastest growing group in the labor force. These factors have tended to increase greatly the job stability of women workers and suggest that dramatically different work patterns are in the process of developing.

However, women are frequently denied the incentives given to male workers to remain on the job. Employer practices that restrict women to low-paying, dead-end jobs and deny them access to training programs serve to raise their turnover rates. The lack of guaranteed maternity leaves forces many younger women to leave their jobs permanently when they become pregnant. Thus, a "vicious circle" may exist whereby employer views of women as unstable workers are constantly reaffirmed without giving women an opportunity to respond to a different structure of incentives.

Prospects for the Future

Even those who recognize the disadvantages women now face in the labor market are often fearful of the impact of remedies upon the structure of the present labor force. A major concern is the effect of an increase in the number of working women upon unemployment rates. How many more women can we expect to enter the labor force? And what kinds of jobs will they seek? By analyzing trends in participation rates, this chapter will provide some tentative answers to these two questions.

A study by Valerie Kincade Oppenheimer identified the increase in the *sex-specific* demand for women workers as the crucial factor in explaining the growth over time of the female labor force between 1940 and 1960.[42] The increasing importance of service industries and white-collar occupations has provided increased job opportunities for women within the framework of a rigidly sex-segregated labor market. Moreover, this expansion, as well as the development of new female occupations in the postwar period, greatly exceeded the potential supply of the young, single women who were the backbone of the labor force in the pre-1940 period. Thus, Oppenheimer has concluded:

the combination of the rising demand for female labor and the declining supply of the typical worker opened up job opportunities for married women and older women that had not previously existed. . . the great influx of older married women into the labor force, was, in good part, a response to increased job opportunities—not a creator of such opportunities.[43]

This analysis of past female labor force growth provides some indication of why projecting future patterns of female labor force participation is not an easy matter. On the demand side, it is not clear whether the demand for women workers will continue to expand as it has in the past and, further, whether there will be a breakdown of occupational segregation by sex in employment, thus creating more job opportunities for women. On the supply side, we would like to know whether women will continue to respond to the variables that determine labor force participation to the same degree as they have in the past. In the absence of definite knowledge, we can, at best, use past trends as a guide to the future.

In order to consider a range of possibilities, two estimates of expected female labor force participation over the next fifteen years are presented. The first set of projections, which is labeled "low estimates," has been prepared by the Bureau of Labor Statistics,[44] and it adopts such a conservative view of the continuation of present trends that by 1969 the proportion of working women sixteen years of age and over had already exceeded its projected level for 1975. The second set of projections, which is labeled "high estimates," presents independent estimates, based to a greater extent on the continuation of past trends.

Even the "high estimates," however, do not take into consideration the possible impact of the women's movements, improved child care facilities, or a continued decline in the birth rate on future employment patterns. It is therefore entirely possible that the growth of the female labor force could surpass even that predicted by the "high estimates." On the other hand, both sets of estimates assume a full-employment economy in the coming years. The entrance of women into the labor force in the past has been highly responsive to changes in the aggregate level of economic activity. If this pattern continues, a period of relatively high levels of unemployment can be expected to slow the growth rate of the female labor force.

With these factors in mind we may proceed to examine the prospects for future growth in the female labor force. According to these estimates, we can expect that from 39.4 million to 43 million women will be working or seeking work in 1985 (Table 1-3). The "high estimates" indicate the possibility that 47 percent of all women will be in the labor force, including 54 percent of women between the ages of sixteen and sixty-four, and that these women will account for nearly 40 percent of the total labor force. If the decline in the labor force participation rates of male workers due to school attendance and retirement continues beyond the level projected by the Bureau of Labor Statistics, the female proportion of the work force can be expected to rise still higher.[45]

The Employment of Women

Because this report is being prepared during a period of less than full employment, the question arises as to whether or not the economy can generate enough jobs to absorb the anticipated increase in the number of women seeking work. Although it is beyond the scope of this paper to evaluate the precise measures needed to provide full employment, we can discuss the magnitude of the task, focusing on the prospects for the next ten years. Only the high estimates of female labor force growth will be used, because they are of greater relevance to the question posed. The projections of the male work force were prepared by the Bureau of Labor Statistics.

Table 1-3
Projections for Female Work Force

	Actual			Projected	
	1960	1969	1975	1980	1985
Labor force participation rate—women, 16 years and over (percent)	37.1	42.7	42.5[a] 44.4[b]	43.0[a] 45.9[b]	43.2[a] 47.1[b]
Female labor force—16 years and over (in thousands)	23,171	30,551	33,916 35,488	37,115 39,560	39,438 43,018
Women as a proportion of total labor force—16 years and over (percent)[c]	32.1	36.3	36.6 37.6	36.8 38.3	36.8 38.8

Sources:
[a]"low estimates"—U.S. Bureau of Labor Statistics.
[b]"high estimates"—independent estimate.
[c]Sophia Travis, "The U.S. Labor Force: Projections to 1985," *Monthly Labor Review* (May 1970), p. 4.

In order to provide enough jobs for the projected increase in the labor force, setting a target of full employment for the year 1980, total employment would have to expand at an average rate of 2.1 percent per year.[46] Between 1960 and 1969, employment grew at an average annual rate of 1.9 percent, roughly comparable to the figure estimated as necessary for the next ten years. Similarly, while the estimates project an average yearly increase of 2.4 percent in the female labor force in the coming years, the actual increase between 1960 and 1969 was 2.5 percent.

The period from 1960 to 1969 was not one of uniform prosperity. The unemployment rate was well over 5 percent at the start of the period. Though between 1960 and 1964 unemployment rates averaged 5.7 percent, the early years of high unemployment did not prevent a sizable employment increase over the whole period. Thus, the high unemployment rates of the early 1970s need not ruin the prospects for the whole decade.

It is not possible to predict whether or not the economy will actually attain full employment; this depends on government policies and their efficacy. On the basis of historical experience, however, this appears to be a feasible goal.

Since women are heavily concentrated in a limited number of occupational categories, the ability of women to find employment depends not only on the aggregate number of jobs available, but on the structure of demand as well. The Bureau of Labor Statistics projections of the occupational distribution of the work force in 1980 indicate that the structure of demand will continue to favor the employment of women, even if the present uneven distribution of women among occupations persists into the future. Above average rates of increase in employment are anticipated in the professional and technical, clerical and service categories that accounted for 70 percent of women workers in 1969. The rate of employment increase projected for those occupations, under conditions of full employment, exceeds the anticipated 2.4 percent annual rise in the female labor force (Table 1-4).

The aggregate statistics do, however, conceal certain problem areas. For example, employment in elementary and secondary school teaching, in which 36 percent of all professional women were involved in 1969, is not expected to grow as rapidly as it has in the past. The Bureau of Labor Statistics projections indicate that the number of people seeking to enter the noncollege teaching profession could be as much as 75 percent above projected requirements.[47] Such shifts in demand are not unusual in a dynamic and changing economy. Under conditions of full employment, the decline in the need for teachers would be offset by expanding employment opportunities in other areas. However, given the sex segregation of the labor market and the long period of training required for most professional jobs, this shift in demand could pose serious problems for college-educated women. Present projections indicate that other traditionally female professions will not expand sufficiently to compensate for the poor prospects in elementary and secondary education. Those professions in which

Table 1-4
Occupational Distribution of the Labor Force (1969 and projections for 1980)

| Major Occupational Group | Percent Distribution | | | | Average Annual Employment Change 1969-80 |
	1969 Male	1969 Female	Total	1980 Total	
Total Employed	100.0	100.0	100.0	100.0	2.1
White-collar workers	40.1	59.4	47.3	50.5	2.7
Professional and technical	13.8	13.8	13.8	16.3	3.6
Managers, officials and proprietors	13.8	4.3	10.2	10.0	1.8
Clerical	7.0	34.4	17.2	18.2	2.6
Sales	5.5	6.9	6.0	6.0	2.0
Blue-collar workers	49.7	17.1	36.2	32.7	1.1
Craftsmen and foremen	20.2	1.2	13.1	12.8	1.9
Operatives	20.2	15.4	18.4	16.2	0.9
Nonfarm laborers	7.2	0.5	4.7	3.7	0.2
Service workers	6.7	21.6	12.2	14.1	3.4
Private household	0.1	5.5	2.1	–	
Other	6.6	16.1	10.1	–	
Farm workers	5.6	2.0	4.2	2.7	2.0

Sources:

[1]U.S. Department of Labor, Manpower Administration, *Manpower Report of the President*, March 1970, p. 2. Washington, D.C.: U.S. Government Printing Office.

[2]U.S. Department of Labor, Bureau of Labor Statistics, "The U.S. Economy in 1980: A Preview of BLS Projections," *Monthly Labor Review* (April 1970).

[3]Rate of employment change—independent estimate.

demand is expected to expand rapidly—medicine, dentistry, architecture, science, and engineering—have not traditionally employed large numbers of women.[48] If no efforts are made to encourage a substantial change in the type of training acquired by women at the college and graduate level, the consequence could well be serious underemployment of college-trained women. If, in the absence of sufficient professional opportunities, women college graduates begin to compete for jobs that have in the past been held by women with less education, the latter group will be adversely affected as well.

While the continued trend toward a service economy and white-collar employment does not in general indicate a worsening of the economic position of women, it does not necessarily imply an improvement. Lower earnings and higher unemployment rates will probably continue to plague the female work force as long as occupational segregation by sex persists. For this reason, the goal of equal employment opportunity is crucial to the economic welfare of women.

The evidence presented in the preceding sections shows that until women have more occupational mobility, it is extremely unlikely that the pay differentials between female and male workers will be substantially reduced. Although it is not possible to predict exactly what the distribution of female employment would be if there were complete equality of opportunity in the labor market, it can reasonably be expected that women would be much more evenly distributed throughout the occupational structure.

The size of the effort needed to substantially change the occupational distribution of women workers should not be underestimated. Not only are women heavily concentrated in a small number of occupations, but they comprise nearly 40 percent of the civilian labor force. Nonetheless, the projections shown in Figure 1-2 indicate that a great deal can be accomplished in the near future by concentrating on the *new* jobs created by the growth and replacement needs of the economy. For the purposes of this example, we have allocated 40 percent of the new jobs in each occupational category to women and 60 percent to men. The particular ratio employed is, of course, purely illustrative, but the results do give some indication of what the impact on the occupational distribution of women workers would be if new jobs were distributed differently than they have been in the past.

It appears as though fairly large changes would be forthcoming. The proportion of female managers, officials, and proprietors would increase from 16 to 26 percent, the proportion of craftsmen and foremen from 3 to 16 percent.

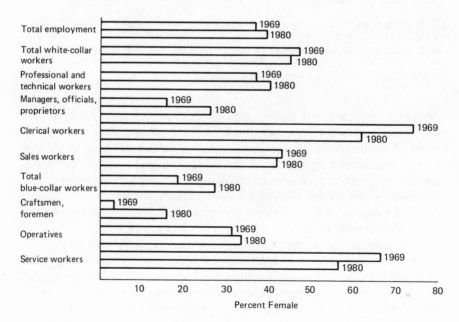

Figure 1-2. Women as a Percent of Total Employment in Major Occupation Groups 1969 and Projected 1980

Similarly, the proportion of women would decline from 74 to 61 percent of all clerical employees and from 66 to 56 percent of service workers.

An assessment of the future prospects for women in the labor market would be incomplete without some consideration of the impact of the level of unemployment on women's economic status. The adverse effect of periods of high unemployment on women cannot be overemphasized. First, since the unemployment rate of women is generally higher than that of men, women bear a disproportionate share of unemployment. Second, in times of high unemployment, many women become discouraged and drop out of the labor force; others postpone their entry until economic conditions improve. This kind of "hidden unemployment" is a particular problem for women. Finally, the level of unemployment will undoubtedly affect the social acceptance of programs designed to increase the opportunities for women in what are presently predominantly male jobs.

An unavoidable consequence of the effort to expand the employment opportunities open to women is that men will face a new source of competition. Thus, some men may find that they are unable to obtain employment in their preferred occupation. However, under conditions of full employment, they can always find employment elsewhere. Further, buoyant demand conditions combined with a new mobility for women workers would tend to reduce earnings differentials between occupations that were once predominantly male or female. Thus, the price paid by men for being unable to enter the occupation of their choice may not prove to be very great. On the other hand, during a period of high unemployment, public support for a fundamental change in women's employment status may diminish. Moreover, since it is the new jobs that become available in a growing, healthy economy that are most likely to become available to women, the maintenance of full employment is important if we are to move rapidly toward the goal of economic equality for women.

Notes

1. Eleanor Flexner, *Century of Struggle: The Women's Rights Movement in the United States* (New York: Atheneum, 1968), p. 9.

2. Edith Abbott, *Women in Industry* (New York: D. Appleton and Co., 1910), p. 11.

3. Ibid., chapters 4 and 5.

4. Janet Neipert Hedges, "Women Workers and Manpower Demands in the 1970's," *Monthly Labor Review*, June 1970, p. 21.

5. U.S. Department of Labor, Manpower Administration, *Manpower Report of the President*, April 1971 (Washington, D.C.: U.S. Government Printing Office), p. 234.

6. Ibid., March 1972, p. 195; U.S., Women's Bureau, *1969 Handbook on Women Workers*, Bulletin 294 (Washington, D.C.: U.S. Government Printing Office, 1969), p. 23.

7. Elizabeth Waldman, "Marital and Family Characteristics of the U.S. Labor Force," *Monthly Labor Review*, May 1970, p. 25.

8. Ibid.

9. "Why Women Start and Stop Working: A Study in Mobility," *Monthly Labor Review*, September 1965, pp. 1077-82, cited in Vera C. Parella, "Women and the Labor Force," *Special Labor Force Report No. 93*, February 1968, p. 4.

10. *Manpower Report of the President*, March 1972, p. 162.

11. Elizabeth Waldman, "Women at Work: Changes in the Labor Force Activity of Women," *Monthly Labor Review*, June 1970, p. 12.

12. Gertrude Bancroft McNally, "Patterns of Female Labor Force Activity," *Industrial Relations*, May 1968, p. 209.

13. *Manpower Report of the President*, March 1973, p. 145.

14. This definition is similar to that used by Victor Fuchs in *The Service Economy* (New York: National Bureau of Economic Research. 1968).

15. *1969 Handbook on Women Workers*, p. 110 and U.S., Department of Labor. Women's Bureau, *Background Facts on Women Workers in the United States*, 1970, p. 14.
Facts on Women Workers in the United States, 1970, p. 14.

16. Elizabeth Waldman and Beverly McEaddy, "Where Women Work," *Monthly Labor Review*, May 1974, p. 6.

17. *1969 Handbook on Women Workers*, p. 114.

18. Janet Neipert Hedges and Stephen Beims, "Sex Stereotyping in the Skilled Trades," *Monthly Labor Review*, May 1974, p. 16

19. Computed from Equal Employment Opportunity Commission, *Report No. 1: Job Patterns for Minorities and Women in Private Industry, (1966), and* Manpower Report of the President (1966), p. 172.

20. Hedges, "Women Workers," p. 19.

21. Valerie Kincade Oppenheimer, "The Sex-Labeling of Jobs," *Industrial Relations*, May 1968, p. 220.

22. Edward Gross, "Plus Can Change . . . ? The Sexual Structure of Occupations Over Time," *Social Problems*, Fall 1968, p. 202.

23. National Manpower Council, *Woman Power*, p. 91, cited in Valerie Kincade Oppenheimer, *The Female Labor Force in the United States* (Berkeley: Institute of International Studies, University of California, 1970), p. 66.

24. Oppenheimer, "The Sex-Labeling of Jobs," p. 222.

25. Computed from Equal Employment Opportunity Commission, *Report No. 1: Job Patterns for Minorities and Women in Private Industry* (1966), p. 164.

26. U.S., Department of Labor, Bureau of Labor Statistics. *Wages and Related Benefits*, part 2, p. 79.

27. U.S., *Economic Report of the President*, January 1973, p. 103.

28. U.S., Women's Bureau, *Facts on Women Workers of Minority Races*, p. 9.

29. U.S. Department of Labor, *Fact Sheet on the Earnings Gap* (1970). For a discussion of the impact of union membership on the earnings gap, see Edna Raphael. "Working Women and Their Membership in Labor Unions," *Monthly Labor Review*, May 1974, pp. 27-33.

30. In addition, full-time hours for women tend to be less than those of men on the average. For the effect of adjustment for this factor on the earnings differential, see *Economic Report of the President*, January 1973, table 28, p. 104.

31. Barbara Bergmann, "The Effect on White Incomes of Discrimination in Employment," *Journal of Political Economy*, March-April, 1971, pp. 294-313.

32. U.S., Women's Bureau, *Why Women Work*, July 1972, p. 1.
1972, p. 1.

33. *Economic Report of the President*, January 1973, p. 108.

34. *1969 Handbook on Women Workers*, p. 130.

35. Frank S. Endicott, "Trends in Employment of College and University Graduates in Business and Industry," Northwestern University, 1970.

36. Oppenheimer, *The Female Labor Force in the United States*, pp. 100-101.

37. See Isabell Sawhill, "The Economics of Discrimination Against Women: Some New Findings," *Journal of Human Resources*, Summer 1973, for a review of this research.

38. U.S., Bureau of Labor Statistics, *Facts on Absenteeism and Labor Turnover Among Women Workers*, August 1969, p. 2.

39. It is important to note that since a higher proportion of women than men are relatively new entrants into the labor force, not all of the difference in job tenure is attributable to higher turnover rates.

40. U.S., Civil Service Commission, President's Commission on the Status of Women, *Report of the Committee on Federal Employment*, Appendix F, October 1963.

41. Ibid., p. 24.

42. See Oppenheimer, *The Female Labor Force in the United States.*

43. Ibid., p. 187.

44. Sophia Travis, "The U.S. Labor Force Projections to 1985," *Monthly Labor Review*, May 1970, pp. 3-12. The Bureau of Labor Statistics has issued a new set of projections that are somewhat less conservative. See Denis Johnston, "Population and Labor Force Projections," *Monthly Labor Review*, December 1973, pp. 8-17.

45. Estimates of the projected size of the male labor force used in this computation are from Travis, "Labor Force Projections."

46. Full employment is here defined at a 3 percent level of unemployment, an extremely low rate.

47. Hedges, "Women Workers," p. 22.

48. Ibid.

2 Employer Attitudes and Practices

Traditional beliefs and continuing social norms have encouraged employers to treat women and men differently. Sometimes this differential treatment reflects an explicit policy; more often it represents the attitudes of employers toward women in general and working women in particular. In many cases, women themselves fail to recognize this differential treatment and its effects. The continuing inequality between women and men in the work force is often accepted as both natural and unimportant.

From recruitment to retirement, sex discrimination appears in every phase of the employer-employee relationship. Recent legislation has outlawed many discriminatory practices, but tradition and economic self-interest make the implementation and enforcement of such legislation difficult. Before women achieve equal opportunity, deeply embedded attitudes encouraging discrimination must first change.

This chapter demonstrates that much of the basis for sex discrimination lies in the motivations and attitudes of both employers and employees. After describing some prevailing beliefs about women who work, the chapter shows the manner in which these beliefs translate into discriminatory policies and practices in the areas of recruitment, benefits, and working hours. Finally, the practices of one of the country's largest employers, the federal government, will be discussed.

Employer Attitudes Toward Women Workers

The preceding chapter described the sex-segregated structure of the labor market, which prevents women from competing with men for the same jobs. The attitudes of employers, reflecting deeply rooted beliefs about the social and economic roles of women and men, help to maintain this sex-segregated structure. While most employers now admit that there are fewer differences between women and men than they once believed, and that the differences between two individuals of the same sex are often more significant than the differences between women and men, many employers still continue to view women in stereotyped ways that limit women's opportunities for employment and promotion.

Four stereotypes underlie many of the traditional beliefs about women workers. The first is that a woman's primary commitment is to her family and

65

that this commitment limits her effectiveness on the job. In *The Female Labor Force in the United States*, Valerie Oppenheimer lists a number of factors that help account for the sex segregation of the labor market, four of which are derived from this first stereotype. They are (1) that women's work life will be characterized by interruptions rather than career continuity, (2) that women will lack the geographical mobility necessary for many jobs, (3) that women will have lower career aspirations than men and will therefore be less productive, and (4) that for the three reasons just listed, women will not be good candidates for on-the-job training.[1] On the assumption that women will or should place home and family first, employers also conclude that women will have high rates of turnover and absenteeism, and that they work best at jobs that draw upon the same skills as homemaking. Because of these beliefs, women are frequently considered to be generally less qualified workers and are excluded from jobs that require on-the-job training, career continuity, geographical mobility, strong motivation, or skills outside the traditional realm.

A second assumption that encourages sex segregation in the labor market is that women are suited by temperament and skill for certain jobs and not for others. As Oppenheimer explains:

The sex linked traits in question may not even be proven traits of one sex or the other—it is sufficient that employers believe they are, or believe that one sex has an advantage over the other in some important respect. . . . Women are supposed by many employers to have greater manual dexterity than men. This may or may not be true, but that is not particularly important. What is important is the extent to which employers believe it, and let this belief guide their hiring policies.[2]

It is ironic that dexterous female hands are required for the manufacture of transistor radios but not for surgery. Similarly, women are told they should not apply for some jobs because the jobs require working at night; yet female telephone operators and nurses routinely work at night. The inconsistencies are apparent, but the same excuses persist. Caroline Bird wryly observed that employers justified the sex typing of jobs "in the tone of voice a teller of fairy tales uses to warn his audience that what he says is not to be taken literally."[3] It is not surprising, therefore, that following a 1962 order requiring federal appointing officers to give reasons for requesting an employee of a particular sex, the number of requests for applicants of a specific sex dropped to 1 percent of their former volume.[4]

A study by Georgina Smith of changes in the supply and demand of women workers in a large New Jersey county between 1953 and 1961 identified reasons why specific jobs shifted from being men's jobs to women's jobs during this period. The explanations given by employers were surprisingly uniform. A spokesman for a large manufacturing firm said:

Most technological changes were of a type that would tend to increase the percent of women. For example, we have broken down the alignment of components and simplified jobs and, *as the jobs called for less skill, they became women's work.*[5]

Another manufacturer explained:

In assembly, we have one job . . . which was formerly performed by men. We decided that the job was simple enough so that there was no point in continuing to recruit men for it. So we made it a woman's job. We couldn't redesign it; it was already too simple.[6]

A third employer stated:

We feel that jobs requiring manual dexterity call for women. Also this work is particularly tedious and painstaking—definitely a woman's job.[7]

Similarly, jobs entailing much physical strength tend to be automatically labeled male.[8] For example, a study of hiring practices in New Haven, Connecticut, and Charlotte, North Carolina, revealed that about 90 percent of employers preferred men for common laboring jobs—those in which physical strength is more likely to be needed—and about 75 percent required men; women were preferred only for cleaning jobs.[9]

In certain jobs, femininity itself is considered to be an important factor.[10] For example, in a 1960 National Office Management Association study, about 28 percent of the two thousand companies surveyed indicated that sex appeal is a qualification on some office jobs and that it is given serious consideration in the employment of receptionists, switchboard operators, secretaries, and stenographers.[11] While employers may no longer explicitly claim that women are better suited for some jobs than others, their attitudes and practices have changed little.

The third and fourth social beliefs about women and work were identified by Theodore Caplow in his examination of the relationship between cultural attitudes and the inferior position of women in the labor force.

Women are barred from four out of every five occupational functions, not because of incapacity or technical unsuitability, but because the attitudes which govern interpersonal relationships in our culture sanction only a few working relationships between men and women, and prohibit all the others on grounds that have nothing to do with technology.[12]

Caplow believes that, except in family or sexual relationships, our social values dictate that men should not be subordinate to women, and that "intimate groups, except those based on family or sexual ties, should be composed of either sex but not both."[13] These deeply embedded perceptions explain the tenacity with which some companies as well as police and fire departments have insisted on keeping certain jobs sex segregated. In addition, emotion is often aroused when the question of a female supervising male workers is discussed. The desire to prevent women from moving to positions of responsibility becomes in some cases a justification for defining whatever work women do as low-level work.

The relationship of these stereotypes to reality is interesting. When one female employee conforms to the stereotype, an employer is likely to generalize his experience and conclude that all women will exhibit similar behavior; paradoxically, however, the deviation of individual women employees from the stereotypes does not undercut the mythology. For example, Smith reported that even when individual women held "men's" jobs and did them well, they were often not fully accepted by their employers and co-workers. In fact, the successes of these women were sometimes held against them. More than half of the firms Smith surveyed answered that women currently held jobs that the employer would prefer to fill with men.[14] This opposition to a woman in a high-paying "male" position was evident for both blue- and white-collar jobs. One employer said of a relatively highly paid blue-collar woman who had been employed by his company since World War II: "The men want us to get rid of her. They want her out because she's too good; she's a pace-setter. I would say that the day she quits, all the men are going to go out and get cockeyed drunk."[15]

Popular beliefs that women workers have higher rates of turnover and absenteeism are another example of the persistence of sex stereotypes in the face of alternative explanations of reality. They also illustrate the self-reinforcing nature of sex stereotypes. For, as explained in Chapter 1, there is evidence that age, grade level, type of job, and length of employment are better predictors of job success and retention than the single factor of sex. Thus, women may on the average have higher turnover and absenteeism rates because they are on the average in low-pay, low-status jobs, not because they are women. Because of the stereotype that women as a group have higher rates of turnover and absenteeism than men, individual women are probably denied the higher status and better-paying jobs that might give them the incentives to stay on their jobs longer and cut down their rates of absenteeism.

Employer Practices

The attitudes described above are easily translated into practices that place women at a disadvantage in the work force. The most common areas of discrimination include hiring, job assignment, promotion, pay and benefits. Concrete examples of discrimination are described in Chapter 3, which discusses specific cases brought against employers under antidiscrimination laws. Here the systematic discrimination of a major private employer and of the federal government, as well as several recent settlements in major challenges to employer discrimination, are briefly discussed to highlight the sheer magnitude of the problem of sex discrimination by employers.

The AT&T Case

The most complete and recent documentation of discriminatory employment practices is a 1972 study of the American Telephone and Telegraph Company (AT&T) by the Equal Employment Opportunity Commission (EEOC).[16] The EEOC study showed that in 92.4 percent of the jobs within the Bell System, 90 percent or more of the employees in that job were of one sex. In thirty cities, 54 percent of all employees worked in jobs that were 100 percent segregated at the time of the EEOC study.[17] As was to be expected, women were concentrated in the lower ranks of the Bell System. Thus although 41.1 percent of the company's managers were women, 94 percent of the women managers were at the first level of management.[18]

Sex segregation began with recruitment. The pictures and pronouns made it clear to any potential employee which jobs were male and which jobs were female.[19] Handbooks describing "opportunities for young women in the telephone business" and brochures describing "beginning entry jobs for men" were used in high schools. In 1965, all the Bell companies maintained separate hiring offices for men and women; women interviewers spoke to applicants for traditionally female jobs, while men interviewers talked to candidates for positions in Bell-defined male jobs. Women applicants were asked questions about family, marriage and children, while men were asked whether they had a valid driver's license and were given a security test. The form for women applicants asked for grades in English, math, typing, bookkeeping, stenography, business machines, and art, while men were asked about their prior work in English, algebra, plane geometry, solid geometry, trigonometry, physics, mechanical drawing, shop courses, and languages.[20]

Much of Bell's recruitment was done through word of mouth. The EEOC believes that the Bell System's reliance on this method of recruiting had "serious implications for women and minorities" in the context of Bell's sex, race, and ethnically segregated labor force:

The implication is only too apparent. Females traditionally confined to "female" jobs, will have limited familiarity with "male" jobs. They will be unaware of vacancies in craft jobs and will be able to offer no encouragement to their female friends and relatives in this area. . . . Employee recruiting, the major Bell system recruitment technique, can have only one result. Females will continue to flow into "female" jobs and males into "male" jobs.[21]

Although some Bell companies had been sued for discriminatory recruitment and hiring, few companies had actually changed their practices by the time of the EEOC investigation.[22]

The two largest departments in the Bell System are plant and traffic. Men who entered the Bell System usually worked first in the plant department as frameworkers, earning a starting salary of $7500 or $8000. Women who joined the system usually worked as operators in the traffic department, earning from $5000 to $6000.[23] Since the majority of the 200,000 people employed each year by Bell are unskilled and trained by Bell, differential abilities cannot excuse such a wide difference in wages. Opportunities for women in the plant department, and in craft jobs in particular, have theoretically been available since the passage of Title VII. However, in 1966, two years after the passage of Title VII, only three companies had women in craft positions; subsequently, all companies reported that more than 1 percent of their craft members were women. Women were not told of opportunities in the plant department when they applied for jobs with the company. Since few women who work for the Bell System were themselves aware of these opportunities and of the legislation permitting them to work in other capacities, informal recruitment did not tend to break down sex segregation.

Until recently, Bell relied on state protective laws where they existed to keep women from working at plant jobs. In some states, restrictions made it illegal to require women to work overtime and to lift certain weights. In addition, Bell claimed "that women as a class were unable or unwilling to meet some of the rigors associated with traditionally male jobs."[24]

Bell maintained sex segregation at all levels, keeping men out of women's jobs as much as women out of men's jobs. Operators had to be women, Bell argued, because the company had already invested money in its image of "the voice with a smile." Furthermore, if men were operators, there might be pressure to equalize salaries between the plant and traffic divisions, since men would enter the company in both divisions. Other arguments pointed to the close nature of operators' work, the design of facilities from chairs to rest rooms to lounges, and the fact that men were, by nature, unsuited for operators' jobs. However, since no personality tests are given to deselect women who happen to be noisy and aggressive, this argument, like others, was specious.[25]

A good example of Bell's effort to maintain sex segregation was the job of frameworker, the usual starting job for men. All telephones in an area are connected by wire to routing equipment in central plant locations, and the frameman's job is to change the connections of these individual telephone wires with the central routing equipment to reflect changes in service.[26] Michigan Bell employs women to do this job and calls them switchroom helpers. While for all other companies this job was the first in the male ladder in the plant department, in Michigan this job was treated as a clerical job and the rate of pay was within the clerical rather than the craft range. Promotion, of course, was through the clerical ladder. Switchroom helpers in Michigan were required to be over 5'3" tall; frameworkers in most other companies were required to be over 5'6". In Michigan as well as in every other Bell Company, this job was sex segregated, performed either by men or by women but not by both.

The law has, however, required that Bell open its jobs to members of both sexes. The EEOC report proved that by 1972, there had been little change. A 1965 memorandum may not have been policy, but it was practice: "We are not anxious to place men in jobs that are normally held by women or women in jobs that are normally held by men."[27]

In addition to discriminating in job placement, the opportunities for promotion were greater for men than for women. While Bell publicity talked about beginning a career, the chances were that most women began and ended in the operator's job. Women were promoted to positions where they supervised other women; thus, while opportunities to enter management did exist, women stayed at the bottom of the management ladder. Lower-level male managers were shifted from department to department to gain a better understanding of the entire company operation, but women remained isolated in one department and thus did not develop the broader knowledge required for further promotion. Furthermore, the lack of female managers at upper levels did not encourage women employees to seek higher-level positions.[28]

On the basis of their study, the EEOC petitioned the Federal Communications Commission to deny AT&T a rate increase. In January 1973, AT&T, in an agreement reached with the Department of Labor and the EEOC, announced that it was paying $15 million to employees who had been injured by the employment practices of AT&T and its twenty-four operating companies. Half of this settlement was in the form of back-pay awards. The company also announced that it was adjusting salaries for many of its female and minority employees and altering its promotion policies. These changes alone are expected to cost the company between $23 million and $35 million annually.[29] In addition, AT&T has agreed to change its practices relating to the hiring, promotion, and training of its employees and is in the process of developing an affirmative action plan with specific goals and timetables.

The consent decree settlement has been heralded as unprecedented. To the extent that it has established a model for significant back-pay awards to employees who often did not apply for better paid jobs because they did not believe these jobs to be available, it may have a significant impact on the practices of other employers.[30] On the other hand, the National Organization for Women has criticized the settlement because it believes that the back-pay provisions are insufficient, that the settlement did not require AT&T to establish goals and timetables that NOW considered adequate, and that it did not require AT&T to comply with EEOC guidelines regarding maternity leave.[31] Furthermore, there is reason to wonder whether companies and the government may not use consent decrees as a way of reaching agreements in secret without the full involvement of employees.

Since the initial AT&T settlement, there have been several similar out-of-court settlements that include back-pay awards prior to July 1974. In May 1974, AT&T reached a second agreement with the government and announced that it would award $30 million in back pay to 25,000 first- and second-level managerial employees. In addition, AT&T has agreed to revise its methods of determining salaries in order to eliminate discrimination. AT&T has been charged with violating both Title VII of the Civil Rights Act of 1964 and the Equal Pay Act.[32] (See Chapter 3.)

In April 1974, Bethlehem Steel and eight other steel companies promised to pay $30 million in back pay to 40,000 employees, including 6000 women. However, this agreement has been strongly criticized by women's groups because it requires the government to "enter litigation on behalf of any of the nine defendants and take the position that any further relief to parties charging discrimination is unwarranted" for a five-year period. The agreement does call for women to comprise 20 percent of new hirings in maintenance and production jobs, but it excludes clerical workers from the new seniority system.[33]

In another agreement, Rutgers University announced that it was awarding $375,000 in back pay to women faculty members. Given the financial straits in which most educational institutions find themselves, the Rutgers settlement should serve to encourage educational administrators to cease discrimination, because they cannot afford to risk a high back-pay settlement.[34]

The Federal Government as Employer

The federal government is the country's largest single employer: in 1972, there were nearly 2 million white-collar employees alone.[35] The impact of the federal government's employment policies far exceeds its immediate employee population, however, for the government sets the tone for employment practices. The historical and contemporary evidence of extensive sex discrimination by the government is thus suggestive of what is going on throughout the labor market.

Women have worked in the federal government since its beginning. Records show that the Army employed a number of women during the Revolution and that the Post Office employed some females well before 1800. By the mid-1800s, women had moved into such varied jobs as lighthouse keeper and clerk copyist. But significant numbers of women were not admitted into government positions until 1862, when the Treasury Department began to hire women in order to save money. Female clerks earned $600 a year, while male clerks earned at least double that figure.[36]

In 1870, Congress, after hearing testimony from the Post Office and Treasury Department that women outperformed more highly paid men, passed a bill that *permitted* appointing officers to pay male and female clerks at the same rate.

This legislation, known as Section 165 of the Revised Statutes, was interpreted to give the appointing officers the right to consider only one sex or the other for any given job.[37] Using this interpretation, the agencies often requested men, especially for the higher-level positions.

Even after the passage of the Civil Service Act of 1883 (which stressed competitive examinations and recruitment for all levels), and the 1923 Classification Act (which specifically provided for equal pay for equal work, regardless of sex), the government still excluded women from many high-level positions.[38] It is not surprising that in 1907, when 7.4 percent of all federal employees were women, 95 percent were in the low-paying, clerical, subclerical, and labor classifications. In 1919 the Civil Service Commission officially opened all examinations, but not all positions, to women.[39] It was not until 1962, ninety-two years after its passage, that the President's Commission on the Status of Women finally requested a review of Section 165 of the Revised Statutes. The attorney general declared the prevailing interpretation invalid, and President Kennedy required that all civil-service appointments be made on the basis of merit alone, except "in unusual situations where such action has been found justified by the Civil Service Commission on the basis of objective nondiscriminatory standards."[40] In 1965, Congress repealed Section 165.

In 1971 the Civil Service Commission ruled that agencies would not be able to specify their employees by sex except in certain institutional jobs or when a job requires employees to sleep together in common quarters. Thus, jobs previously open to men only—such as those requiring the carrying of firearms—are now open to women. In 1973, height and weight requirements were removed from several categories of jobs related to law enforcement, thus enabling a larger number of women to compete for these jobs.

In 1967, Executive Order 11375 added sex discrimination to the forms of discrimination in federal employment (race, color, religion, and national origin) prohibited by Executive Order 11246. (See Chapter 3.) This order also created the Federal Women's Program "to provide leadership and direction to the Federal Government's efforts at assuring equal opportunity for women." The intent of the program was to make government agencies more aware of, and responsive to, the concerns of their women employees, to help qualified women advance their careers, to encourage more women to enter federal service at higher levels, and to eliminate attitudes and customs that are prejudicial to women and in conflict with the spirit of the merit system.[41] Each agency received instructions to draw up a formal plan of action, to designate a Federal Women's Program coordinator, and to send periodic progress reports to the Civil Service Commission.

In 1969, President Nixon's Executive Order 11478 strengthened the program established under Executive Order 11375 by requiring that affirmative action plans for equal employment opportunity apply to all employees together. The Federal Women's Program thus officially became part of the overall programs under the director of the Equal Employment Opportunity Program. The director must still maintain on the staff a qualified advisor for the women's program, a person "with empathy for and understanding of the special concerns of women in the employment situation."[42]

In response to the Executive Order and the 1970 recommendations of the President's Task Force on Women's Rights and Responsibilities, the Department of Health, Education and Welfare initiated the Women's Action Program to make recommendations for changes in their employment practices, ways of improving their programs that affect women, and future organizational arrangements for HEW's women's program.[43] In addition, in 1972, the HEW established its own Federal Women's Program to monitor its employment of women. The program is reviewing employment patterns for each occupation within each department of HEW, identifying discrimination in job-training programs, and reporting on the status of minority women in HEW. Officials in the program feel that the very fact that they are monitoring HEW's employment practices helps women employees.

In spite of these steps, the members of Federally Employed Women question the effectiveness of federal programs for female employees. They believe that female employees are often not informed about either the existence of a plan of action for their agencies or the identity of the Federal Women's Program coordinator. Further, many of the program coordinators lack the necessary "special empathy," or they retain a regular full-time position that leaves them no time for the problems of the women's program. Some field establishments ignore the problem entirely.[44]

In 1972, 33 percent of the federal white-collar workers were women. But most of these women were in the lower ranks of the civil service. Well over half of the federal employees ranked at GS 7 and below were women, and over 82 percent of the women employed by the government were in these ranks. At the same time, 4.2 percent of the employees with ranks of GS 13 and above, and less than 2 percent of the federal employees with ranks of GS 16 and above were women. One hundred and ninety-one women had ranks of GS 16 or above, and over 10,000 men were at these grades.[45]

In addition, women were unevenly distributed among the twenty-three occupational groups in the federal service; almost 90 percent of all women worked in just seven of the largest occupational groups. The Civil Service Commission's 1969 report of "Characteristics of the Federal Executive" showed that of the 2 percent of women employees above grade GS 14, most were medical or social scientists.[46] In general, a disproportionately high number of women had clerical and lower-grade technician jobs, and a disproportionately low number of women had professional and relatively high paying jobs.

Similarly, very few women receive high political appointments. Franklin D. Roosevelt appointed Frances Perkins secretary of labor, but Perkins's appointment was hardly a breakthrough.[47] Only one other woman, Oveta Culp Hobby, has since served as a cabinet officer. The number of women in federal elective offices has increased, but not significantly. In the second session of the 92nd Congress, there were only twelve women in Congress, one in the Senate and eleven in the House. In 1973, there were *no* women in the Senate and only sixteen in the House. The number of women in responsible, high-level governmental positions (both elective and appointed) is still disproportionately small. Efforts to train women for these positions are now being sponsored by the Eagleton Institute for Women in Politics at Rutgers University and by the National Women's Political Caucus.

The Foreign Service Officers Corps has hired women with great reluctance. The Foreign Service first admitted women in the 1920s, but only began to appoint them in significant numbers during the Roosevelt administration. Still, by 1954, only 1.3 percent of Foreign Service officers were women, and by 1968, less than 10 percent were women, although women held about half of the staff positions.[48]

The Foreign Service now hires, promotes, and trains women on a more equal basis with men, but inequities still exist. For example, the President's Commission on the Status of Women found that a lower percentage of women qualified in the oral examination because "closer attention is directed toward motivation and marriage plans of women than of men."[49] In 1971, the State Department admitted the denial of assignments to three African embassies to a female Foreign Service officer, Alison Palmer, because of her sex.[50]

Individual or Class:
Identifying Discrimination

Challenges to sex discrimination in employment often emphasize the right of women workers to be judged on the basis of their individual characteristics and performance rather than on average characteristics of women as a class. Paradoxically, however, sex-based averaging is an important tool for identifying sex discrimination and developing remedies to overcome it.

For example, to determine whether employers are treating women fairly, it is necessary to ask how they treat women as a group, compared to men. How many women are in managerial jobs? Do men predominate in some occupations or divisions and women in others? How do women's earnings compare, on the average, with those of men? As indicated in the previous chapter, the answers to questions like these demonstrate overwhelmingly that most employers discriminate against women workers.

Similarly sex-based averaging is used to detect discrimination in the application of rules that are neutral or appear to have no sex bias, but which actually have a differential impact on women and men. Law schools, for example, have a "sex-neutral" preference for hiring law professors who have clerked for Supreme Court justices. However, as of 1974, fewer than ten women had ever been employed in that capacity, so the policy is actually sex discriminatory. Similarly, police departments have often set minimum height and weight requirements which appear to be "neutral" on the surface but which actually disqualify many more women than men. Generally, employers develop policies to suit the needs and interests of white male workers. Since women workers *on the average* are different from men workers *on the average* in some ways, policies set in this manner are likely to harm more female workers than male workers. For example, services that many companies provide often assist men more than women. They may help their staff procure theater tickets, make travel reservations, or provide cocktail lounges for entertainment, but few companies provide day care centers or locate baby-sitters. When companies develop extra services, they rarely take into account the fact that women employees often prefer or require different services than men.

Both the right of a woman worker to be judged on her individual qualities and the right of women workers as a group to have their needs taken into account must be protected if sex discrimination in employment is to be eliminated. The next two sections of this chapter concern employee benefits and work hours, both aspects of sex discrimination.

Employee Benefits

Over the last two decades, "fringe" benefits for the American working man have increased more than twice as fast as wages and salaries. In 1967 alone, U.S. companies spent over $100 billion on employee benefits.[51] Benefits currently play a crucial role in any wage settlement and are either written into contracts at the bargaining table or are recommended by the employers.

Because many employee benefit programs discriminated against women by either providing obviously different benefits for male and female employees or failing to meet the needs of women, in April 1972 the EEOC issued guidelines regarding benefit policies toward females. Common practices with which the EEOC was concerned include unequal protection for different categories of employees (such as clerical versus professional), a practice that results in de facto discrimination when jobs are sex segregated; the exclusion or provision of only minimal coverage for part-time workers, many of whom are women; and the provision of death benefits and comprehensive health insurance to wives of male employees but not for the husbands of female employees, or even for the female employees themselves. (Such policies are based on the myth that the husband is, or should be, the primary "wage earner.") Some companies have mandatory life insurance programs that are often of less importance to women and single employees than to married men. In addition, retirement programs often pay women less per year than men at retirement because of actuarial tables based on life expectancy. For example, Teachers Insurance and Annuity Association

(TIAA) pays women 10 to 20 percent a year less than men who have contributed the same amount of money to the retirement fund, because women are expected to live longer on the average. If this principle were taken to its logical conclusion, blacks would receive higher annual retirement benefits than whites, because, on the average, they have a considerably shorter life expectancy. Present policies deny equity to women workers by assuming that each one shares the average characteristics of her sex. Instead, all workers should receive benefits based on the average life expectancy of all workers regardless of sex.

TIAA, however, intends to continue its present practices until there is a court ruling on the subject,[52] even though the policy was officially prohibited by the EEOC under its April 1972 guidelines.[53] Presently, it is also illegal to provide different benefits to families of male and female employees and to extend benefits to families of employees without giving these same benefits to employees themselves.[54]

Benefits that most often affect women are those related to childbearing and child rearing. It is not uncommon for benefit programs to treat maternity as "special" and provide less coverage for the costs of childbirth than for other medical conditions. Employers claim that the cost of giving mothers temporary disability benefits while they are having a child would be prohibitive. In fact, Aetna Life and Casualty Company estimates that the typical cost to employers to provide full maternity coverage would add an additional 9 percent, and about 80 percent of that increase would be due to the cost of covering wives of male employees.[55] One reason why employers may think the cost of temporary disability benefits for pregnancy-related disabilities is too high is the common failure to distinguish between childbearing and child-rearing leave. Under a temporary disability plan, pregnant women would receive benefits only while they were physically disabled. In most cases, this would be two to three weeks.[56]

Most benefit programs now require that a woman be married in order to receive maternity benefits, and refuse to cover the cost of abortion, regardless of the woman's marital status. Some companies have offered more restrictive maternity benefits to female employees than to wives of male employees. For example, in 1970, one insurance broker's own plan covered maternity benefits "for an employee's wife if pregnancy commences after the effective date of her insurance." However, for a female employee, maternity benefits were available only if pregnancy commenced after her insurance had been in effect for at least fifteen months. Often a woman is required to leave her job and lose both seniority and benefits after the fourth or fifth month of pregnancy, regardless of her health or ability to perform her job.

The Equal Employment Opportunity Commission's interpretation of Title VII is that a woman must be allowed leaves for childbearing and must be reinstated "to her original job, or to a position of like status and pay, without loss of service or credits."[57] But as the next chapter shows, the EEOC has a backlog of cases, and enforcement of these laws is limited.

A number of employers follow the example of a large department store that "maintains a policy of terminating the employment of pregnant women at the discretion of the management."[58] While these women may be rehired, the company is not bound to do so. Many education systems also have had a mandatory maternity leave, generally requiring a teacher to leave her job after the fifth month of pregnancy. Thus, while a teacher with a serious, chronic heart condition can decide whether or not to continue working, a pregnant teacher in good health generally has not had the same choice. Many people feel that this decision should be made by each individual woman and her doctor, not by an arbitrary administrative fiat. But those favoring the five-month rule maintain that they are protecting the women from the "pointing, giggling, and snide remarks" of students, that they are protecting the health of the woman and her unborn child, and that such a policy is an administrative necessity. Opponents of this policy maintain that this rule is arbitrary, deprives teachers of their livelihood and the pursuance of their chosen profession, disrupts the education of the students, and denies women equal protection under the Fourteenth Amendment.[59] Further, no medical reason exists for such a policy; in fact, the incapacity of pregnant women most likely occurs during the *early* stages of pregnancy.

The five-month rule has been challenged in the courts, and in January 1974 the Supreme Court held that such a practice was unconstitutional.[60] However, many school systems still maintain either official or unofficial policies requiring an interruption of teaching when the pregnancy reaches a specific stage. Although these rules vary somewhat in detail, their discriminatory effects are the same. Pregnant teachers often lose seniority, opportunities for sabbaticals, and chances for promotion.

Closely related to the five-month rule are policies prohibiting women from returning to the classroom as soon as they and their doctors feel that they are able. These policies can cause women unnecessarily to lose teaching credit, tenure, and the benefits of group insurance policies. It is ironic that previous court action allows pregnant students to return to school much more quickly than pregnant teachers.[61]

In March 1972 the EEOC ruled that childbirth and pregnancy complications are, for employment purposes, temporary disabilities that should be subject to the same leave and wage replacement benefits as other temporary disabilities.[62] Rhode Island, New Jersey, and Puerto Rico already include childbirth in temporary disability plans enacted by their legislatures. This policy has long been advocated by the Citizen's Advisory Council on the Status of Women, which argued against giving special treatment to women because in the long run such treatment would only provide an excuse for employers not to hire or promote women.[63] Furthermore, special treatment for pregnancy-related disabilities has often meant less rather than more favorable treatment.

Linked with maternity leave policies are leaves for the purpose of child rearing. While some employers, such as City College of New York, permit men to take such leaves, others limit them to women. For example, the New York City Board of Higher Education allowed women but not men to take a year's leave without loss of seniority for the purpose of child rearing. This policy was successfully challenged as a violation of the Fourteenth Amendment.[64] More equitable policies governing child-rearing leaves are required. Such a policy might permit each working parent to take up to one year of leave for each of two children without loss of benefits or seniority.

Flexible Working Hours

In many cases, employers do not directly discriminate against women. The nature of the work environment itself, however, is often designed for the life styles of most men rather than women. In many professional situations, men conduct business after office hours in bars and clubs. Many women feel uncomfortable in such situations, while others complain because male colleagues rarely invite them to join this type of session.

Work schedules are another way in which the work environment accommodates men more easily than women. Flexible working hours and vacation schedules are of particular importance to working parents. However, both employers and unions have been reluctant to explore the potential of flexible work schedules.

Hours per day, days per week, and weeks per year are measurements of working time. A full-time worker normally works eight hours a day (counting lunch and coffee breaks), five days a week, and fifty-two weeks a year, including appropriate vacation time. Employers believe that full-time workers have a relatively permanent commitment to working.

Arrangements of part-time employees vary. Some work eight hours a day for fewer than five days a week; others work every day of the week for fewer than eight hours, or forty hours a week for fewer than fifty-two weeks a year. In 1972, one worker out of seven had a part-time or part-year job. Nearly 80 percent of part-time or part-year workers in 1967 were women, although a rising percentage of men have expressed interest in part-time work.

Employers argue that being permitted to work on a permanent part-time basis is, in and of itself, a benefit. Furthermore, they argue that part-time workers are less committed to their jobs than full-time workers. Employers also often confuse regular part-time employees with temporary employees. This belief does not accurately reflect the commitment or the productivity of many part-time employees. Studies show that in some cases part-time workers are more efficient than full-time workers. In one such study, employers in fifteen federal government agencies reported that their part-time workers were at least as productive per hour as full-time employees, and in some situations were *more* efficient.[65]

Another study by the Massachusetts Department of Social Services revealed that half-time social workers carried 54 percent of the average full-time case load, averaged 58.9 percent of the productivity of the full-time staff, and devoted more individual attention to each case. Their attrition rate was "about one-third of that of full-time workers in the department."[66] These experiences demonstrate that part-time schedules and serious commitment to the job are not mutually exclusive; high-quality work depends on considerations other than the number of hours in the work week.

Many people would prefer to work part time but are unable to do so because of inflexible job situations. Twenty-seven percent of the women surveyed by the Bureau of Labor Statistics in 1968 said they preferred part-time work, but two-thirds of these women held full-time jobs.[67] On the other hand, a high proportion of women workers would like to work full time but can only find part-time or part-year jobs. According to Carolyn Shaw Bell:

While more women than men work only part of the year or less than 40 hours a week, only one out of five does so by choice. Of the 33 million women in the labor force, only six million are on a *voluntary* part-time basis. . . . Involuntary part-time work, including short work-weeks, layoffs for a day or two, and the like, greatly exceeds 20 per cent; like recent rates for unemployment, these figures run considerably higher among women workers than men.[68]

Those women who do have part-time jobs face a number of disadvantages. They are frequently excluded from benefit programs such as health and pension plans. An employee who works for a company three days a week for ten years may be eligible for fewer benefits than one who works five days a week for two years. Employers argue that the overhead required to administer a benefit program for part-time workers is costly, but the widespread use of computers suggests that most benefits can easily be calculated on a pro rata basis.

Promotion is another concern for part-time workers. In failing to consider most part-time workers for promotion, employers explain that they can assume only limited responsibility, because they are not always available to provide necessary supervision. There is little evidence to either support or contradict this statement. In some jobs, these objections may be valid, but in the vast majority of cases they probably are not. Finally, some employers are uncertain as to whether their basis for promotion should be qualitative or quantitative: should a part-time worker work twice as long as a full-time worker before being promoted? Clearly this does not make sense, but many employers are reluctant to revise their promotion policies.

In 1967, the federal government took steps to encourage part-time work opportunities when John Gardner, then Secretary of the Department of Health, Education and Welfare, announced the creation of a Professional and Executive Corps that would utilize the skills of talented people in the civil service who did not wish to work a forty-hour week. The program was designed as a model for other employers, and by May 1969 it included forty women. Questionnaires distributed among these women revealed that most had small children and could not work on a full-time basis. Yet many of these women, over half of whom were employed at the level of GS 12-GS 15, commented that they contribute well over half of their time to their jobs. These professional women, with Ph.D.s, were most disturbed about the lack of opportunity for promotion.[69]

There are other steps the government could take to encourage the employment and fair treatment of part-time workers. The failure to distinguish between temporary and permanent part-time workers discourages employers from acknowledging the contribution of part-time permanent workers to overall productivity. If the federal government required that information about permanent part-time workers be included in affirmative action plans, employers would be forced to acknowledge this contribution and redefine their employment categories. Furthermore, the government could require that salaries of part-time employees be based on the salary of full-time employees with comparable experience, doing comparable work, and that benefits also be provided on a pro rata basis.

Some companies are now experimenting with a variety of schedules to promote part-time work. Some argue that a system of two five-hour shifts a day can alleviate rush-hour traffic and simplify employees' planning family responsibilities.[70] A few employers, notably educational institutions, have hired husband-and-wife teams to share full-time positions.

Some private employment agencies are now promoting part-time work and placing part-time workers. One example is Catalyst Inc., founded in 1962 to assist female college graduates in finding part-time work. Catalyst pioneered such ideas as job sharing in high-school teaching and part-time residencies for women doctors.

Another alternative is the option of full-time employment based on the four-day, forty-hour week. A recent study of twenty-seven firms that converted to this schedule shows that they did so with no particular concern for women, but benefits to women may be a byproduct. Specifically, women found the four-day week saved them baby-sitting and commuting money and enabled them to spend more time with their children. In 1973, 1500 firms using this schedule had been identified.[71]

The acceptance of part-time employees into organizations that remain bound to the forty-hour week will not be easy. Because of high unemployment, most employees accept whatever terms employers dictate, including full-time work schedules. At the same time, during a recession, part-time work and proportionately lowered salaries appear preferable to extensive layoffs. In any event, the elimination of discrimination against part-time workers will enable both women and men with multiple commitments to join the labor force, and will make alternatives such as more flexible working hours realistic possibilities.

Conclusion

As this chapter demonstrates, attitudes of employers about women workers influence policies that employers have designed and implemented, and have helped to ensure that few women move into positions of responsibility at work.

In the past several years, some employers' policies and practices have changed. In some cases, these new practices will encourage new attitudes. Employers who find that women are effective in positions of responsibility will be more willing to give such responsibility to other women. In other cases, changing practices are not helping to form new attitudes. Some employers resent women who are asking for equal pay for equal work, and resent the federal government for requiring it. Other employers express sympathy for the goal of equal opportunity for women and believe that they do not discriminate against women. However, learning new jargon and changing patterns of behavior are two different things. As the initial interest in, and sometimes amusement at, the women's movement declines with time, it will be easy to see which employers are actually committed to equal opportunity.

Notes

1. Valerie Kincade Oppenheimer, *The Female Labor Force in the United States* (Berkeley: Institute of International Studies, University of California, 1970), pp. 104-5, 109-14.

2. Ibid., p. 103.

3. Caroline Bird, *Born Female* (New York: Pocket Books, 1969), p. 69.

4. Ibid.

5. Georgina M. Smith, *Help Wanted—Female: A Study of Demand and Supply in a Local Job Market for Women* (New Brunswick: Institute of Management and Labor Relations, Rutgers University), p. 11.

6. Ibid., p. 24.

7. Ibid.

8. Valerie Kincade Oppenheimer, "The Sex-Labeling of Jobs," *Industrial Relations*, May 1968, pp. 226-27.

9. E.W. Noland and E.W. Bakke, *Workers Wanted: A Study of Employers' Hiring Policies, Preferences and Practices in New Haven and Charlotte* (New York: Harper, 1949), pp. 184-85. In a study of job opportunities for women as technicians, the Women's Bureau found that in the electronics field, for example, "firms producing large electronic units often require their technicians to lift and move heavy equipment; they may, therefore, refuse to hire a woman for such work if they think it is beyond her strength" ("Careers for Women as Technicians," Women's Bureau Bulletin 282 [Washington, D.C., 1962]), p. 3.

10. Oppenheimer, "The Sex-Labeling of Jobs," p. 227.

11. Charles E. Ginder, "Factors of Sex in Office Employment," *Office Executive*, February 1961, p. 11.

12. Theodore Caplow, *The Sociology of Work* (Minneapolis: University of Minnesota Press, 1954), p. 137.

83

13. Ibid., p. 238.

14. Smith, *Help Wanted—Female*, p. 25.

15. Ibid., p. 26.

16. U.S., Congress, Senate, *Congressional Record*, 92nd Cong., 2nd sess., 1972, 118, pp. E1242-58.
E1242-58.

17. Ibid., p. E1252.

18. Harvey Shapiro, "Women on the Line, Men on the Switchboard," *New York Times Magazine*, May 20, 1973, p. 26.

19. *Congressional Record*, p. E1246.

20. Ibid., p. E1253.

21. Ibid., p. E1252.

22. Ibid., pp. E1249-50.

23. Ibid., p. E1244.

24. Ibid., p. E1250.

25. Ibid., p. E1249.

26. Ibid., p. E1244.

27. U.S., Equal Employment Opportunity Commission, *Equal Employment Opportunity Commission Finding*, no. 2288 (1965).

28. *Congressional Record*, pp. E1254-56.

29. *Women Today*, Vol. 3, No. 3, February 5, 1973; Shapiro, op. cit.

30. *Spokeswoman*, Vol. 3, No. 8, February 15, 1973.

31. *Women Today*, Vol. 3, No. 4, February 19, 1973.

32. *New York Times*, May 31, 1974.

33. *Spokeswoman*, Vol. 4, No. 11, May 15, 1974.

34. "Wages and Women," *Time*, June 17, 1974, p. 90.

35. U.S., Civil Service Commission, Manpower Statistics Division, prepared for Federal Women's Program, *Study of Employment of Women in the Federal Government* (1973), p. 7.

36. President's Commission on the Status of Women, *Report of the Committee on Federal Employment* (1963), pp. 8-9.

37. Ibid., pp. 7-8.

38. Ibid., pp. 8-9.

39. Ibid., p. 13.

40. Ibid., p. 12.

41. U.S., Congress, House Committee on Education and Labor, Special Subcommittee on Education, *Statement of Irving Kator*, July 31, 1970, p. 3.
Assistant Executive Director, U.S. Civil Service Commission, July 31, 1970, p. 3.

42. Ibid., p. 13.

43. U.S., Department of Health, Education and Welfare, *Report of the Women's Action Program*, January 1972, p. 1.

44. U.S., Congress, House Committee on Education and Labor, Special Subcommittee on Education, *Statement of Mrs. Daisy B. Field*, June 29, 1970, pp. 6-9.

45. *Study of Employment of Women in the Federal Government,* 1972, p. 13.

46. *Report of the Women's Action Program,* p. 74.

47. *Report of the Committee on Federal Employment,* pp. 51-55.

48. U.S., Department of Labor, Women's Bureau, *1969 Handbook on Women Workers,* p. 121.

49. *Report of the Committee on Federal Employment,* p. 45.

50. "Foreign Service: Tally's Triumph," *Time,* September 6, 1971, p. 20.

51. T.J. Gordon and R.E. LeBleu, "Employee Benefits, 1970-1985," *Harvard Business Review,* January/February 1970, p. 4.

52. Carnegie Commission on Higher Education, *Opportunites for Women in Higher Education: Their Current Participation, Prospects for the Future, and Recommendations for Action* (New York: McGraw-Hill, 1973), pp. 145, 146.

53. Erica Grubb, "Love's Labors Lost: New Conception of Maternity Leaves," *Harvard Civil Rights–Civil Liberties Law Review* (1972), p. 27.

54. For a discussion of how the Social Security system discriminates against women workers, see Carolyn Shaw Bell, "Women and Social Security: Contributions and Benefits," a paper prepared for the hearings of the Joint Economic Committee on the Economic Problems of Women on July 25, 1973, and Carolyn Shaw Bell, "Social Security: Society's Last Discrimination," *Business and Society Review,* Autumn 1972, p. 45.

55. Grubb, "Love's Labors Lost," p. 27.

56. See the Testimony of Dr. Andre E. Hellegers Before the Federal Communications Commission, Docket No. 19143. In the Matter of Petitions filed by the Equal Employment Opportunity Commission February 14, 1972. Dr. Hellegers was a Professor of Obstetrics-Gynecology at Georgetown University Hospital who testified that women need not cease working during a normal pregnancy until the onset of labor, and that the period of disability following childbirth was seven to ten days at a minimum, two to three weeks on the average, and six weeks at a maximum.

57. *Equal Employment Opportunity Commission Decision* # 71-562, December 4, 1970, and # 71-144, March 1971.

58. Grubb, p. 270.

59. "Discriminating Against the Pregnant Teacher," *Today's Education,* December 1971, p. 33.

60. *Cleveland Board of Education et al v. LaFleur et al.,* 94 S.Ct. 791 (1974).

61. John Carmody, "Fighting the Five Month Rule," *The Washington Post,* December 23, 1971, p. C2.

62. EEOC Guidelines, Title 29, Labor, Chapter XIV, Part 1604 as amended, March 31, 1972. *Geduldig v. Ajello,* 42 U.S. L.W. 4905 (June 17, 1974), a Fourteenth Amendment decision about temporary disabilities caused by pregnancy and childbirth is discussed in chapter 3.

63. Address by Jacqueline Gutwillig, chairwoman, Citizens' Advisory Council on the Status of Women, to the Conference of Interstate Association of

Commissions on the Status of Women, St. Louis, Missouri, June 19, 1971, p. 5.

64. *Danielson v. Board of Higher Education*, 4 FEP Cases 885 (S.D.N.Y. 1972).

65. Federally Employed Women, *ABC's of Your Job: A Handbook on Personnel Management Matters*, "Fact-Sheet #2: The ABC of Part-Time Work" (Washington, D.C.: F.E.W., Inc., June, 1971), p. 1.

66. Lawrence Podell, *Evaluation Research Report on the Catalyst Demonstration Project to Employ Mature, College-Graduated Women as Caseworkers in Public Welfare in Boston* (Boston: Catalyst, Inc., June 1970), pp. 18-22.

67. *1969 Handbook on Women Workers*, pp. 63-66. *Workers*. Bulletin 294, pp. 63-66.

68. Carolyn Shaw Bell, "Age, Sex, Marriage and Jobs," *The Public Interest*, Winter 1973, p. 79.

69. Marjorie Silverberg and Lorraine B. Eyde, *Career Part-time Employment: Personnel Implications of the Health, Education, and Welfare Professional and Executive Corps* (Washington, D.C.: U.S. Government Printing Office, 1970), p. 10.

70. E.C. Weiss, "Here Comes the Two-Shift, Five Hour Work Day," *Advertising Age*, August 10, 1970.

71. Riva Poor, *Four Days, Forty Hours* (New York, 1973), p. 39.

3 Employer Sex Discrimination and the Law

In the 1960s and early 1970s a number of federal laws prohibiting sex discrimination in employment were enacted and existing legislation was modified to cover sex discrimination. Increasing numbers of women have been seeking to use them to force employers to change discriminatory practices, with greater success under some statutes than others. The following is a brief account of some of the laws, their scope, the developing case law interpreting them, and the advantages and disadvantages of each.

The Equal Pay Act of 1963

The Equal Pay Act (EPA) is the oldest federal legislation prohibiting discrimination on the basis of sex. Enacted in 1963 as an amendment to the Fair Labor Standards Act of 1938 (FLSA), it prohibits differential rates to pay for women and men who:

do equal work on jobs, the performance of which requires equal skill, effort, and responsibility, and which are performed under similar working conditions, except where such payment is made pursuant to (i) a seniority system; (ii) a merit system; (iii) a system which measures earnings by quantity or equality of production; or (iv) a differential based on any other factor other than sex.[1]

If an unjust wage differential is found, employers must raise the wage rate of the lower-paid group. Wage reduction, in an attempt to comply with the act, is illegal. Furthermore, labor unions are forbidden from causing or attempting to cause an employer to violate the act.

Coverage

Until July 1972, the Equal Pay Act applied only to those employees who were covered by the minimum-wage requirements of the Fair Labor Standards Act. Because this act only covers employees who work for establishments that do business of at least $250,000 a year, many employees (including those in small retail establishments, restaurants, and beauty shops) were not protected. Employees in agriculture, seasonal amusement or recreational establishments, motion-picture theaters, certain small newspapers, hotels, motels, and laundries were also specifically excluded from coverage. In 1972, of the 11.3 million workers who were excluded from protective coverage under the FLSA, approximately 5 million were women.

The Education Amendments of 1972[2] amended the act to cover executive, administrative and professional employees (including teachers), and outside sales employees, all of whom had previously been excluded from coverage.

Equal Work

The interpretation of the phrase "equal work" is crucial to an understanding of the act.[3] In the landmark case of *Shultz v. Wheaton Glass*, the Third Circuit Court of Appeals explained: "Congress in prescribing 'equal' work did not require that the jobs be identical, but only that they must be *substantially equal.* Any other interpretation would destroy the remedial purpose of the Act"[4] (emphasis added). In determining whether or not the work involved is substantially equal, the courts must analyze jobs in terms of the four factors specifically set out in the Equal Pay Act itself: skill, effort, responsibility, and similar working conditions. The most important of these factors is equal effort. In case after case, employers have tried to justify higher wages for men because the men are assigned a few extra lifting duties. Most courts have rejected this contention.

In a case comparing the jobs of male orderlies and female nurse's aides in a hospital, the Fifth Circuit Court of Appeals concisely summarized the standards to be used in determining whether or not equal effort is involved in jobs compared under the EPA:

The equal effort criterion has received substantial play in the reported cases to date. As the doctrine is emerging, jobs do not entail equal effort, even though they entail most of the same routine duties, if the more highly paid job involves additional tasks which (1) require extra effort, (2) consume a significant amount of the time of all those whose pay differentials are to be justified in terms of them, and (3) are of an economic value commensurate with the pay differential. We are persuaded that this approach to the application of the statutory "equal effort" criterion is in keeping with the fundamental purposes of the Equal Pay Act, and adopt it here. Employers may not be permitted to frustrate the purposes of the Act by calling for extra effort only occasionally, or only from one or two male employees, or by paying males substantially more than females for the performance of tasks which command a low rate of pay when performed full time by other personnel in the same establishment.[5]

Affirmative Defenses to Equal Pay Suits

The Equal Pay Act permits pay differentials between male and female employees if these differentials are based on a seniority system, a merit system, a system that measures earnings by quality or quantity of production, or "any other factor other than sex." The first three factors have been of relatively little significance in EPA litigation.[6] However, under "any other factor other than sex," companies have raised a number of issues. For example, in *Hodgson v. Behrens Drug Co.*,[7] the Fifth Circuit Court of Appeals considered a claim that wage differentials between male "sales trainees" and female "order clerks" (who had been held to be doing equal work) were justified because the men were enrolled in a bona fide training program. Although the court found some substance to the claim, it was not accepted as justification for wage discrimination, because, among other things, women were arbitrarily excluded from the program. The court commented, "In light of . . . the clear purpose of the Equal Pay Act, a training program coterminous with a stereotyped province called 'man's work' cannot qualify as a factor other than sex."[8]

A particularly troubling case is *Hodgson v. Robert Hall Clothes, Inc.*[9] The Secretary of Labor challenged differentials in pay between salespersons (all women) selling women's clothes and salespersons (all men) selling men's clothes. Robert Hall claimed that the men's higher wages were based on the higher average profits per sales-hour earned in the men's clothing department. However, the greater profits were in a large part because there was a greater markup on men's clothes; men's clothes were also more expensive and had a lower turnover. Therefore, the bonuses for men's sales were higher due to factors related to the goods being sold and not to any demonstrable difference in the selling performance of the men. Furthermore, on at least some occasions, some women sold a higher dollar volume of merchandise per hour than some men; yet their wages were lower because they were based on the lower female wage and incentive structure. Therefore, female employees were discriminated against on two accounts. First, their work assignments, which were determined according to sex, were less profitable, and second, because their wages were based on a sex-based profit average, their earnings remained low, even if their individual performance was exceptional. It seems likely that the court was moved to rule in favor of Robert Hall Clothes by its conclusion that the sex segregation of jobs was justified by privacy. However, in another case, *Wirtz v. Midwest Mfg. Corp.*,[10] the court refused to allow higher wages for men performing equal work with women, despite the company's contention that it cost more to employ women due to higher insurance costs.

In general, it appears that courts are prepared to use the EPA to maximize the remedial effects of the Act. The judicial doctrines interpreting equal work and "any other factor other than sex," in particular, encourage courts to look carefully at the facts of each case, rather than to accept stereotypes and excuses as justifications for wage discrimination against women.

Enforcement

As part of the minimum wage provisions, the Department of Labor's Wage and Hour Division has the authority to enforce the Equal Pay Act. The Wage and Hour Division can issue interpretive opinions, investigate companies or unions to uncover violations, and bring suit to enjoin violations by employers and unions to recover unpaid wages from employers. The division has over one thousand compliance officers throughout the country who routinely visit employers to check their compliance with the EPA, the federal minimum-wage standards, and other laws within the division's purview. Equal pay complaints were brought against 385 establishments in fiscal year 1969, 736 in 1970, 1203 in 1971, and 1115 in 1972.[11] While the Wage and Hour Division only records the number of establishments against which complaints are made, the Equal Employment Opportunity Commission (EEOC) tabulates each individual complaint. In 1971 the EEOC received over 5800 sex-discrimination complaints and over 26,600 actionable complaints altogether, and seems, even with the different method of counting complaints, to be dealing with many more cases than the Wage and Hour Division.[12]

Although some corrective measures have been taken, Morag Simchak, special assistant to the assistant secretary of labor for employment standards, estimated that from June 1964 through fiscal year 1972, employers paid only about a third of the $47 million that the Wage and Hour Division has found owing to almost 113,000 employees, almost all of whom were women. About $4 million of this estimated $15.7 million had been recovered through court action or through out-of-court settlement of suits.[13] More recently, in the six months between July 1 and December 31, 1973, employers paid over $3 million to employees as a result of court cases brought under the EPA.

Back-pay awards may cover a three-year period in cases where "willful violation" is found and two years where the violation is "not willful." Decisions on back wages serve as an incentive for individuals to bring suit and as a deterrent to employers who might otherwise risk violating the law. However, the greatest impact of Equal Pay Act enforcement will be to raise the level of the take-home pay of women workers to equal that of men and to eliminate sex-based wage classifications.

If the secretary of labor does not take action after it has been requested, individual employees may bring suit. As of December 1974, over six hundred suits had been brought to court under the act, most of which were filed by the secretary of labor, rather than by individuals. Less than a dozen suits to enjoin labor union practices have yet been filed.[14]

In terms of enforceability, the Equal Pay Act is one of the better pieces of federal employment legislation. Unfortunately, the employment patterns of women are such that the legislation has a much smaller impact than one might expect. First, gaps in coverage mean that many women are not protected against sex-based wage discrimination. Second, in industrial jobs, an important area of women's employment, positions are frequently sex segregated both by company and by job categories. Thus, women are often paid less because they are assigned to "women's" jobs that pay less, rather than because they are paid less for the same work. When both men and women do have the same occupation, it is still common for individual establishments to employ only workers of the same sex in a given occupational category. For example, some companies employ either male or female elevator operators, not both. Those that employ only women elevator operators generally pay less for the same work than companies that employ only, or predominantly, men; yet they cannot be sued for violation of the Equal Pay Act.

Title VII of the Civil Rights Act of 1964

The federal legislation that covers the most workers and the widest array of discriminatory practices is Title VII of the 1964 Civil Rights Act. In March 1972, a number of substantial changes in the enforcement mechanisms and coverage provisions of Title VII were enacted. This section focuses on the present scope of the law; references to previous provisions of the act are included to highlight the most significant of the recent changes.[15]

Coverage

From June 1967 until March 24, 1972, the act covered private employers with twenty-five or more employees for twenty or more weeks in the current or preceding calendar year and labor unions with twenty-five or more members. Employers who were exempt from coverage were educational institutions with regard to educational personnel, certain religious institutions with regard to the employment of individuals of a particular religion, bona fide private membership clubs, Indian tribes, and government-owned corporations.[16]

As of March 24, 1972, Title VII's coverage was expanded to include those employed by educational institutions, governmental agencies, and state and local governments, with the exception of elected officials and some staff members. The increased coverage allowed employees of the federal government to bring civil suits against the heads of their departments, agencies, or units under certain circumstances.[17] As of March 24, 1973, employers hiring between fifteen and twenty-five employees as well as labor unions with fifteen to twenty-five members were covered under Title VII.[18]

Both public and private employment agencies are subject to the provisions of the act if they deal with covered employers. Thus, as the number of employers covered by Title VII increases, the number of employment agencies covered also increases.

Unlawful Practices

An employer covered by Title VII may not discriminate in hiring or firing, wages, terms, conditions or privileges of employment, or in training, retraining, or apprenticeships. Further, an employer may not "limit, segregate or classify his employees or applicants for employment" in a discriminatory manner because of race, color, religion, sex, or national origin. An employer, labor union, joint labor-management committee supervising apprenticeship or training, or employment agency cannot advertise discriminatory preferences, limitations, or specifications for employment, membership, training, or referral. Nor can employers or employment agencies discriminate in receiving and processing applications or in referring people to jobs. Labor unions cannot exclude or expel from membership, discriminate against any individual, limit, segregate, or classify membership, or refer or fail to refer for employment or attempt to cause employers to discriminate on the basis of race, color, religion, sex, or national origin. Further, no organization covered by Title VII may discriminate against any person because he or she has opposed any unlawful practices or participated in any action under Title VII.[19]

Exceptions to Title VII occur when religion, sex, or national origin (but not race) is found to be a bona fide occupational qualification that is "reasonably necessary to the normal operation of that particular business or enterprise."[20] In addition, employees may be treated differently if they work in different locations, if there is a bona fide seniority or merit system, or if a system measures earnings by quantity or quality of production. Employers may also discriminate when filling positions relating to national security, and no employer can be required to employ members of the Communist party or certain other organizations.

Some of these provisions have been litigated extensively over the past few years; both judicial and administrative rulings on the major issues that have been raised are discussed below.

Enforcement

Under Title VII of the Civil Rights Act of 1964, there were three instrumentalities of enforcement: the aggrieved individual, the Equal Employment Opportunity Commission (EEOC), and the attorney general.[21] Prior to the 1972 amendments, the aggrieved party assumed "the primary responsibility for enforcing Title VII through the mechanism of a private action in federal district court." This "private action was specifically endowed with public interest characteristics," including provisions for "Justice Department intervention, . . . appointment of counsel at the discretion of the court, and for the discretionary award of attorney's fees to victorious litigants," and for "discretionary relief in the form of affirmative action and back pay."[22]

In addition to private enforcement with possible Justice Department intervention, the attorney general was empowered to bring suit in the government's name when a pattern or practice of discrimination had occurred. On the other hand, the EEOC, a five-member body appointed by the president, had no power to go into court on the behalf of the government or the aggrieved individuals, although the EEOC general counsel's office played a role as a "friend of the court" in many private Title VII suits. Instead, the EEOC was limited to using "conference, conciliation and persuasion." Title VII's enforcement was further weakened by the requirement that the EEOC defer to state enforcement proceedings for at least sixty days in those states having an antidiscrimination law and enforcement agency.[23] Private court action, in turn, was delayed an additional sixty days after the EEOC took jurisdiction of the complaint to allow time for EEOC conciliation procedures.

Unfortunately, EEOC conciliation procedures have been notoriously unsuccessful: in fiscal year 1966, 82 percent of the 68 conciliation attempts were successful or partially successful; by fiscal 1969, this figure had declined to 49 percent of the 774 conciliation attempts.[24] Furthermore, the EEOC was unable to handle investigatory and conciliatory functions for the enormous volume of complaints it received. Soon the commission had a backlog that created an average delay of four or five months before an investigation began, and another twenty months before the conciliation process was completed.[25]

Substantial changes were enacted in 1972 due to widespread dissatisfaction with the original enforcement mechanisms of Title VII.[26] Of particular importance are provisions empowering the EEOC to intervene in private actions brought under the act and to go directly into federal district court to seek judicial enforcement of Title VII against private employers, if conciliation efforts fail. The attorney general is granted the power to seek judicial enforcement of Title VII against state governments, agencies, and political subdivisions if EEOC conciliation efforts fail. The pattern and practice enforcement power of the attorney general was transferred to the commission in March 1974. In addition, although the federal government as an employer is still exempt from the provisions of Title VII, federal employees and applicants for federal employment who believe they have suffered employment discrimination by the federal government may bring civil suit in federal district court 180 days after filing a complaint with the Civil Service Commission or the relevant department, unit, or agency.[27] One other significant change in Title VII is the extension of the time within which a charge must be filed or a civil action brought. Before March 24, 1972, a charge had to be filed within ninety days of the alleged violation, and suit had to be brought within thirty days after the EEOC notified the complainant of his or her right to sue. This time limit has now been extended to 180 days for filing a charge, and ninety days after EEOC notification to file a civil action in federal court.[28] The EEOC may go to court within thirty days after it has received the initial complaint or within ninety days after the complaint was filed with a state enforcement agency. A private party, however, may not sue until 180 days after the filing of the charge with the EEOC (unless the case is dismissed by the EEOC at an earlier date), although he or she may intervene in any suit brought by the attorney general or the EEOC before that time expires.[29]

Under the old provisions of Title VII, the EEOC did develop some imaginative substitutes for the enforcement procedures it lacked. In addition to filing *amicus curiae* briefs in private suits, the commission issued interpretive guidelines that have been given considerable weight by the courts, held hearings on employment discrimination problems, testified before state and federal legislative committees, and filed charges of discrimination with other federal administrative agencies, notably against the American Telephone and Telegraph Company in rate increase hearings before the Federal Communications Commission. Presumably the commission will continue these activities.

Bona Fide Occupational Qualifications

As we mentioned earlier, Title VII does have one major exception: an employer may discriminate on the basis of religion, sex, or national origin if the factor can be shown to be a bona fide occupational qualification (BFOQ) that is reasonably necessary to the normal operation of his or her business. The EEOC and the courts have clarified the definition of BFOQ and taken a very strong position on its interpretation.

EEOC sex discrimination guidelines state: "The bona fide occupational qualification exception as to sex should be interpreted narrowly. Labels—"Men's jobs" and "Women's jobs"—tend to deny employment opportunities unnecessarily to one sex or the other."[30]

"Stereotyped characterizations of the sexes," "preferences of coworkers, the employer, clients or customers," the existence of state laws and regulations that prohibit or limit the employment of females, or the fact that the employer may have to provide separate restroom facilities for a person of the opposite sex are not sufficient reasons for sex discrimination.[31] The only situation in which the commission recognizes that sex differentiation might be permitted is "where it is necessary for the purpose of authenticity or genuineness.[32] Actors and actresses, for example, can be employed according to sex.

There have also been numerous court interpretations of this provision. The Fifth Circuit Court of Appeals gave the first broadly applicable judicial interpretation of the BFOQ provision in the case of *Weeks v. Southern Bell Telephone & Telegraph Co.*[33] In *Weeks*, a female employee of nineteen years bid for the job of switchman, which was granted to a male with less seniority, ostensibly on the ground that a Georgia weight regulation, prohibiting any woman from being required to lift over thirty pounds, forbade awarding the job to Weeks. The district court accepted this argument. After the district court had ruled, Georgia repealed its weight limitation. However, on appeal, the company relied on the district court's finding that the job was strenuous and on its right to use a private restrictive thirty-pound weight policy for women, even in the absence of state law to this effect. The Fifth Circuit reversed the lower court, saying that "the employer has the burden of proving that he has reasonable cause to believe, *that is a factual basis* for believing, *that all or substantially all* women would be unable to perform safely and efficiently the duties of the job involved"[34] (emphasis added). It held that the company had failed to meet this burden, because it had submitted no evidence on the issue, but rather had relied on unproven stereotypes about the lifting abilities of women.

A district court first applied the *Weeks* BFOQ standard in *Cheatwood v. South Cent. Bell Tel. & Tel. Co.*[35] The court heard detailed medical testimony from both parties concerning the differences between the ability of men and women to lift heavy weights and determined that selecting applicants for that particular job on the basis of sex was unlawful because at least 25 to 50 percent of all females could do the job.

The Seventh Circuit Court of Appeals followed the *Weeks* lead in *Bowe v. Colgate-Palmolive Co.*[36] by invalidating another company-imposed weight restriction that applied to women only. Colgate-Palmolive had promulgated a weight limit of thirty-five pounds only for women shortly after the passage of Title VII in order to maintain their sex-segregated job system under the guise of protecting women. The court held that, although the weight requirement was invalid if it applied only to women, the company had the options of retaining a weight-lifting limit if they were willing to apply it to all employees, both male and female, or if they instituted individual testing of weight-lifting ability for both male and female workers. The *Bowe* court's definition of the BFOQ was much narrower than that set forth in the *Weeks* case, although its practical effect, the abolition of the weight-lifting limit for women, was the same.

The trend toward narrowly defining the BFOQ provision was continued in *Rosenfeld v. Southern Pacific Co.*[37] Leah Rosenfeld, an employee for twenty-two years, bid for the position of agent-telegrapher with Southern Pacific. Although she was the most senior employee bidding for the job, it was awarded to a male with less seniority on the grounds that awarding the job to the plaintiff would violate both company policy and the California hours and weight laws restricting the employment of women. The district court held in favor of the plaintiff. In the appeal by the company and the State of California, which had intervened in the case, the Court of Appeals for the Ninth Circuit ruled that the physical requirements of the job of agent-telegrapher, allegedly involving long hours (especially during harvest season), strenuous work (climbing in and around boxcars), and lifting heavy objects did not establish a BFOQ. The court set forth the following interpretation of the BFOQ provision, basing its holding on its understanding of the legislative history and on the EEOC's sex discrimination guidelines: "sexual characteristics, rather than characteristics that might, to one degree or another, correlate with a particular sex, must be the basis for the application of the BFOQ exception."[38]

The court used wet nurses, actors, and actresses as examples of jobs to which the BFOQ exception might apply, thus making clear that the "sexual characteristics" to which the opinion referred were physical characteristics unique to one sex rather than "characteristics generally attributed to the group." The court equated this with the *Bowe* court's holding that both male and female employees can only be excluded from jobs upon a showing of individual incapacity.

The case of *Dias v. Pan American World Airways, Inc.*[39] is important for several reasons. At issue was whether or not an airline could restrict the position of flight cabin attendant to the female sex on the grounds that sex was a BFOQ for the job. The district court held that the defendant's practice was based on a BFOQ and was not in violation of Title VII. The court based this decision, which was in contradiction to previous court decisions, on the testimony of Pan American's expert witness, a psychiatrist, that women were psychologically better equipped than men to handle the unusual anxiety, boredom, and excitement that various passengers experienced as a result of air travel, and the testimony of Pan American officials that the extreme difficulty of identifying the few men who were psychologically equipped to do the job as well as women made it a business necessity that only women be considered for the job. The district court also held (despite the EEOC's position to the contrary) that Title VII's legislative history demonstrated that Congress intended customer preference to be a permissible basis for finding a BFOQ and took the customer preference for female flight attendants documented by a Pan American customer survey into account in deciding the case.

The circuit court reversed the district court decision, stating that "discrimination based on sex is valid only when the *essence* of the business operation would be undermined by not hiring members of one sex exclusively."[40] Thus, the court held that customer preference can only be considered in situations where the essential nature of the business is the satisfaction of certain customer preferences.[41] The court found that the "primary function of an airline is to transport passengers safely from one point to another," not to satisfy customer preference for female flight attendants, and that although the characteristics of stewardesses may be important, they "are tangential to the essence of the business involved."[42]

State Protective Labor Laws and Title VII

The position of the EEOC and the court decisions described here have made it apparent that the provisions for equality of employment opportunities under Title VII of the Civil Rights Act of 1964 and the impending ratification of the ERA supersede restrictive, "protective" legislation on the state level, and that in no instance does the existence of such state laws justify using sex as a BFOQ exception.

While there are many types of labor laws applicable to women only, they can be broken down into three broad categories: laws that confer supposed *benefits*, such as minimum wage, a day of rest, a meal, a rest period, or the provision of chairs during rest periods; laws that *exclude* women from certain jobs, such as mining or bartending, or from employment in any job before or after childbirth; laws that *restrict* women's employment under certain conditions, such as laws that prevent women from working at night, from working more than a certain number of hours, or from being hired for jobs that require lifting weights over a set limit.

The last two categories, laws that exclude or restrict, are clearly discriminatory. However, even laws providing benefits such as a minimum wage or rest periods can operate to discriminate against either women or men, or both. Men are discriminated against whenever these laws deny them benefits. Women are discriminated against when an employer uses the "special" status or the "special" benefits they have (such as rest periods) as a rationalization to pay them less, to deny them access to certain jobs, or to lay them off first. Title VII has paved the way for the repeal of exclusionary and restrictive state "protective" laws that apply to women only and the extension of benefit laws to cover men as well as women.

The EEOC position regarding state protective laws that exclude women from certain jobs or restrict women's employment under certain conditions is strong. The 1972 guidelines declare:

Such laws and regulations do not take into account the capacities, preferences, and abilities of individual females and, therefore, discriminate on the basis of sex. The Commission has concluded that such laws and regulations conflict with and are superseded by Title VII of the Civil Rights Act of 1964. Accordingly, such laws will not be considered a defense to an otherwise established unlawful employment practice or as a basis for the application of the *bona fide* occupational qualification exception.[43]

Comparable language was included in the 1969 guidelines.[44] Court decisions, such as the *Rosenfeld* case, described earlier, are in congruence with these guidelines.[45]

Similarly, both the EEOC and the courts have advocated extending to men benefits, such as special rest or meal periods, that applied only to women. This policy is clearly preferable to denying the benefits to women. The Equal Pay Act, for example, expressly requires that wage differentials be eliminated by raising the lower rate of pay to the higher. EEOC guidelines specify that provision of benefits to one sex only will be a violation of Title VII.

The cases at the district and state court levels have been divided on the question of whether benefit-conferring laws will be struck down or extended to men under Title VII; and at least one state attorney general has ruled that a law conferring benefits on women only was invalid under Title VII.[46] However, in July 1972 a landmark decision was handed down by the Eighth Circuit Court of

Appeals in the case of *Hays v. Potlatch Forests, Inc.*,[47] which may well settle the issue in favor of the extension of benefits.

In the *Potlatch* case, the issue was a state law requiring that women be paid time and a half for overtime. The union filed a complaint under Title VII alleging that male employees at Potlatch were paid less than female employees for overtime. Therefore, the employer went into court separately to obtain a ruling on the validity of the state law. The employer, the EEOC, and the union all agreed that Title VII required that men and women be paid at the same rate. The employer sought the invalidation of the state law so that he would not have to pay time and a half for overtime to either male or female employees.

The district court ruled that there was no conflict with Title VII because the employer could comply with both state law and Title VII by paying the overtime premium rate to both male and female employees.[48] The circuit court upheld the decision.[49]

In reaching the conclusion that Title VII required the extension of benefits rather than the invalidation of the law, the court relied in part on the precedents set under the Equal Pay Act and the EEOC's position. The circuit court quoted the lower court's statement that "it certainly does not 'impede' or 'frustrate' the purpose of [Title VII] to require an Arkansas employer to eliminate discrimination by paying its male employees more than it would pay them ordinarily in order to equalize their pay with that of women"[50] and pointed out that, unlike laws that restrict the employment of members of one sex (e.g., maximum hours and weight-lifting laws), "no unreasonable burdens are imposed [on the employer] by extending the benefits of the Arkansas statute to male employees."[51]

The Equal Rights Amendment and Title VII

The effect of the Equal Rights Amendment on protective labor legislation has been hotly debated. The constitutional amendment, which passed Congress in 1972 after being introduced to every session since 1923, has, as of June 1974, been ratified by thirty-three states. Five more must ratify the amendment before it can become law. Even some people who favor the concept of equal rights for women and men have been concerned that the amendment would cause working women to lose gains or concessions they fought hard to achieve during the late nineteenth and early twentieth centuries. It has become evident, however, that although these laws were originally enacted to prevent unscrupulous or thoughtless employers from exploiting working women, they have often become barriers both to equal employment opportunity for women and to improved working conditions for men. The effect of these laws has been more repressive than protective. The uneven coverage, the wide variation among states, the number of exceptions for jobs, and the outright exclusion of women from many lucrative jobs dramatizes this.

The Equal Rights Amendment stresses the need for "a consistent theory and program for women's equality on a national level, in order to finally dislodge discriminatory laws, doctrines, attitudes and practices which are deep set on our legal system."[52] Until recently, the need to ratify a constitutional amendment to affect the necessary changes towards reaching this goal was never taken seriously. The ratification of the Equal Rights Amendment will have only a limited impact on the situation of most women workers in relation to protective labor legislation, since Title VII has already caused many of the so-called protective laws to be declared invalid or to be extended to men. But the passage of the amendment is important for psychological and political reasons, and its impact on family law and military service will be considerable.

The fundamental legal principle underlying the Equal Rights Amendment is that the law must deal with particular attributes of individuals, not with classifications based on sex. Therefore, if passed, the Equal Rights Amendment will in many ways accelerate present trends toward legal equality.

"Sex Plus"

An argument that some employers have tried to use as a defense to a Title VII prosecution is that they discriminate not against men or women as such, but only against a subclass of men or women. For example, an employer may discharge women, but not men, upon marriage, or refuse to hire men, but not women, with long hair. The employer would argue that he doesn't discriminate against all women, but only against women who are also married; or not against all men, but only against men with long hair. In other words, he tries to get the court to agree that, while Title VII prohibits discrimination on the basis of sex, it does not affect discrimination on the basis of "coalescence" of sex and another factor, e.g., "sex plus" marriage or "sex plus" long hair.

A case based on the issue of "sex plus" was the first sex-discrimination case to reach the Supreme Court under Title VII—*Phillips v. Martin Marietta Corp.*[53] On September 6, 1966, Ida Phillips, a woman with preschool children, applied for one of a hundred positions at Martin Marietta as an assembly trainee. She was told by a receptionist that female applicants with children of preschool age would not be considered for the job. However, both the district court and the Fifth Circuit Court agreed that Title VII applied to "discrimination based *solely* on one of the categories, i.e., in the case of sex, women vis-à-vis men"[54] (emphasis added). The court reasoned that "when another criterion of employment is added to one of the classifications listed in the Act, there is no longer apparent discrimination based solely on race, color, religion, sex, or national origin."[55] Contrary to the legislative history of Title VII, of which the lower courts were apparently unaware, the courts argued that Congress could not have possibly intended to preclude any considerations by employers of the differences between the relationships of working fathers and working mothers to their preschool children.[56] In his dissent from the decision of the Fifth Circuit Court of Appeals denying a petition for a hearing in the *Phillips* case, Judge Brown said, "If 'sex plus' stands, the Act is dead. Free to add nonsex factors, the rankest sort of discrimination against women can be worked by employers."

The U.S. Supreme Court vacated and remanded the decision of the court of appeals, stating in a *per curiam* opinion that "under Title VII, persons of like qualifications must be extended equal employment opportunities irrespective of sex. The Court of Appeals therefore erred in reading this section as permitting one hiring policy for women and another for men—each having preschool age children."[57]

There are several other areas in which the issue of "sex plus" either has arisen or can be expected to arise in the near future. One of these areas is "sex plus" marriage. Some employers, specifically airlines, have traditionally refused to hire married stewardesses. With only one exception (*Cooper v. Delta Airlines, Inc.,*[58] a case decided before the Supreme Court ruled in the *Phillips* case) the courts have held that refusing to hire an employee because of the combination of sex and marital status is in violation of Title VII. In *Lansdale v. United Air Lines, Inc.* and *Lansdale v. Air Lines Pilots Ass'n.,*[59] the Fifth Circuit Court of Appeals reversed the district court's finding for the defendant.[60] Other courts have also held that, without a BFOQ showing, a marriage ban cannot be applied to women employees only. It is unlikely that BFOQ standards would allow discrimination in such situations.

The EEOC has taken a stand on several other "sex plus" issues, including discrimination against men (but not women) with long hair[61] or against unwed mothers (but not fathers)[62] and unequal treatment of women or men of the same age.[63] In general, the courts are following the lead of the EEOC in finding that discrimination based on "sex plus" some neutral factor is in violation of Title VII.[64]

Pregnancy and Childbirth

Many employers have policies that treat pregnancy and childbirth differently from other temporary disabilities, as was discussed in the section on employer practices. According to the EEOC guidelines, these policies violate Title VII of the Civil Rights Act of 1964. The 1972 guidelines clearly state: "A written or unwritten employment policy or practice which excludes from employment applicants or employees because of pregnancy is prima facie violation of Title VII."[65]

The EEOC also contends

Disabilities caused or contributed to by pregnancy, miscarriage, abortion, childbirth, and recovery therefrom are, for all job-related purposes, temporary disabilities and should be treated as such under any health or temporary disability insurance or sick leave plan in connection with employment.[66]

In addition, the EEOC guidelines state:

Where the termination of an employee who is temporarily disabled is caused by an employment policy which is insufficient or no leave is available, such a termination violates the Act if it has a disparate impact on employees of one sex and is not justified by business necessity.[67]

That is, if female employees are disproportionately affected by the lack of an adequate temporary disability program, the employer is in violation of Title VII.

It is important to note that these guidelines are specific to medical leaves for *childbearing*, which, because of the unique physical characteristic of pregnancy, apply only to women. This section of the guidelines does not refer to leaves for *child rearing*, for which both men and women can and should be eligible.

No cases concerning pregnancy and childbearing have arisen directly from Title VII. However, the issue was touched in *Doe v. Osteopathic Hospital of Wichita*.[68] The court found that the dismissal of an unmarried, pregnant employee was improper sex discrimination under Title VII. The court stated that the dismissal of the woman was discriminatory because of "an absence of any evidence that the plaintiff's marital state *or her pregnancy* had any relationship at all to the performance of her duties"[69] (emphasis added).

Other cases regarding pregnancy and childbirth have been brought under the Fourteenth Amendment equal protection clause. On January 21, 1974, in *La Fleur v. Cleveland Board of Education*,[70] the U.S. Supreme Court held unconstitutional the rules of two school districts, one in Cleveland, Ohio, and one in Chesterfield County, Virginia, requiring teachers to take unpaid maternity leave commencing five and four months respectively before expected childbirth. The Cleveland rule also prohibited the teacher from returning to work until the next regular semester after her child became three months old, while the Virginia rule required as a condition of reemployment that the teacher submit a written notice from a physician that she was physically fit for reemployment and that she give assurances that the care of the child would cause minimal interference with her job responsibilities. The Supreme Court pointed out that these rules penalized the pregnant teacher for deciding to bear a child, and held them to be an undue interference with the teacher's freedom of personal choice in matters of marriage and family life, a right protected by the due process clause of the Fourteenth Amendment. The school boards had attempted to justify the rules on two grounds. First, they argued that firm cutoff dates were necessary to obtain qualified substitutes and thus insure continuity of classroom instruction. Second,

the school boards seek to justify their maternity rules by arguing that at least some teachers become physically incapable of adequately performing certain of their duties during the latter part of pregnancy. By keeping the pregnant teacher out of the classroom during these final months, the maternity leave rules are said to protect the health of the teacher and her unborn child, while at the same time assuring that students have a physically capable instructor in the classroom at all times.[71]

The court observed that the early cutoff dates in fact often hindered the maintenance of continuity, by requiring a teacher who was able to complete a school year to leave earlier in the term, and found that the rules therefore were not rationally related to the first state interest asserted. As to the second concern advanced by the state, the court held that the rules swept too broadly. A narrower rule, such as one permitting individual determinations of physical capability, would also serve the state's interest, with less intrusion on the rights of individual teachers. The court also invalidated the Cleveland school board's three-month-age return provision, but upheld the Chesterfield County rule requiring teachers who had recently given birth to submit evidence of physical competence to return to work.

Despite the vindication of women's right to teach if physically capable of doing so, the *La Fleur* decision is a disturbing one. Other mandatory maternity leave decisions, have focused on the sex discriminatory aspects of treating pregnancy-related disabilities differently from other temporary disabilities, rather than dealing with childbirth leave as a unique problem as the Supreme Court did.[72] The former approach is preferable—first, it often dramatically illustrates the extent to which employers are discriminating on the basis of sex rather than making objective decisions about the employment situation. Second, it helps undercut the idea that pregnancy is such a unique situation that special treatment is warranted, an idea that is at the heart of much discrimination against women.

A subsequent decision confirmed the openness of the Supreme Court to the idea that pregnancy is unique. In *Geduldig v. Aiello,*[73] the Court, in a 6-3 decision, upheld the exclusion of disabilities caused by normal childbirth from coverage under California's state disability insurance program on the grounds that the exclusion of pregnancy-related disabilities was reasonable in that it lowered the costs of the program. In response to the charge that excluding pregnancy was sex discriminatory, the Court stated, "There is no risk from which women are protected and men are not,"[74] and in a footnote, argued:

The California insurance program does not exclude anyone from benefit eligibility because of gender but merely removes one physical condition—pregnancy—from the list of compensable disabilities. While it is true that only women can become pregnant, it does not follow that every legislative classification concerning pregnancy is a sex-based classification. . . . Normal pregnancy is an objectively identifiable physical condition with unique characteristics. Absent a showing that distinctions involving pregnancy are mere pretexts designed to effect an invidious discrimination against the members of one sex or the other, lawmakers are constitutionally free to include or exclude pregnancy from the coverage of legislation such as this on any reasonable basis, just as with respect to any other physical condition.[75]

The Court did not explain how the unique characteristics of pregnancy were related to the purpose of the California legislation—protecting employees from loss of income due to temporary inability to work caused by physical conditions. In his opinion for the three dissenting justices, Mr. Justice Brennan commented:

Despite the Act's broad goals and scope of coverage, compensation is denied for disabilities suffered in connection with a "normal" pregnancy—disabilities suffered only by women. . . . Disabilities caused by pregnancy, however, like other physically disabling conditions covered by the Act, require medical care, often include hospitalization, anaesthesia, and surgical procedures, and may involve genuine risk to life. Moreover, the economic effects caused by pregnancy-related disabilities are functionally indistinguishable from the effects caused by any other disability: wages are lost due to a physical inability to work, and medical expenses are incurred for the delivery of the child and for post-partum care. In my view, by singling out for less favorable treatment a gender-linked disability peculiar to women, the State has created a double standard for disability compensation: a limitation is imposed upon the disabilities for which women workers may recover, while men receive full compensation for all disabilities, suffered, including those that affect only or primarily their sex, such as prostatectomies, circumcision, hemophilia, and gout. In effect, one set of rules is applied to females and another to males. Such dissimilar treatment of men and women, on the basis of physical characteristics inextricably linked to one sex, inevitably constitutes sex discrimination.[76]

Fortunately, the Supreme Court observed in a footnote in *La Fleur* that the practical impact of their decision might have been somewhat lessened by the extension of Title VII to cover teachers, and the issuance by the EEOC of regulations requiring pregnancy-related disabilities to be treated similarly to other temporary disabilities. It appears that most maternity issues in the future will be resolved under Title VII, and it is hoped that the strict EEOC guidelines will have a more powerful effect on development of the law in this area than the Supreme Court decisions.

Executive Order 11246

Executive Order 11246, issued in 1965, forbids federal contractors and subcontractors and employers on federally assisted construction to discriminate in employment on the basis of race, color, religion, or national origin. Executive Order 11375, which took effect on October 13, 1968, amended this to include discrimination based on sex.[77] The executive order establishes the practice and policies that government contractors must follow in order to receive federal monies. The courts have affirmed that the government has the right to set the terms of its contracts with contractors.

Coverage

The executive order covers all contractors who have $10,000 or more in federal construction or other contracts with the federal government, including those awarded to colleges and universities. If any part of an institution has a federal contract, the entire institution is covered. Unions are not directly bound by the executive order; state and local governments are exempt from the obligations of the order.

In 1966 an estimated 24 million persons (one-third of the total labor force) were working for companies holding government contracts.[78]

Affirmative Action and Guidelines
for the Executive Order

The executive order requires federal contractors to practice nondiscrimination in all aspects of their employment activity. The key section reads:

The contractor will not discriminate against any employee or applicant for employment because of race, color, religion, sex, or national origin. The contractor will take affirmative action to ensure that applicants are employed, and that employees are treated during employment, without regard to their race, color, religion, sex, or national origin. Such action shall include, but not be limited to the following: employment, upgrading, demotion, or transfer; recruitment or recruitment advertising; layoff or termination; rates of pay or other forms of compensation; and selection for training, including apprenticeship.[79]

A nondiscrimination clause to this effect must be included in each contract with the federal government. Government contractors and those subcontractors working on the project that is receiving federal funds are required to institute affirmative action programs to eliminate discrimination based on sex. Private federal contractors and subcontractors with contracts totaling $50,000 or more and with fifty or more employees must develop *written* affirmative action plans within 120 days from the commencement of a contract. With the exception of educational institutions and medical facilities, public institutions with federal contracts are obliged not to discriminate, but are not required to have written affirmative action plans unless they are found to be in noncompliance. Educational institutions and medical facilities must have written plans.

The guidelines require affirmative action to rectify the effects of past discrimination. Even if an employer does not discriminate at the time of the compliance review, he can be found in noncompliance if he has not acted positively to eliminate the effects of his previous practices. Without such compensatory action, those who have been discriminated against in the past might never be able to move into a competitive position.

In 1965, when the Office of Federal Contract Compliance (OFCC) issued the first set of rules and regulations implementing Executive Order 11246, sex was not included. Therefore, these guidelines did not specifically prohibit sex as a basis of discrimination. Instead, they referred throughout to undefined "minority employment."[80] In January 1970 the OFCC issued Order No. 4, "Affirmative Action Guidelines," which set forth employers' obligations in great detail.[81] However, because these guidelines did not deal explicitly with discrimination based on sex, there was some confusion about the interpretation of the executive order with regard to sex discrimination.

Guidelines for implementation of the executive order with regard to sex discrimination were issued by the Department of Labor in June 1970. These guidelines required employers to take affirmative action to recruit women for jobs from which they had previously been excluded. They specified that both sexes must have equal access to all training programs and that contractors must maintain written personnel policies stating clearly that they do not discriminate on the basis of sex. Specifically, these guidelines prohibited employers from making any distinctions based on sex in employment opportunities, wages, hours, or other conditions of employment (including fringe benefits and pension plans); making any distinction between married and single persons of one sex but not the other; advertising in sex-segregated help-wanted columns unless sex is a bona fide occupational qualification; denying employment to women with young children unless the same policy applies to men with young children; terminating an employee of one sex upon reaching a certain age, but not an employee of the other sex; penalizing women because they require time away from work for childbearing (childbearing must be considered justification for a leave of absence for a reasonable period of time, whether or not an employer has a leave policy); maintaining seniority lists based solely on sex; or denying a female employee the right to any job she is qualified to perform because of state "protective" legislation.[82]

Revised Order No. 4, effective December 4, 1971, strengthened the guidelines, outlined the requirements for written affirmative action plans under the executive order as amended, and made it clear that sex discrimination was included in its coverage. Revised Order No. 4 requires that a contractor analyze the work force to determine if women and minorities are underemployed and set numerical goals and timetables by job classification and organizational unit to correct any deficiencies.

Because there has been some controversy about the differences between quotas and numerical goals and timetables, an explanation of the distinctions is in order. Quotas are rigid limits that serve to restrict a specific group from a particular activity. Goals, on the other hand, are numerical targets that aim to help increase the number of *qualified* women and minority representatives. The difference between the two is significant. Goals are affirmative, rather than exclusionary or discriminatory. Unlike quotas, they are flexible, and the failure to meet certain goals does not constitute noncompliance *if* good faith has been present in efforts to meet them. Goals must reflect the characteristics of the female or minority work force, such as the percentage of such workers in the relevant labor market. A goal can never be used to force a contractor to hire an unqualified person or to discriminate against any qualified person on the basis of race, color, sex, or national origin. In line with this, the courts have ruled that numerical target goals are not in conflict with Title VII of the 1964 Civil Rights Act (which forbids preferential treatment that results in discrimination) or with the Fifth Amendment.

There has been a great deal of controversy about whether or not affirmative action plans should be available to the public. Good personnel practices require that policies as significant as the affirmative action plans be made public. Women and minorities have maintained that they can neither evaluate an affirmative action plan realistically nor judge the effectiveness with which it is implemented if they do not know its content. Furthermore, these plans, which are general in nature, usually do not contain any information that could be harmful to an institution if made public. Presently, HEW, which has developed its own guidelines relating to the executive order, requires educational institutions to make their affirmative action plans public.

The OFCC has not yet adopted this policy. Noting that affirmative action plans contain commercial and financial information, the OFCC has argued that the plans are "confidential investigatory files compiled for law enforcement purposes."[83] The OFCC is now revising its policy to permit a more liberal disclosure of data by the OFCC itself, however.

The policy of the Department of Labor as of July 1972 reads:

That we [OFCC] disclose Affirmative Action Plans to the extent that the information does not affect the commercial and/or financial status of a private contractor having Federal contracts. If disclosure will harm the competitive advantage or position of a contractor, that portion of the Affirmative Action Plan affecting the competitive position is not releasable under present policy. The names and salaries of individual employees are also not releasable.[84]

Revised guidelines that will conform with existing legislation and explain the requirements of the executive order are now being developed by the OFCC. Among other things, these guidelines are expected to identify for the first time the specific data and information that institutions must gather in order to document their good faith in recruiting women and minorities. In the past, the type of information requested during compliance reviews has varied considerably from contractor to contractor.

Enforcement: Complaints and Compliance Reviews

The Department of Labor, through the Office of Federal Contract Compliance, has the overall responsibility for developing program policy under the executive order and for ensuring that it is enforced consistently. The OFCC itself does few compliance reviews. Instead, it has delegated to certain federal agencies the responsibility for ensuring that the establishments covered by specified industrial classification codes comply with the order. For example, the Department of Health, Education and Welfare's Office for Civil Rights has been designated by the OFCC as the agency responsible for enforcing all contracts with colleges and universities. Construction contracts are reviewed by the agency awarding or administering the contract.

In all, although the OFCC office itself only has a small staff, there were nearly one thousand contract compliance officers in the various compliance agencies in 1974.[85] The lack of personnel and other resources in the OFCC itself has several undesirable consequences. For example, the OFCC does not publish an annual report, and with so few people in the central office, it is difficult for the staff, no matter how competent, to adequately train and monitor all of the compliance officers in the field.

According to Executive Order 11246, as amended, the secretary of labor or the designated contracting agency has the power to publish the names of noncomplying contractors or unions; to recommend suits by the Justice Department to compel compliance; to recommend action by the EEOC or the Justice Department under Title VII of the Civil Rights Act; to recommend criminal actions by the Justice Department for furnishing false information; to suspend or cancel the contract of a noncomplying employer; or to blacklist a noncomplying employer from future government contract work until he has demonstrated a willingness to comply with the order.

Although the executive order is potentially a powerful tool, its major weapons—contract cancellation and the loss of future government contracts—have not yet been used by the OFCC in a sex-discrimination case.[86] The principle means of enforcement has been through compliance review and voluntary solutions worked out with contractors. Individual complaints are now sent to the Equal Employment Opportunity Commission (EEOC). The OFCC deals directly only with pattern and practice complaints.[87]

Thus far, colleges and universities have come under the strongest criticism for discrimination against women. The Women's Equity Action League (WEAL) and other women's groups have filed complaints against over four hundred institutions of higher learning. Until these charges were filed, the executive order had not been enforced with regard to sex, and it appears that the executive order will not be enforced until organized groups or individuals in different industries demand its enforcement.

Conclusion

Federal legislation, as interpreted by enforcement agencies and the courts, establishes the principle of equal rights for women workers. But the laws are not followed by many employers. In addition, many women are not aware of the legislation that does exist for their protection; others are reluctant to begin the time-consuming and costly process of litigation. They are afraid of reprisals and want to avoid the controversy a court case can bring.

In many situations it is not always easy to make a clear-cut case to prove sex discrimination. In white-collar jobs, and administrative work in particular, it is difficult to define equal work and to identify the precise reasons for promoting one person over another. For example, the factors that contribute to a decision to promote a university professor to the tenured rank are many and complex. Employers often take refuge behind the complexity of the situation to avoid confronting the possibility of sex discrimination.

Nonetheless, employers are beginning to discover that they will have to answer in court if they discriminate against women. Recently, women's organizations have assumed the responsibility of informing women workers of their legal rights, explaining the procedures required to file a complaint, and providing assistance to those who bring charges. This is an encouraging development, because it is only through the actions of aggrieved individuals and through political pressure brought by organizations that represent them that the law will become a significant force in eliminating sex discrimination on the job.

Notes

1. 29 U.S.C. 206 (d) (1) (1964).

2. Pub. L. 92-318, Title IX, § 906 (b) (1), 86 Stat. 375.

3. In preparing this and the following section, the authors have relied heavily on the work of Susan C. Ross.

4. 421 F. 2d 259, 265 (3rd Cir.) *cert. denied* 398 U.S. 905 (1970).

5. Hodgson v. Brookhaven General Hospital, 436 F.2d 719 (5th Cir. 1970). The Fifth Court of Appeals remanded the case to the District court for a new factual determination, whereupon the district court found that the work of the aides and orderlies required equal effort. 66 CCH Lab. Cas. 32,520, 20 Wage & Hour Cas. 54 (N.D.Tex. 1971). The hospital appealed once more and lost. 470 F.2d 729 (1972). For an aide-orderly case that reached a different result, see Hodgson v. Golden Isles Convalescent Homes, Inc., 468 F.2d 1256 (5th Cir. 1972).

Other instructive cases ruling on the issues of effort and the other three factors are Shultz v. Wheaton Glass, *supra*; Hodgson v. Daisy Manufacturing Co., 317 F. Supp. 538 (W.D.Ark. 1970) 445 F.2d 823 (8th Cir. 1971) (mental effort); Hodgson v. Good Shepherd Hospital, 327 F. Supp. 143 (E.D.Tex. 1971) (skill effort and responsibility); Hodgson v. Corning Glass Works, 474 F.2d 226 (2d Cir. 1973); (Similar working conditions; work at night); Hodgson v. Miller Brewing Co. 427 F.2d 221 (7th Cir. 1971) (comparison of working conditions in two laboratories).

6. On seniority, see e.g., Kilpatrick v. Sweet, 262 F. Supp. 561 (M.D.Fla. 1967); Hodgson v. Corning Glass Works, 474 F.2d 226 (2d Cir. 1973); on merit systems, see Hodgson v. Brookhaven General Hospital, 436 F.2d 719, 726 (5th Cir. 1970) and Wirtz v. First Victoria National Bank, 63 CCH Lab. Cas. § 32,378, 19 Wage & Hour Cas. 684 (S.D. Tex. 1970), aff'd *per curiam, sub nom* Hodgson v. First Victoria National Bank, 446 F.2d 47 (5th Cir. 1971).

7. 70 CCH Lab. Cas. § 32,844, 20 Wage & Hour Cas. 1152 (5th Cir. 1973).

8. 70 CCH Lab. Cas. § 32,844, p. 45,806–45,807, 20 Wage & Hour Cas. 1152, 1156 (5th Cir. 1973).

9. 473 F.2d 589 (3rd Cir. 1972).

10. 58 CCH Lab. Cas. § 32,070, 18 Wage & Hour Cas. 556 (S.D.Ill. 1968).

11. U.S. Dept. of Labor, Employment Stds. Admin., *Equal Pay Act Findings* (July 1972).

12. Telephone conversation with Mr. Jeffrey Geilich, Deputy Director of Public Information, EEOC (May 4, 1972).

13. U.S. Dept. of Labor, Employment Stds. Admin., *Equal Pay Act Findings* (July 1972); telephone conversations with Morag Simchak, Wage and Hours Division, Department of Labor (May 4 and August 1, 1972 and February 1, 1974).

The Department of Labor also obtained wage increases, averaging twelve dollars a week in 1969, for more than six thousand women employed in a variety of jobs; this figure includes wage increases obtained on the basis of the minimum wage provisions of the Fair Labor Standards Act as well as through enforcement of the Equal Pay Act. BNA Manpower Inf. Svc. Current Reports, No. 18, at 7 (May 20, 1970) and news release, U.S. Dept. of Labor, 11-242, May 27, 1970, WH70-1102.

14. Simchak, *supra* n.12. An attempt was made by the employer defendant in Wirtz v. Hayes Industries, Inc., 58 CCH Lab. Cas. § 32,058 (N.D.Ohio 1968), to enjoin the union as a third-party defendant and recover compensation from the union if the employer was found to be in violation of the act. The employer based this action on the fact that the contract governing wages paid to employees was negotiated jointly with the union. The court dismissed the motion to join the union, holding that the act provided an action for recovery of unpaid wages only against the employer. Relief against the union could only be injunctive and based on the section of the act specifically regulating union activity.

15. For a more complete discussion of Title VII prior to the 1972 amendments, see "Developments in the Law—Employment, Discrimination and Title VII of the Civil Rights Act of 1964," 84 *Harvard Law Review* 1109 (1971). (Hereinafter Developments—Title VII.)

16. Title VII of the Civil Rights Act of 1964, Pub. L. No. 88-352, § 701 (b) and (e), 702, 78 Stat. 253.

17. Title VII of the Civil Rights Act of 1964 as amended by the Equal

Employment Opportunities Act of 1972 (hereinafter Title VII), Pub. L. No. 92-261, § 701(b), 702, 718, 83 Stat. 103.

18. Title VII § 701 (b) and (e).

19. Ibid., § 703-704.

20. Ibid., § 703 (e).

21. Developments—Title VII at 1196.

22. Ibid., at 1197.

23. As or 1972, the EEOC did not defer to at least seven states because these states either did not have a state agency to administer existing statutes preventing discrimination or did not provide for effective enforcement.

24. Developments—Title VII at 1200, n. 39.

25. Developments—Title VII at 1201-2 and telephone conversation with Seymour Snyderman, Office of Conciliation (February 7, 1974).

26. One commentator listed three main limitations of Title VII enforcement procedures: failure to adequately compensate the complainant for the wrong suffered, time-consuming procedural requirements, and lack of effective sanctions to deter employers from pursuing discriminatory practices. Avery, *Title VII of the 1964 Civil Rights Act—A Prayer for Damages*, 5 *California Western Law Review* 224 (Spring 1969).

27. Title VII, § 706.

28. The time limit for individuals who file first with a state or local agency is three hundred days after the complaint is filed with the state or locality, or thirty days after receiving state or local notification of the termination of state or local proceedings, whichever is earlier. Title VII § 706 (e).

29. Time limits are set forth in Title VII. § 706.

30. 29C.F.R. § 1604.2 (a) [issued November 24, 1965, last amended April 4, 1972].

31. Ibid., § 1604.2 (a)(1) & (b)(5).

32. Ibid., § 1604.2 (a)(2).

33. 408 F.2d 228 (5th Cir. 1969) *reversing in pertinent part*, 277 F. Supp. 117 (S.D.Ga. 1967).

34. 408 F.2d at 235.

35. 503 F. Supp. 754 (M.D.Ala. 1969).

36. 416 F.2d 711 (7th Cir. 1969).

37. 444 F.2d 1219 (9th Cir. 1971).

38. 444 F.2d at 1255 (oth Cir. 1971).

39. 442 F.2d 385 (5th Cir.) *cert. denied*, 404 U.S. 950 (1971).

40. 442 F.2d at 388.

41. 442 F.2d at 389.

42. 442 F.2d at 387.

43. 29 C.F.R. 1604.2(b) (2) [issued November 24, 1965; last amended April 5, 1972].

44. For a history of the EEOC's earlier positions on state protective laws and

regulations, see the discussion in *The Harvard Law Review*'s "Developments—Title VII," *supra*, n. 17, at 1187-88.

45. 314 F. Supp. 171 (E.D.Cal. 1970), upholding California job exclusion law (bartending), Butsee Krauss v. Sacramento Inn, appeal pending.

46. Hays v. Potlatch Forests, Inc., 318 F. Supp. 1368 (E.D.Ark. 1970), aff'd, 4 FEP Cas. 1037 (8th Circ., July 20, 1972 [Extending benefits] : Ridinger v. General Motors Corp., 325 F. Supp. 1089 (S.D.Ohio 1971), Jones Metal Products Co. v. Walker, 29 Ohio St.2d 173, 4 FEP Cas. 483, 4 EPD #7746 (Ohio Sup. Ct. March 15, 1972), and Burns v. Rohr Corp., 4 FEP Cas. 939, 4 EPD #7924 (S.D.Calif. June 20, 1972) [All invalidating sex-based benefit laws] : and Op. Att'y Gen. No. 72-22, CCH EPG #5062 N.M. May 13, 1972). Cf. Bastardo v. Warren, 4 EPD #7635 (W.D.Wis. March 30, 1970); 332 F. Supp. 501, 4 EPD #7636 (W.D.Wis. October 7, 1971). In the Rohr Case, the court described ten-minute rest breaks that were given to women only without loss of pay as "restrictive," a description that is confusing at best.

47. 4 FEP Cas. 1037 (8th Cir., July 20, 1972).

48. 318 F. Supp. 1368 (E.D.Ark. 1970).

49. 4 FEP Cas. 1037 (8th Cir., July 20, 1972).

50. 4 FEP Cas. at 1038, citing 318 F. Supp. at 1375.

51. 4 FEP Cas. at 1039.

52. Barbara A. Brown, Thomas I. Emerson, Gail Falk, Ann Freedman, "The Equal Rights Amendment: A Constitutional Basis for Equal Rights for Women," *The Yale Law Journal*, vol. 80, no. 5 (April 1971): 884.

53. 400 U.S. 542 (1971).

54. 411 F.2d 1, 3 (5th Cir. 1969).

55. 411 F.2d at 3-4.

56. A proposed Senate amendment to Title VII to insert the word *solely* before the proscribed categories of discrimination—race, color, religion, sex, national origin—was defeated by a roll-call vote. (110 Cong. Rec. 13837-13838 [1964].)

57. 400 U.S. 542, 544 (1971) rev'g and remanding 411 F.2d 1 (5th Cir. 1969). The three paragraph *per curiam* opinion of the U.S. Supreme Court for the Phillips case, while correctly holding that "sex plus" was not an acceptable affirmative defense, struck a blow at the BFOQ exception. The opinion stated, "(t)he existence of . . . conflicting family obligations, if demonstrably more relevant to job performance for a woman than for a man, could arguably be a basis for distinction under § 703 (e) [BFOQ exception] of the Act." Justice Marshall, although concurring with the decision, strongly objected to this suggestion, saying, "I cannot agree with the Court's indication that a *bona fide* occupational qualification reasonably necessary to the normal operation of Martin Marietta's business could be established by a showing that some women, even the vast majority, with preschool age children have family responsibilities that interfere with job performance and that men do not usually have such

responsibilities." Fortunately, it seems unlikely that the lower court will pick up on the Supreme Court's suggestion, in light of previous Fifth Circuit interpretations of the BFOQ provision, discussed earlier.

58. 274 F. Supp. 781 (E.D.La. 1967).

59. 437 F.2d 454 (5th Cir. 1971) rev'g 2 FEP Cas. 462 (S.D.Fla. November 28, 1969) and 430 F.2d 1341 (5th Cir. 1970), rev'g 2 FEP Cas. 461 (S.D.Fla, November 28, 1969).

60. See, e.g., Sprogis v. United Air Lines, Inc., 444 F.2d 1194 (7th Cir. 1971).

61. See EEOC Decision No. 71-1529, CCH EPG § 6231 at 4410 (April 2, 1971); EEOC Decision No. 71-3003 (July 2, 1971); and EEOC Decision No. 71-2343, CCH EPG § 6256 (June 3, 1971). Also see Roberts v. General Mills, Inc., F. Supp., 3 FEP Cas. 1080 (N.D.Ohio, September 21, 1971) and Dodge v. Giant Food, Inc., F. Supp. 3 FEP Cas. 374 (D.D.C. April 16, 1971).

62. EEOC Decision No. 71-332, CCH EPG § 6164 (September 28, 1970); cf. EEOC Decision No. 71-562, 3 FEP Cas. 233 (December 4, 1970).

63. Dodd v. American Airlines, Inc., CCH EPG § 6001 (June 20, 1968); cf. EEOC Decision No. 70-145, CCH EPG § 6066 (September 9, 1969) Rosen v. Public Serv. Elec. Co., 2 FEP Cas. 1090 (D.N.J. 1970); EEOC Decision No. 70-706, 2 FEP Cas. 684 (April 20, 1970); EEOC Decision No. 69-9-183E, CCH EPG § 6022 (June 26, 1969).

64. For a more complete discussion of areas in which the issue of "sex plus" is relevant, see Oldham, "Questions of Exclusion and Exception Under Title VII–'Sex Plus' and the BFOQ," 23 *Hastings* LF 62-75 (1971).

65. 29 C.F.R. § 1604.10 (a) [issued November 24, 1965, as amended April 5, 1972].

66. Ibid., § 1604.10 (b). See also U.S. Dept. of Labor, Citizen's Advisory Council on the Status of Women, *Job-Related Maternity Benefits*, November 1970 and Koontz, "Child Birth and Child Rearing Leave: Job-Related Benefits," 17 *N.Y. Law Forum* 480 (1971).

67. 29 C.F.R. § 1604.10 (c) [issued November 24, 1965, as amended April 5, 1972].

68. 3 F.E.P. Cas. 1128, 4 E.P.D. § 7545 (D.Kans. October 18, 1971).

69. 3 F.E.P. Cas. at 1131, 4 E.P.D. at 5191.

70. 42 LW 4186.

71. 42 LW at 4189.

72. See e.g. the district court opinion in Cohen v. Chesterfield County School Board, 326 F. Supp. 1159 (2b. Va. 1971). This decision, which was first affirmed by the 4th Circuit, 467 F.2d 262 (1972) and then reversed on rehearing en banc 474 F.2d 395 (1973), was then consolidated for Supreme Court consideration with the La Fleur case, discussed above. See also Green v. Waterford Board of Education, 473 F.2d 629 (2d Cir. 1973).

73. 42 L.W. 4905 (June 17, 1974).

74. 42 L.W. at 4908.

75. 42 L.W. at 4908, n. 20.

76. 42 L.W. 4909-4910.

77. Part I, dealing with nondiscrimination in government employment, effective November 12, 1967, was superseded by Executive Order 11478, signed August 8, 1969.

78. Statement by Senator Walter F. Mondale before the Subcommittee on Administration Practice and Procedures of the Senate Judiciary Committee, March 27, 1969, cited in "Note: Executive Order 11246: Anti-Discrimination Obligations in Government Contracts," 44 *New York Univ. L. Rev.* 590 (1969).

79. Executive Order 11375, Amending Executive Order No. 11246, 32 FR 14304 (October 17, 1967).

80. 41 C.F.R. S 60-1.1 *et seq.*

81. 41 C.R.F. S 60-20 *et seq.*

82. Summary of provisions from Betty Pryor, American Council on Education, "Laws and Regulations on Sex Discrimination," A.C.E. Special Report (April 20, 1972), p. 4.

83. Freedom of Information Act–5 USC 553, 45 C.F.R. S 577.

84. Quoted in a July 1972 letter from Frederick L. Webber, special assistant for legislative affairs of the U.S. Department of Labor, to Senator Edward Kennedy.

85. Telephone conversation with Morag Simchak (January 1974).

86. According to the Webber-Kennedy letter of July 1972, these sanctions have been used in only four instances. Edgely Air Products, Inc., had its contract terminated and was disbarred from future government contracts. Aro Incorporated was ordered to adopt a remedy for its seniority system. Randeb Incorporated and Russell Associations were disbarred from future contracts. However, HEW has temporarily withheld funds from eleven universities for failure to comply with the Executive Order.

87. In his July 1972 letter to Senator Edward Kennedy, Frederick Webber explains the relationship between the two agencies in this manner:

Concerning complaints, the OFCC and the Equal Employment Opportunity Commission (EEOC) concluded an agreement in May 1970, designed to reduce duplication of efforts. (The EEOC administers Title VII of the Civil Rights Act of 1964.) Under this agreement, complaints filed with the OFCC are transmitted to the EEOC for investigation. The EEOC then acts on behalf of both agencies and conducts an investigation. If the EEOC determines that there is reasonable cause to believe a Government contractor has violated his obligations, it notifies the OFCC. The OFCC will then undertake whatever conciliatory action is required, and if that fails will follow the required procedures and apply sanctions. The basis for this agreement is that most Government contractors are also subject to Title VII. The other possible remedy is for the individual to bring suit under Title VII or for the EEOC to file suit. This agreement is referred to as the "Memorandum of Understanding."

This was not always the case: originally, priority was given to individual complaints.

4 Sex Discrimination in the Trade Unions

Over the past century, the labor movement has stressed the importance of unity and equality among workers. To reinforce this policy, federal legislation based on the principle that similarly situated workers should be treated similarly has been passed. But in many cases, neither the rhetoric nor the law has changed discriminatory attitudes or practices. In fact, most individual labor unions not only have failed to mount an effective challenge to the discrimination by employers and society, but also have tended to mirror these same attitudes by underrepresenting women at the bargaining table and by discouraging their participation in union activities. Some unions, particularly those for the skilled trades, have, in the past, even advocated discrimination against women on the job and within the union itself.

Some patterns of trade union discrimination are obvious. Women are underrepresented in the leadership of trade unions, even in unions where a majority of the members are women. The jobs, occupations, and industries where women form a large portion of the work force are generally unorganized or underorganized. In general, unions reflect the interests, style, and preferences of working men, treating women at best as "minority group" members.[1]

Historical Perspective

The earliest trade unions in America developed from workmen's social clubs: their language was male and their meeting place was the neighborhood saloon.[2] The first American trade unions were established in the 1820s among the printers, shoemakers, and carpenters, occupations in which there were no women. At the same time, almost seventy thousand women were employed in New England cotton mills.[3] That these women had serious grievances and the ability to organize was demonstrated in 1828 when the cotton-mill workers of Dover, New Hampshire marched out of work to protest a reduction of wages. They eventually won their strike, and labor activity among women grew during the next three decades. This growth, however, was parallel to, rather than a part of, the development of men's trade unions. Labor organizers took no interest in working women, so women formed a few segregated "sister" unions. Separate women's unions were started among the collar workers, tailoresses, seamstresses, umbrella sewers, capmakers, textile workers, printers, laundresses, and furnishers.[4]

115

The nineteenth-century women's unions were unable to sustain themselves very long, however. Working women then, as now, frequently carried a double burden—responsibility for a home and family as well as for a job. Furthermore, they lacked the funds for organizational efforts—dues, strike funds, and spreading the word to other women—because they were generally paid only a fraction of what men were paid for the same work and were employed almost entirely in unskilled jobs.[5] Moreover, women, traditionally isolated from one another in the home, were inexperienced as organizers, unaccustomed to thinking of themselves as workers, and not used to working in groups.[6]

Thus, a vicious cycle began, a cycle that still continues in modified form today: men excluded women workers from fully participating in their unions, and women were unable to organize strong unions of their own; women, lacking bargaining power, were forced to work at lower wages under inferior working conditions; employers used women workers to undercut the wages and organizational efforts of men, thus increasing the hostility between the two groups.

Very slowly a few men in the trade unions began to see that women were in the work force to stay and that the interests of men workers lay in joining with their women co-workers, rather than excluding them. In 1868, the National Labor Union (NLU), a short-lived federation of national unions, passed a resolution favoring equal pay for equal work. However, women were still not treated equally. For example, at its first convention in 1866, the NLU had solicited the "hearty cooperation of women," but did not offer to organize them.[7]

Even more than today, working women in the nineteenth century were confined to unskilled and semi-skilled jobs. It is not surprising then that the first wide-scale organizing of women was done in the 1880s through the Knights of Labor, a national organization dedicated to the organization of all workers, unskilled and skilled. The history of the early years of the Knights indicates that discrimination against women was inherent even in an organization philosophically committed to the interests of all workers. In 1879, a resolution admitting women to membership and permitting them to form assemblies on the same basis as men was defeated,[8] even though the preamble to the constitution, adopted in 1878, listed as one of the order's principle objectives: "To secure for both sexes equal pay for equal work."[9] Not until 1882 did the convention vote to permit the initiation of women.[10] The Knights organized men and women in the same assemblies and also chartered separate women's assemblies; however, most efforts of the Knights to help and organize women workers were probably sparked by a small group of women within the organization.[11] By 1886, at the height of the Knights of Labor's membership, 121 women's assemblies existed and the order had about fifty thousand women members who formed 8 to 9 percent of its total membership.[12] (Women formed between 15 and 17 percent of the total work force at this time.)[13] However, that same year, less than 3 percent of the 660 delegates to the annual convention were women. Still, the

Knights were more strongly committed to organizing women than any other labor organization of their day, and their swift decline in the late 1880s seriously impeded the unionization of women.

The period between 1885 and 1930 is especially interesting because the patterns that developed were significant in shaping the present situation. The American Federation of Labor (AFL) began to grow in the late 1880s just as the Knights of Labor was declining. Perhaps because of competition with the Knights, the federation early showed an interest in women; in 1891, the AFL endorsed women's suffrage.[14]

As the twentieth century began, the labor movement was dominated by the skilled craft unions of the AFL, many of which openly excluded women. Although this practice gradually died when men's unions felt serious competition from nonunion working women, seven AFL internationals still officially opposed the admission of women members as late as 1924.

There were many ways of excluding women without explicitly barring them from a union. High dues were exclusionary in a period when many women's wages were below subsistence levels, averaging about half that of male co-workers. Moreover, few women had the qualifications needed to make them eligible for skilled craft unions. The prevailing social myths discouraged women from entering the skilled trades by defining craftsmen's work as "men's work." Even when economic necessity pushed women into many trades previously considered "men's work," they were still prevented from acquiring craftsmen's skills by the rigid sets of regulations that excluded them from apprenticeship and other training programs.[15]

Exclusionary policies were only the most clear-cut discriminatory practices. Once women were admitted to trade unions, they were generally treated as unwanted poor relations or, at best, as second-class citizens. In the 1920s, a number of international unions required lower dues and lower initiation fees for women.[16] At that time many unions made the amount of benefits received contingent upon the amount of dues paid, so that working women received lower strike, sickness, and death benefits than working men.

Unions generally recognized that women were more effective than men at organizing women workers; yet, as late as 1924, only eight national unions had women organizers.[17] Even unions like the International Ladies' Garment Workers Union (ILGWU), Amalgamated Clothing Workers, and the Cap Makers, which emphasized female leadership and had a heavily female membership, hired only about one woman organizer for every three men organizers in the 1920s.[18] Women officers were also virtually nonexistent in the higher levels of the union hierarchy, even in unions with large female memberships.

Union leaders justified their discriminatory policies on the grounds that working women did not have time to be active union members because they had, in effect, two jobs: one at work and one at home. Their lack of interest in having female members was shown by the fact that there was little concern with disturbing the social tradition that had created this condition. Demands for benefits, such as child care, that might have eased the dual burden were never made, nor were male union members encouraged to share home responsibilities.

The result of these traditions and discriminatory policies was that women were discouraged from joining unions. In 1929, one estimate was that one in nine wage earners was organized, but only one in thirty-four women workers was a union member.[19] If anything, this was an overestimate.[20]

The small number of women union members was only partially due to overt discriminatory practices by unions. Large numbers of women worked in occupations traditionally thought of as hard to organize, such as housekeeping, clerical work, and agriculture. Furthermore, most women were working in unskilled and semi-skilled jobs, and the labor movement generally underrepresented low-skilled workers, regardless of sex. Finally, most women workers accepted the social myths about women who work: they failed to think of themselves as permanent workers; they considered working a cause for shame; and they feared that identifying with a union was, or would be considered unfeminine.[21] Most unions did not want women members, and women generally did not join unions, thus establishing the myth that women could not be organized.

With the growth and federal protection of unionism in the 1930s, unions became "respectable," and more unskilled, semi-skilled, and white-collar workers, male and female, became unionized. But the huge employment rate of the Depression put a premium on jobs, and women, pictured as secondary workers, were the primary target in the struggle to limit the size of the labor force. Union leaders and rank-and-file workers were among those who argued that it was obviously wrong for women to have jobs when married men were out of work. Many unions adopted policies, some of which remain in effect today, against helping working women, especially married women workers.

During World War II, the labor situation reversed. Women flowed into the work force to meet labor shortages, and by 1944 union membership of women reached a high of 21.9 percent. The war experience stimulated greater sensitivity to the problems and interest of women, as evidenced by the establishment of equal pay for equal work clauses,[22] maternity leave and maternity benefits, day care, and in general a greater show of concern for employer discrimination against women by such unions as the UAW, Amalgamated Clothing Workers, United Electrical Workers, and the National Federation of Telephone Workers.[23]

However, in 1943, even at the height of the war effort, the American Civil Liberties Union counted twenty-five national unions that excluded women. In addition, those unions that supported equal pay for equal work generally accepted sex segregation of jobs and used separate seniority lists for men and women.[24] In even the most liberal unions, women were still underrepresented in administrative and leadership positions.[25]

The improved status of working women brought by the war years proved short-lived; it faded as the need for working women diminished after the war. Returning veterans received preference not only for new job openings but also for jobs that had been filled by women during the war years. As a result, women were pushed into lower-paying jobs or back into their homes. The proportion of women labor union members declined in the postwar years, and labor union concern for the interests of women fell almost to the vanishing point during the following two decades.

Present Practices[a]

The ranks of women trade unionists have grown in the past two decades, as have the total numbers of working women in this country. In 1954, 2.8 million women belonged to labor unions; by 1968, this figure had increased to 3.7 million.[26] During the decade from 1958 to 1968, the overall number of trade unionists grew by 2 million, and 600,000 of those were women.[27] Nevertheless, women have not become active union members as fast as they have joined the civilian labor force. While 14.1 percent of all working women were unionized in 1954, the figure had declined to 12.5 percent by 1968,[28] and 10.3 percent by 1970.[29] This decline in percentage of union membership among female blue-collar workers has been accompanied by an increase in the earnings gap between male and female blue-collar workers.[30] Although there has been a similar decline in unionization among male workers, the decline has been less substantial, from 31.4 percent in 1966 to 28.5 percent in 1970.[31]

The reasons for the relative underorganization of women are complex, and raise the chicken-and-egg question of whether employers or unions are responsible. While employers in no sense should be exonerated of culpability for sex bias in the job market, the responsibility of labor unions must also be acknowledged. Employers, particularly in the skilled trades, have correctly contended that exclusion or discrimination can begin with union-controlled apprenticeship programs, which are often the only means of entry into active membership.

Those unions that control the 300,000 apprenticeships that open up each year in effect control access to the highest-paying job categories: electricians, plumbers, tool and die-setters, etc. Traditionally, they have been able to restrict admission or give preference to the sons or nephews of current members, whether by formal rules or merely by requiring that new members be sponsored by old ones. The exclusionary techniques, well-known methods of discriminating against blacks, have also been effective against women.[32] Unfortunately, the litigation prior to 1970 challenged racial or ethnic but not sex discrimination in apprenticeship and referral programs.[33]

Exclusionary apprenticeship programs are not the only problem. Until

[a]The section on present trade union practices was prepared by Erica Grubb.

recently, unions often exercised control over bargaining units in ways that clearly undermined the interests of working women. For example, the bargaining units were defined to separate women workers from their male co-workers or to exclude women's jobs altogether. Unions have also been suspiciously selective in deciding which workers to organize. Documenting clear-cut sex bias in such decisions is difficult, however, because the factors involved in organizing workers are subtle and complicated. The underorganiztion of so-called women's jobs—especially clerical, sales, and domestic occupations—and their notably low pay scales suggests that they have been ignored or forgotten. However, some people have argued that defensible explanations exist. They point to the difficulty of organizing workers who are "scattered over small units" and the "legal impediments to organizing that have been set up in the postwar period, when the labor force participation rate of women has been increasing most rapidly."[34]

Whatever the reason, the fact remains that a far greater proportion of women than men are denied the *option* of union participation. While it is true that there are disadvantages as well as advantages to unionization, most thoughtful proponents of women's rights argue that the "pros outweigh the cons."[35] The choice ought to be a real one, for only then can women's treatment *within* the union be improved.

Until the early 1970s, even those women who belonged to labor unions may have found that their interests were not represented as thoroughly as possible, probably because their representatives and leaders were male. It is still true that women do not generally play an active role in internal union affairs. The largest proportion of women officers is found at the local level. In the intermediate bodies—joint boards and district councils—very few women are officers, and almost none appear on major negotiating teams, national executive boards, national staffs, or rosters of national officers.[36] Until very recently, most unions with large female memberships routinely placed one, or at most two, women on national executive boards, a token gesture that did not even approach proportional representation.[37]

Once again, there is no consensus about the causes of female underrepresentation in union leadership. Doubtless, one factor is that domestic and family duties have traditionally been allotted to women, leaving them no time to engage in activities that could be stepping stones to union leadership. Another factor could be that some women take ten to fifteen years away from the labor force when their children are small. This is likely to mean nonparticipation in union affairs during their twenties and early thirties, the time when young men often take their first leadership positions.[38]

Psychological and social barriers are perhaps the strongest factors. Both men and women have been taught to underrate the competence of women. Both might vote for male candidates because, according to the stereotype, they will be "tougher" at the bargaining table, or because it is more "appropriate" for men to hold positions of authority. Similar stereotypes operate to discourage women from voting regularly in union elections or from seeking leadership positions themselves.

The past several years have seen a marked increase in union women's active demand for equal hiring practices, seniority, equal pay, nondiscriminatory promotions, day care, and social insurance. The following discussion of specific union practices relating to women demonstrates some recent progress.

United Auto Workers

The best-known union program for women's rights has been sponsored by the United Auto Workers. The UAW has over 200,000 women members, and it has represented them in an enlightened fashion for longer than any other union.[39] Close to 1000 women hold elective office at local levels, and many more have appointive positions. In 1967, when the women's movement was barely touching organized labor, the UAW had three female department directors, one executive board member, and sixteen international representatives. At the present time, the international has one woman vice-president, Olga Madar, who has been an articulate and vigorous advocate of the Equal Rights Amendment, affirmative action plans, economic equality for women, and increased political activity for women's rights.[40]

The UAW constitution requires that every local have a women's committee.[41] These committees have helped the women's department and the political action department to formulate strong legislative programs. Women's auxiliaries for wives of workers function actively at some locals, and regional women's councils sponsor classes and area conferences that alert delegates to issues of sex discrimination. The National Advisory Women's Council (NAWC), composed of one woman from each region, has convened to devise policy recommendations to the international. It was at the insistence of NAWC that each local received detailed explanations of developing fair employment legislation during the late 1960s.

The most noteworthy women's agency within the UAW is the women's department, directed by Caroline Davis and located at union headquarters in Detroit. This department was established twenty-five years ago, long before comparable bodies were formed in other unions. It has conducted regional women's conferences on an annual basis for a number of years and generally serves as a coordinator/clearinghouse for the local women's committees. The department staff assists with drives to organize women, teaches at union summer schools, researches and publishes materials about working women, and lobbies internally for women's interests. In addition, the women's department has been instrumental in seeing that fair employment legislation gets passed and implemented, by filing charges with FEP agencies[42] and also by acting as consultant to parties involved in grievance proceedings.

The UAW's legal department has also taken enlightened stands against sex discrimination, through appearing in friend of the court briefs in litigation involving protective laws[43] and maternity leave.[44] The legal department has also issued administrative letters interpreting the Equal Pay Act and Title VII of the Civil Rights Act of 1964,[45] and has coordinated with the women's department in filing charges of dsicrimination with the EEOC.

At the UAW's twenty-first constitutional convention in April 1970, the union adopted resolutions favoring increased powers for the EEOC, extended coverage of Title VII and the Equal Pay Act, and statutory mandates for maternity leave, child care, and temporary disability benefits for childbirth. The convention reaffirmed the need to repudiate discriminatory state labor laws and extend truly "protective" laws to men. And it urged locals to exert pressure on companies that still maintain discriminatory hiring practices.[46]

This action was supplemented at the union's twenty-third constitutional convention in April 1972. There a resolution was adopted that, among other things, urged ratification of the ERA, amendment of the Equal Pay Act to expand its coverage, passage of voluntary overtime legislation, renegotiation of contracts to ensure job security during maternity leaves, and development of comprehensive child care facilities.[47]

International Union of Electrical,
Radio, and Machine Workers

A somewhat smaller, but very active proponent of women's rights is the International Union of Electrical, Radio, and Machine Workers (IUE). Women comprise over 35 percent of the IUE membership, and representatives from each district and conference board constitute the union's official women's council. Although women have not attained proportional representation on the executive board, the elected chairwoman of the women's council participates with and advises the board on all matters of concern to women members. At the international's office in Washington, D.C., women have held high appointive positions—such as assistant comptroller, associate general counsel, and director of education and women's activities—for a number of years.

As early as 1951, the IUE convention unanimously adopted a resolution on women workers that stated in part:

A fundamental principle of our International Union is the equality of all workers regardless of race, color, creed, sex, or national origin. . . . Women workers should be provided not only with the opportunity for equal pay for equal work, but also assured of the safeguard of their health and the provision of community facilities to aid them in carrying out their family responsibilities.[48]

The IUE supported enactment of Title VII of the 1964 Civil Rights Act, as well as legislation designed to extend the power and jurisdiction of EEOC, which enforces Title VII.[49] Earlier than most labor organizations, the union recognized that protective laws were outmoded and in need of revision. It recommended that the states reexamine such legislation, repealing those laws that discriminated against women and extending to men those that were indeed beneficial.

In 1974 the union adopted a resolution in support of the Equal Rights Amendment which reflected similar goals. In the spirit of implementing these commitments, an IUE resolution in March 1973 called for the examination, local by local, of contracts and plant policies to determine where race and sex discrimination may persist. The union's legal department has worked closely with the social action department in pursuing the project.

The general counsel's office of the IUE filed a friend of the court brief in litigation challenging such protective laws.[50] It also initiated litigation against General Electric's denial of disability benefits to women on leave for childbearing or complications of pregnancy.[51] At the present time, the IUE is litigating twenty-two lawsuits under Title VII and the Equal Pay Act. Another issue that has received the IUE's active support is child care, and this support has continued despite President Nixon's veto of the Child Development Act of 1971.

The IUE has sponsored national women's conferences since 1957, biennially since 1967. Several regional women's conferences are held each year; in 1971, six of the IUE's nine districts held them in 1971. These meetings concentrate on issues that concern women workers, both within and outside the union. Delegates have been both male and female, and their policy recommendations are submitted to the executive board for approval. The conferences also serve to inform locals about recent developments in the area of equal rights. Biennial surveys have revealed that as women's participation in union politics increases, the network of their activity also grows.[52]

But the real evidence of women's progress in the labor movement comes from unions that had not shown great concern for their women members prior to the 1970s.

The Communications Workers of America

The Communication Workers of America (CWA), half of whose 500,000 members are women, began several efforts on behalf of women's rights in the early 1970s. A department of women's activities and consumer affairs was established in 1971 to coordinate and encourage greater female participation in local union activities. The department also analyzes union contracts to ensure just treatment for women, works with the EEOC on Title VII issues raised by union members, prepares testimony for congressional hearings on legislation affecting women, and writes articles for the CWA newspaper.

In April 1972, CWA filed sex-discrimination charges with EEOC against twenty-eight Bell System operating companies and subsidiaries. These charges alleged that policies on maternity disability were not applied on the same terms and conditions as other temporary disabilities.[53] In December of 1973, the EEOC found reasonable cause to believe that the union's charges against one of the twenty-eight Bell System companies were true.[54] CWA has not waited for the EEOC to act with regard to all the remaining charges; it requested right-to-sue letters from the EEOC and has filed lawsuits of its own against six Bell System companies.[55]

Perhaps the most significant issue of concern to CWA is the affirmative action program to be implemented by AT&T. Despite the extensive favorable publicity about the consent decree signed by AT&T in 1973 and negotiated by the EEOC, Department of Labor, and Justice Department, advocates of minority and women's rights were disappointed with the agreement (see Chapter 2). CWA attempted to challenge the implementation of this consent decree, after it had been reached and approved by a federal district court. CWA reasoned that since it has been excluded from negotiations conducted by the governmental agencies, it should not be bound by AT&T's bargain. The federal district court denied CWA's right to intervene, asserting that the union could have entered at an earlier stage of the negotiations had it so desired.[56] Although the union disputes this contention and has attempted to appeal the ruling, it has pressed on in urging AT&T to negotiate about affirmative action provisions in upcoming bargaining talks.[57]

Other Unions

Other unions that have recently actively supported issues relating to women include the American Newspaper Guild (ANG), which sponsored a three-day conference on "Sex Discrimination and Women's Rights in the Industry" and which has lobbied vigorously within the AFL-CIO, urging that body to endorse the Equal Rights Amendment.[58] The ANG locals have also acted on behalf of their women members by filing charges with the EEOC and pursuing cases to litigation where conciliation efforts fail.[59]

The American Federation of State, County and Municipal Employees (AFSCME) has, at its 1970 and 1972 conventions, passed resolutions to advance the position of women. These resolutions were directed specifically at training programs, recruitment, equal representation, and low pay scales and poor organization of women in public employment.[60] An interim committee on sex discrimination has been established and the international's department of program development launched a survey in 1973 of all state councils and locals in an effort to determine the numbers of women active in local union affairs, their leadership status (as stewards, or bargaining representatives), and the extent to which women's rights affect negotiating priorities. The results of the survey are not yet complete, but its function was as much to educate and prod the locals as it was to glean data for the international.[61]

Along similar lines, the union has reviewed all its collective bargaining contracts, in an effort to pinpoint those job classifications that are egregiously sex segregated. Since AFSCME's membership includes large numbers of clerical and hospital workers, there is likely to be significant adjustment of segregated job categories at the next negotiating sessions.[62]

The program of the Amalgamated Clothing Workers of America, a union that has been reluctant to support the Equal Rights Amendment, but which has been particularly active in establishing child care centers, is discussed in Chapter 6. Similarly, the activities of the American Federation of Teachers, which stem from the 1971 appointment of a Women's Rights Committee, are considered in Chapter 5.

AFL-CIO

The Executive Council of the AFL-CIO has traditionally allowed male biases to dominate despite the fact that many affiliates have always had large female memberships. But the recent activity by certain of those affiliates appears to have had an impact on the tradition-bound AFL-CIO council. During the 1970s, various state labor councils sponsored women's conferences and began to mobilize AFL-CIO bodies in support of equality for working women.[63]

In October 1973, the AFL-CIO resolved to endorse the Equal Rights Amendment, a position that can have considerable impact on the chances of ratification of the amendment. The preliminary clauses of the resolution noted that the United States economy vitally needs women's skills; that 22 percent of today's heads of households are women; that protective laws and other sex-differentiating legislation are consistently being struck down by the courts; and that "women continue to be one of the most discriminated against and exploited groups of workers in the nation." The final clauses then resolved:

That this 10th Biennial Convention of the AFL-CIO endorses the Equal Rights Amendment to the U.S. Constitution as precisely the kind of clear statement of national commitment to the principle of equality of the sexes under the law that working women and their unions can use to advantage in their efforts to eliminate employment discrimination against women, and be it further

RESOLVED: That state labor federations, in states which have not yet ratified the Equal Rights Amendment, urge their legislatures to act favorably upon the measure.[64]

Despite these recent developments, the historical patterns of discrimination persist. Both labor and management could be acting with more speed and vigor than has been characteristic. However, some groups within both groups have been doing the kinds of work that deserve praise and recognition. Those unions that have been discussed here fall in that category. Some women and men in their staffs and memberships have devoted time and energy to insuring fair treatment for working women. They were instrumental in founding the Coalition of Labor Union Women (CLUW) which sponsored a national conference attended by over three thousand union women in Chicago in March 1974.[65] They do not seem likely to abandon the cause.

Unions and the Law

The current statutory and regulatory arsenal seems to present an impressive variety of weapons for attacking discriminatory practices of unions. Federal fair employment laws and regulations (including the Equal Pay Act of 1963, Title VII of the Civil Rights Act of 1964, the Age Discrimination Act of 1967, Executive Order 12246 as amended by Executive Order 11375, and Labor Department regulations for registered apprenticeship programs) are all enforceable against labor unions. The federal labor relations laws, as interpreted by the courts and the NLRB, and the fair employment laws of some states bar sex discrimination by unions.

But for the most part these remedies are little more than possibilities. Some have never been applied to protect women in unions; most are applied only rarely. Some are too unwieldly to provide effective vehicles for broad-scale relief. Others provide such unsatisfactory relief that most aggrieved persons will not bother to make complaints, let alone follow through. Aspects of three of the major laws are discussed below: Title VII of the Civil Rights Act of 1964; the National Labor Relations Act, with its amendments, the Labor Management Relations Act of 1947 (Taft-Hartley) and the Labor Management Reporting and Disclosure Act of 1959 (Landrum-Griffin); and the Equal Pay Act of 1963.

Title VII of the Civil Rights Act
of 1964

Of the possible sources of legislation barring discrimination, Title VII is the broadest and clearest in terms of the numbers of workers and types of practices covered. Under Title VII, unions cannot exclude or expel any individual because of his or her race, color, religion, sex, or national origin. Nor can a union limit, segregate, or classify its membership on these bases. The language of Title VII is broad enough to cover virtually all discriminatory practices by unions, including access to apprenticeship programs, employment opportunities, and membership. As the act is discussed fully elsewhere, only a few areas pertaining specifically to unions are included here.

Seniority Systems. Seniority systems present a crucial component in the overall picture of sex discrimination against women. Job security, advancement, rate of pay, level of benefits, and position within the union may all hinge on the details of a seniority system. Because women are usually the last hired and the first fired, their chances for seniority rights are limited. Unions frequently discriminate overtly against women by negotiating sex-segregated promotion and transfer ladders and separate lines of layoff and rehiring priorities for men and women.

One major case, *Bowe v. Colgate Palmolive*,[66] challenged a whole seniority system as discriminatory against women. In *Bowe*, an example of a technique that employers and unions have used exclusively against women, the plaintiffs claimed that the new post-act seniority system actually exacerbated discrimination against women. Women first entered the work force at the Indiana plant during World War II. When the men came back, the company agreed that certain jobs should be reserved exclusively for women, and the rest given to men. Separate seniority lines for men's jobs and women's jobs were established under the collective agreement, and, as of 1963, the highest pay rate for women was less than the lowest pay rate for men. After Title VII went into effect, the contract was modified to make men eligible for all jobs in the plant. The women, however, were still confined to women's jobs because Colgate-Palmolive instituted a thirty-five-pound weight-lifting limit for women and defined all the men's jobs as requiring them to lift thirty-five pounds or more. This requirement allowed the men to compete for the women's jobs, but did not allow the women to compete for the men's jobs. Although all proceedings in *Bowe*, which began in 1965, have still not been concluded, the district judge has ordered the company to stop treating women employees differently, to pay back wages to women laid off as a result of the job and seniority system, and to give women who want to change into departments that were previously sex segregated the option of doing so without forfeiting their departmental seniority.

Another Title VII case involved the seniority rights of a woman who became pregnant. The collective agreement provided for all pregnant women to be terminated after their fourth month of pregnancy. The complainant wanted to continue working after her baby was born. The case was the subject of an opinion of an Equal Employment Opportunity Commission, which wrote that an employer could be required to preserve the "recall rights" of a woman who takes a maternity leave.[67] The opinion contains this interesting language:

Though a woman who has just had a child is unlikely to return immediately to work, this is not sufficient reason for depriving those women who should wish to so return from enjoying the same rights that a man would enjoy should he wish to return to the labor force after a period of sustained illness or convalescence. Most of the women who will want to return to their jobs will do so because they must do so to provide for themselves and their children. It is in the national interest that children be born. But there is little benefit to anyone to make mother and baby public charges or to force her to seek other work. An arbitrary rule that severs her rights of tenure and seniority is neither desirable nor fair.

Issues of seniority are difficult and complex, because, more than any other term or condition of employment, seniority raises the question of what is to be done about the existing effects of past discrimination. Before the Civil Rights Act of 1964 was passed, much was made of the fact that Title VII was not intended to allow reverse discrimination or preferential hiring of minority groups or women. However, in the first seniority case under Title VII, *Quarles v. Philip Morris, Inc. (and Local 203 Tobacco Workers International Union),*[68] the court said, in answer to the argument that Congress did not intend to require reverse discrimination, "It is also apparent that Congress did not intend to freeze an entire generation of Negro employees into discriminatory patterns that existed before the Act." The act, said the court, does not condone present differences that are the result of a past intent to discriminate. In the Philip Morris plant, seniority lines followed departmental lines, and departments had been segregated on racial lines before Title VII was passed. The court ordered, without delay or interference, that qualified black workers who had more seniority than the whites in line for the jobs would be invited to bid for the better-paying jobs in the white departments. Subsequent decisions have broadened this interpretation.[69]

Sex segregation of seniority systems is a common phenomenon. Just as invidious as racial discrimination, it links low pay with low responsibility and menial or difficult work. Unfortunately, the few cases that have been litigated have taken so long between initial complaint and adequate redress that women seeking to challenge seniority systems in the future may well be discouraged.

Sex-Segregated Union Locals. The practice of segregating locals has a long history, but only recently has it been the subject of suit under Title VII. In *Evans v. Sheraton Park Hotel,*[70] a district court ruled against both a hotel and a union for discriminating against waitresses who were organized into one local, and in favor of waiters who were organized into another local of the same international union. The discrimination had the result of giving waiters longer hours, larger total hourly compensation, larger gratuities, and fewer menial tasks. The court observed:

The discrimination in reception assignments is a classic example of the abuse inherent in maintaining and recognizing separate female and male locals for co-workers performing the same duties. It is inevitable in such a situation that not only will controversy and suspicion arise between males and females, but that the more dominant group, in this case the male, will gain privileges of various kinds. The failure of Local 507 (the all-women local) to support plaintiff's justifiable official complaints concerning uneven and unfair assignments demonstrates the inability of a Janus-headed union to safeguard sex-equality.[71]

The court went on to rule that the maintenance of sex-segregated locals was a per se violation of Title VII, and awarded damages to the waitress who had filed the suit.

Affirmative Action Against Discrimination. Title VII makes it illegal for a union to fail to process grievances because of a member's sex or race. In addition, recent decisions of the National Labor Relations Act (NLRA) have held that a union has a duty to press members' complaints of discrimination under the law.

In 1969 two black men filed complaints of job discrimination because their company operated a white-only pool and racially segregated teen clubs. The union was no help. It claimed that it was unaware of racial discrimination, that it had no machinery to process racial grievances, that it was ignorant of Title VII, that it had never discussed the questions with management, and that it had no instructions from the international union to process racial grievances. However, the EEOC held, "The union not only has the power, it has the *obligation* to process racial discrimination matters. By its refusal to do so, it violates Title VII" (emphasis added).[72] The Fifth Circuit reached a similar result under the NLRA in the *Rubber Workers* case.[73] There the court held that unions had a duty to process grievances about facilities segregated in violation of Title VII.[74]

Unions may now file complaints with the EEOC as aggrieved parties.[75] They may also sponsor class action suits under Title VII.[76] This duty to press grievances about discrimination could be of great significance. Unions have the money to press individual complaints; they have the potential to develop sensitivity to, and expertise in, issues of employment discrimination; they are in touch with workers at the point of discrimination; they are in a position to follow through the lengthy complaint process; and they are situated in a way that allows them to bring class action suits. Moreover, without backing by a union or some equivalent institution, few women's cases will be pressed. Women have had nothing analogous to the NAACP Legal Defense Fund, which presses job-discrimination complaints, and few working women have the money, stamina, or knowledge to press a complaint on their own. The National

Organization for Women (NOW) brought the original appeals in *Bowe, supra* and *Weeks v. Southern Bell Telephone and Telegraph Co.*[77] because "none of the working women involved could afford to appeal on their own and were able to get help from their unions."[78]

Enforcement. Two factors have minimized actual enforcement of Title VII against unions that discriminate against women. The first is the relatively small number of complaints that women have made against unions. In fiscal 1972 the EEOC received a total of 419 complaints against union practices and 335 joint complaints against unions, employers, and employment agencies as compared with 9056 complaints against employers; similarly the California Fair Employment Practices Commission (FEPC) reported that only 5 percent of all complaints received in 1972 were against unions.[79] It may be that unions no longer discriminate against women, but this seems doubtful. More likely, women do not think of filing complaints against unions for a number of reasons: one, the prevailing social belief that unions are the worker's friend and that to make a complaint against the union is a form of scabbing; two, a failure to see the union's role in the perpetuation of discrimination on the job; three, a lack of information about Title VII's applicability to unions; and four, the absence of a direct economic grievance against the union. With regard to the last of these reasons, it seems likely that where the payment of back wages is probable, a woman might go to the trouble of filing and pursuing a protracted and possibly expensive suit. This arduous course of action does not seem as likely when a place in the union leadership is at stake.

For its part, the Equal Employment Opportunity Commission has increased its efforts to force labor unions to comply with the law, and, as a result, unions are often later joined to an initial complaint against an employer. However, the EEOC can still improve its record. In the *Rosenfeld* case, for instance, it failed to notify the Transportation and Communication Employees Union of the complaint and to include the union in conciliation; when it sought to join the union in the federal court suit, it was too late. Furthermore, the EEOC has not always pushed as hard for enforcement against the union as against the employer; in the brief for the *Rosenfeld* case, the EEOC included only general and unsubstantiated allegations against the union.[80]

National Labor Relations Act and
the Railway Labor Act

The National Labor Relations Act (NLRA) and its major amendments, the Labor Management Relations Act of 1947 (Taft-Hartley Act) and the Labor

Management Reporting and Disclosure Act of 1959 (Landrum-Griffin Act), define the structure and nature of federal regulation of labor relations. The Railway Labor Act (RLA) supplements the NLRA by regulating labor-management relations in the railroad and airline industries. Federal labor laws have preempted the regulation of labor relations in all the areas it touches, so that state labor laws have relatively little vitality now.

The major responsibility for administering the NLRA lies with the National Labor Relations Board (NLRB). The board's many responsibilities include determining bargaining units, holding elections, and adjudicating disputes. Policing labor union discrimination against individual workers or classes of workers takes up only a small part of the board's total attention, and for the most part is not even an explicit part of the authority delegated to the board by Congress. However, as the governmental agency most responsible for shaping the development of labor union practices, as well as the agency with the largest staff and resources for regulating labor unions, the NLRB is in a special position to regulate sex discrimination by labor unions and employers if it so chooses.

Coverage. The NLRA does not cover all workers, and most of the job categories it excludes are in areas with a high percentage of women workers. Workers in agricultural labor and domestic service are explicitly excepted from the NLRA's definition of employee.[81] Two percent of all working women do farm work. Only 7.2 percent of all women workers are paid private household workers; however, 97.6 percent of all domestic workers are women.[82] Also excluded from the NLRA's definition of employers are the federal, state, and municipal governments and nonprofit hospitals. The exclusion of governmental bodies is particularly significant, because government is the fastest growing area of employment for women.[83] In 1968 there were 5.3 million women on government payrolls, and women were 43.5 percent of all government workers.[84] In addition to the huge number of clerical and receptionist jobs filled by women in government, this figure includes schoolteachers (elementary school teaching is the fourth highest occupational category for women) and federal, state, and municipal hospital workers.

Because there are relatively few private proprietary hospitals, the exclusion of workers in nonprofit, federal, state, and municipal hospitals means that most hospital workers are excluded from the NLRA. This too is a very significant exception, because 81.3 percent of all hospital workers, more than 1.3 million workers, were women in 1968.[85]

Altogether, the few categories of workers that are excluded from the NLRA and the Railway Labor Act add up to more than one-fourth of all working women, and because important protections are thus not provided for these workers organizing into a union, these exceptions become discriminatory in and of themselves.

Fair Representation. The NLRA and the RLA make extensive legal attempts to clarify the duty of unions to represent their numbers. A union that has been certified as the recognized agent of a bargaining unit has the power to represent and define the terms and conditions of employment of all employees in the unit, whether or not they are members of the union. Because all employees are bound by the collective agreement that the union negotiates and they may not deal independently with the employer, the courts have determined that unions have a duty to represent all employees fairly.

The duty of fair representation, not explicitly required by statute, was first enunciated in 1944 by the Supreme Court in a case under the Railway Labor Act, *Steele v. Louisville & N.R. Co.*[86] Steele, a black male, was a locomotive fireman; he sued for an injunction and damages against the all-white Brotherhood of Locomotive Foremen and Enginemen, which was trying to replace black firemen with whites and thus force the blacks out of jobs. The Supreme Court held that federal courts had jurisdiction to entertain such a suit and explained in the majority opinion by Chief Justice Stone:

So long as a labor union assumes to act as the statutory representative of a craft, it cannot rightly refuse to perform the duty which is inseparable from the power of representation conferred upon it, to represent the entire membership of the craft. . . . [The statute requires the union] to represent non-union or minority members of the craft without hostile discrimination, fairly, impartially, and in good faith.

In the *Miranda Fuel Co.*[87] case in 1962, the NLRB carried the logic of *Steele* further and found that a violation of the duty of fair representation was an unfair labor practice. Since *Miranda*, the NLRB has found in a number of cases that unfair representation violates the NLRA.[88]

No particular limits have been set to what activities the duty of fair representation covers. *Steele* required fair representation in negotiation of the collective agreement. *Conley v. Gibson*[89] extended the duty to fair administration of the contract, which includes fair processing of grievances arising under the collective agreement. In *Local Union No. 12, United Rubber, Cork, Linoleum and Plastic Workers of America,*[90] the Fifth Circuit held that the union was required to process grievances even if they were not specifically subjects of the collective agreement; in the *Rubber Workers* case the court ordered the union to process grievances concerning segregated rest rooms, showers, dining rooms, and a white-only golf course.

The extent to which the duty of fair representation obligates a union to refuse a discriminatory contract and strike is still uncertain. At least in cases of racial discrimination, the NLRB would probably agree that a union may not accept a contract that offers benefits on discriminatory classifications.[91] Breach of the duty of fair representation has been found and prohibited in nonracial cases where the discrimination has been hostile or arbitrary—for instance, in cases of unfair allocation of seniority when two companies merge.

One might think that union discrimination against women would be considered "hostile" or "arbitrary" and therefore a violation of the duty of fair representation. However, this duty has not yet been applied in any case to protect women, and in at least one state case,[92] a court has found that discrimination against women came within the "wide range of reasonableness" that the Supreme Court said it would allow to unions in deciding the best way to represent their members.[93]

Moreover, while no federal court has ever said that sex discrimination *does not* violate the duty of fair representation, no federal court has ever said that discrimination against women *does* violate the duty either.

There is no reason to think that sex discrimination should not be a violation of the duty of fair representation. Writing in 1959, Archibald Cox, the former solicitor general, concluded that it was "settled that the right of fair representation protects individuals and minorities against all forms of hostile discrimination or oppression at the hands of the bargaining representatives."[94] The Equal Pay Act, Title VII of the Civil Rights Act, and Executive Orders 11246 and 11375 are now all evidence of a federal policy that discrimination on the basis of sex is unacceptable. Moreover, in deciding the proper limits of a bargaining unit, the NLRB has refused in a few cases to approve bargaining units established along sex lines. The board refused a request for bargaining units made up of all women on the first and second shifts in *Cuneo Eastern Press, Inc.*[95] and said that bargaining units split on the basis of sex alone were inappropriate unless significant differences in skills were shown between the men and the women.[96]

The crucial question is not so much whether or not sex discrimination violates the duty of fair representation, but how blatant the discrimination must be and to what extent the NLRB and the courts will go in enforcing remedies against sex discrimination. The answer to this will lie in the development of the case law and in the generally inscrutable politics of the NLRB and labor relations law.

Title VII and the NLRA: Joint Action

While virtually any instance of sex discrimination that would violate the duty of fair representation under the NLRA or the Railway Labor Act would also violate Title VII of the Civil Rights Act, there are sometimes advantages to pursuing remedies under both acts. In the past, the NLRB procedures were cheaper and simpler for the complainant and provided more prompt remedies than those under Title VII;[97] the recent grant of direct enforcement powers to the EEOC has changed this situation. Therefore, the main reasons for continuing to use these procedures is to take advantage of the powerful tools the NLRB has for enforcing the duty of fair representation against unions. Of particular importance is the NLRB's power to refuse to help a discriminating union that wants to be certified as a bargaining representative.[98] For a weak union this is a serious sanction, because an employer does not have to bargain with a union that is not certified, nor are competitor unions prohibited from trying to take over under the usual "contract bar" rule. Since the *Bowe* decision, it has been established that an aggrieved individual may pursue parallel remedies both in court and through arbitration as long as he or she makes an election of remedies after final decision by both tribunals. Therefore, if plaintiffs wish to obtain decertification of a union, they have nothing to lose and a great deal to gain by filing charges under both acts simultaneously.

The Equal Pay Act

The Equal Pay Act, discussed in Chapter 3, makes it unlawful for any labor organization to cause or attempt to cause an employer to violate this act.[99] Covered labor organizations include any organization or agency, employee representation committee, or plan in which employees participate and which exists for the purpose, in whole or in part, of dealing with employers concerning grievances, labor disputes, wages, rates of pay, hours of work, and conditions of employment.[100] This is the same definition of labor organizations covered by the Taft-Hartley Act. It is uncertain how actively a union must "cause or attempt to cause" an employer to discriminate to be liable under the act. Affirmative acts such as picketing an employer to establish a wage differential or demanding discriminatory terms at the collective bargaining table are certainly prohibited.[101]

Courts apparently will not go so far as requiring a union to strike to avoid a discriminatory condition. In *Wirtz v. Hayes Industry*, a suit under the Equal Pay Act, the defendant company moved to have the union held jointly liable as coauthor of the contract. The union president testified that he had attempted to have the discriminatory provisions changed at the contract negotiations and that he had filed a complaint of discrimination with the Wage and Hour Division after the employer refused to change his position. The court held that the union had done all it was legally required to do, and refused to hold the union jointly liable.[102] Similarly, in *Murphy v. Miller Brewing Co.,*[103] the court considered a sex-discriminatory job classification scheme, whereby women laboratory technicians were given a different classification and lower wages than their male counterparts for substantially equal work. However, because the union that represented the women had not proposed the discriminatory provisions of the contract, the court held that the union was not liable under the Equal Pay Act. The fact that the local and international unions refused to strike or picket over the issue of equal wages did not establish that the unions *caused or attempted to cause* employer discrimination.[104]

Another problem in the application of the Equal Pay Act to discriminating unions is that the remedies available against the union are relatively weak compared to the remedies against employers. The only civil remedy available is injunctive relief to restrain unions from causing employers to discriminate, and actions for injunctive relief lie exclusively with the Secretary of Labor. Thus, while employees may maintain actions to recover back wages and liquidated damages from employers, they cannot reach unions at all unless the Secretary of Labor brings suit, and they are unable to obtain financial sanctions against the union even if suit is brought. Only if the employer seeks a contribution from the union to a back-pay award will the union have a financial incentive not to discriminate.

So far, very few Equal Pay Act suits have been brought against labor unions. Yet, even with its limitations, the act probably provides the best relief available for wage discrimination. As with Title VII and the NLRA, employees can pursue remedies under the Equal Pay Act while they are seeking redress under other statutes, so plaintiffs should be encouraged to file suit under the Equal Pay Act against employers and to ask the secretary of labor to file against both the union and the employer whenever wage discrimination has occurred.

Conclusion

While women who are union members usually earn more than women with comparable jobs who are not union members, patterns of discrimination within unions remain. The income gap between men and women, union and nonunion, continues to grow.[105] Some unions are becoming aware of the problems of their women members, but the extent to which this awareness will actually be translated into wages and benefits remains to be seen. If it appears that gains for women will mean losses for men, we can expect employers and unions alike to be reluctant to make meaningful changes. Legislation has been, and can continue to be, used to push unions and employers towards granting women union members what are now their rights, but litigation is costly and time consuming.

The discussion in this and earlier chapters of the status of working women, of employer and union practices, and of the existing laws that deal with sex discrimination demonstrates that women are still a long way from having the rights and opportunities that should be theirs. Changes in these areas will have a direct and immediate impact on the status of working women, but they will not end sex discrimination within society as a whole. The next two chapters discuss areas that are not necessarily a direct responsibility of unions and employers but that affect working women: education and day care. Changes in these areas will ensure that women are better trained to take advantages of the opportunities to work and that they have some of the support services to enable them to work if they wish. Employers and unions can have an important role in bringing about the long overdue improvement in these services.

Notes

1. For example, see M. Danish, *The Story of the I.L.G.W.U.* (New York, Educational Dept. International Ladies' Garment Workers Union, 1951).

2. Theresa Wolfson, *The Woman Worker and the Trade Unions* (New York: 1927), p. 56.

3. Ibid., p. 58.

4. Philip Sheldon Foner, *History of the Labor Movement* (New York: 1947), vol. 1, p. 383.

5. Eleanor Flexner, *Century of Struggle, The Women's Rights Movement in the United States* (New York: Atheneum, 1959), pp. 57-60.

6. S.C. Hewitt, an organizer of the Fall River Mechanics Association, was far ahead of his time in 1844 in believing that women should be members of every labor movement. He discovered that he had to mention women explicitly in his writing and speaking, because when he put out a call for "workingmen," women did not understand themselves to be included.

7. Wolfson, *The Woman Worker*, p. 59.

8. Ibid., p. 61.

9. Foner, *History of the Labor Movement*, vol. 2, p. 61.

10. Ibid. Even then, the very name of the organization must have discouraged some women.

11. Flexner, *Century of Struggle*, p. 195.

12. Foner, *History of the Labor Movement*, vol. 2, p. 61.

13. Flexner, *Century of Struggle*, p. 193.

14. Foner, *History of the Labor Movement*, vol. 2, p. 190.

15. Sarah Simpson to Samuel Gompers, quoted in Foner, *History of the Labor Movement*, vol. 3, p. 227.

16. Wolfson, *The Woman Worker*, p. 80. Wolfson lists twelve international unions with such policies.

17. Ibid., p. 104.

18. Ibid., p. 140.

19. Theresa Wolfson, "Trade Union Activities of Women," *Annals of the American Academy of Political and Social Sciences, May 1929, p. 120. She* estimated that 8,500,000 women were gainfully employed in 1927 and that 260,095 of these women were union members.

20. G. Dickason, "Women in Labor Unions," *Annals of the American Academy of Political and Social Science*, May 1947, p. 70. Dickason estimates 10,297,000 women in the labor force and 260,000 women trade union members in 1930. This comes to about one woman in forty.

21. For an excellent discussion of the ways these social myths interacted with working women's experiences, see S. Eisenstein, "Bread and Roses—Working Women's Consciousness Develops, 1905-1920," in *The Human Factor, Journal of the Graduate Sociology Student Union of Columbia University*, Fall 1970, p. 33.

22. Dickason, "Women in Labor Unions," p. 78.

23. Ibid., p. 73.

24. Ibid., p. 109.

25. Ibid., p. 73. In 1949, Dickason was able to count only twenty women officers of state labor organizations and twenty directors of education and research, which was the traditional woman's job. At the time Dickason wrote her article, the Women's Bureau of the United Auto Workers, started during the war, was developing a questionnaire about women officers of unions.

26. Abbott L. Ferriss, *Indicators of Trends in the Status of American Women* (New York: Russell Sage Foundation, 1971), p. 177.

27. Ibid.

28. Ibid.

29. Edna Raphael, "Working Women and Their Membership in Labor Unions" *Monthly Labor Review*, May 1974, pp. 27-28.

30. Ibid.

31. Ibid.

32. Approximately 3 percent of all apprentices in 1968 were black, and fewer than 1 percent were women. U.S. Department of Labor, Women's Bureau, *1969 Handbook of Women Workers*, p. 83.

33. It remains to be seen whether the EEOC National Programs Unit in Washington, D.C., which is considering certain labor unions for broad-based national litigation efforts, will focus on sex as well as racial bias.

34. Dorothy Haener, "Women into Unions," *Trial*, Nov./Dec. 1973, p. 15.

35. Ibid.

36. Alice Cook, "Women and American Trade Unions," *Annals of the American Academy of Political Science*, January 1961, p. 132.

37. Ibid., p. 130. In a recent effort to remedy this situation, the American Federation of State County, and Municipal Employees (AFSCME) now employs the same proportion of women on the professional staff as there are women in the union's membership—40 percent. (Telephone Interview with Linda Tar-Whelan, Deputy Director, Program Development, AFSCME, February 1, 1974.)

38. Recent figures show that the trend since 1948 for women with children reflects increasing labor force participation. Thus, this "factor" may carry less weight than traditionalists might wish. See A. Feriss, *Indicators of Trends*, pp. 103-4.

39. U.S. Women's Bureau, *1969 Handbook on Women Workers*, p. 83.

40. See generally, Testimony Presented by Olga M. Madar in Hearings before Subcommittee No. 4, of the Committee on the Judiciary, House of Representatives, 92d Congress, 1st Sess. (April 1971).

41. Article 43, International Constitution on Standing Committees, UAW.

42. In October 1972, the UAW filed "pattern and practice" charges of sex discrimination with the EEOC, accusing Ford, General Motors, and Chrysler of failing to give women employees sickness and accident benefits for pregnancy-related disabilities comparable to benefits available for other nonoccupational disabilities. In sending copies of the charges to all local women's committees, Caroline Davis stated that the Women's Department had "cooperated closely with the Legal Department in pushing this matter. This is an issue the Women's Department has been pursuing for many years." (Letter from Caroline Davis to all women's committee chairwomen and members, October 27, 1972.)

43. Bowe v. Colgate-Palmolive Co. 416 F.2d 711 (7th Cir. 1969).

44. Cleveland Bd. of Educ. v. LaFleur; Cohen v. Chesterfield County School Board, 6 FEP Cases 1253 (U.S. 94 U.S. 791 (1974)).

45. Administrative Letter #10, vol. 21 (Nov. 6, 1969).

46. UAW, *Women's Resolution*, April 22, 1970.

47. UAW, Resolution on *Women's Rights and Child Care*, adopted by UAW 23d Constitutional Convention, April 23-28, 1972, Atlantic City, New Jersey.

48. IUE testimony before the House Judiciary Committee, April 1971. Hearings published under the title *Equal Rights for Men and Women* (1971), p. 596.

49. Equal Opportunity Act of 1972. Pub. L. 92-261, 86 Stat. 103 (March 24, 1972), 42 U.S.C. § 2000e *et seq.* (Supp. II, 1972).

50. Ridinger et al. v. General Motors, F.2d (6th Cir. 1972).

51. Gilbert et al. v. General Electric, No. 142-72-R (E.D.Va., filed March 15, 1972); Grogg et al. v. General Motors, 73 Civ. 63 (S.D.N.Y., filed 1974).

52. The surveys are conducted and evaluated by Gloria Johnson, Director of Education and Women's Activities, IUE.

53. *CWA News*, April 1972, p. 2.

54. *CWA News*, January, 1974, p. 15.

55. Ibid.

56. EEOC et al. v. American Telephone and Telegraph Company et al., No. 73-149, (E.D.Pa., October 5, 1973). Decision denying right to intervene reported in BNA's *Daily Labor Report*, no. 201 (October 17, 1973).

57. *CWA News*, January 1974, pp. 2 and 9.

58. Letter from ANG to the House Judiciary Committee, April 16, 1971, *Equal Rights for Men and Women*, 1971, p. 634. Telephone Interview with Yetta Riesel, Research and Information Associate, ANG, January 29, 1974.

59. For example, in the fall of 1973 the ANG filed a broad based sex-discrimination charge against the Associated Press.

60. Lucretia M. Dewey, "Women in Labor Unions," *Monthly Labor Review*, February 1971, pp. 42-48. Telephone Interview with Linda Tar-Whelan, Deputy Director, Program Development AFSCME, on February 1, 1974.

61. Ibid.

62. Ibid.

63. See *Minutes of Women's Conference*, held by the Wisconsin State Labor Council, Wisconsin Rapids, Wisconsin, on March 7, 1970.

64. Equal Rights Resolution, Tenth Constitutional Convention of the AFL-CIO, October 1973.

65. This group has the potential for significant policy-making and lobbying power within the existing labor movement, and should be watched with interest. (Telephone Interviews with Yetta Riesel, Research and Information Associate, ANG, and Catherine Conrol, International Representative, CWA, on January 29, 1974.)

66. 272 F. Supp. 332; *modified* at 416 F.2d 711; order entered 2 FEP Cases 463 (S.D.Ind. 2/25/70).

67. Opinion of EEOC commissioner, B.N.A. Fair Employment Practices Reporter 401:2001.

68. 279 F. Supp. 505, 516 (E.D.Va. 1968). See also Robinson v. Lorillard, 444 F.2d 91 (4th Cir. 1971).

69. U.S. v. Paper-makers Local 189, 232 F. Supp. 39 (E.D.La.); *aff'd.*, 416 F.2d 980 (5th Cir. 1969) dealt with discrimination at Crown Zellerback's Bogalusa, La., plant, where the pay for the highest of the black jobs was lower than the pay for any of the white jobs. After the 1964 Civil Rights Act went into effect, the progression lines were merged on the basis of pay, with the result that blacks, no matter what their seniority in terms of length of service, were still at the bottom of all the progression ladders. The court ordered that a seniority system should be instituted based solely on length of service in the mill.

And in Dobbins v. International Brotherhood of Electrical Workers, 292 F. Supp. 413 (S.D.Ohio 1968), the court held that a referral system based on work experience in the union, which had excluded blacks from membership in the past, was discriminatory and illegal.

70. 5 FEP Cases 393 (D.D.C. 1973).

71. 5 FEP Cases at 395 (D.D.C. 1973).

72. EEOC Decis. No. 70134, 2 FEP Cases 237 (9/5/69).

73. Local Union No. 12, United Rubber Cork., etc. Workers, 150 NLRB 312; *enforcement granted*, 368 F.2d 12 (4th Cir. 1966); *cert. den.* 380 U.S. 837 (1967).

74. However, in Rosenfeld v. Southern Pacific, 293 F. Supp. 1219 (C.D.Cal. 1968) the court said a union was not under an obligation to challenge discrimination that resulted from a state protective law.

75. Auto Workers v. H_____ Corp. and Chemical Workers v. P_____ Corp. BNA Fair Employment Practices Reporter 401:3001; adopted by federal court in Chemical Workers v. Planters Mfg. Co., 1 FEP Cases 39, 63 LRRM 2213 (N.D.Miss. 1966).

76. Quarles and Dobbins, above, were class actions. So was Hall v. Werthen

Bag, 251 F. Supp. 184, 400 F.2d 28 (1968). The Fifth Circuit reversed a lower court ruling that had refused to allow a class action by Negroes working in different parts of the plant.

77. 408 F.2d. 228 (5th Cir. 1969), discussed in Chapter 3.

78. Betty Friedan, *Newsletter to Members of NOW*, November 1969, p. 1, quoted in S.D. Ross, "Sex Discrimination and Title VII," (unpublished paper). Note, however, that the NOW filed a brief as *amicus curiae.*

79. 6th Annual Report, EEOC (1972); M. Tobriner, "California FEPC," 16 Hastings L. Rev. 333 (1965).

80. *Supra*, n. 7.

81. 49 Stat. 449 Sec. 101(2)(3) (1935).

82. *1969 Handbook on Women Workers*, p. 38.

83. Ibid., p. 113.

84. Ibid., p. 113.

85. Ibid., p. 116.

86. 323 U.S. 198 (1944).

87. 140 NLRB 181 (1962).

88. See e.g., *Independent Metal Workers Union, Local No. 1 (Hughes Tool Co.) 147 NLRB 1573 (1964)* theory approved in Local Union No. 12, United Rubber Cork, etc. Workers, 150 NLRB 312; *enforcement granted*, 368 F.2d. 12 (4th Cir. 1966); *cert. den.* 380 U.S. 837 (1967).

89. 355 U.S. 41 (1957).

90. Rubber Workers, *supra* n. 71.

91. See, e.g., Local 1367, International Longshoremen's Assoc., 148 NLRB 44 (1967): "[C]ollective bargaining agreements which discriminate invidiously are not lawful under the Act . . . and both unions and employers are enjoined by the Act from entering into them."

92. Ford Motor Co. v. Huffman, 345 U.S. 330 (1953).

93. Cortez v. Ford Motor Co., 349 Mich. 108, 84 N.W. 523 (Sup. Ct. Mich. 1957). See also Hartley v. Br. of By. and Steamship Clerks, 283 Mich. 201, 277 N.W. 885 (1938).

94. A. Cox, "The Duty of Fair Representation," 2 Vill. L. Rev. 151, 160-61 (1957).

95. 106 NLRB 343 (1953).

96. See also Underwriters Salvage Co. of New York, 99 NLRB 337 (1952); Tom Thumb Stores, 123 NLRB 99 (1959); U.S. Baking Co., 165 NLRB 931 (1961).

97. 34 George Washington L. Rev., 155 ff.

98. In Hughes Tool 104 (NLRB 318), the NLRB indicated that it would be willing to refuse or rescind certification to discriminating unions.

99. 29 U.S.C. Sec. 206 (d) (1), 1964.

100. 29 C.F.R. Sec. 800, 109.

101. 29 C.F.R. Sec. 800, 106.

102. 58 Labor Cases, § 32,085 (9/68).

103. 307 F. Supp. 829 (E.D.Wis. 1969).

104. 307 F. Supp. at 839.

105. Edna Raphael, "Working Women and their Membership in Labor Unions," *Monthly Labor Review*, May 1974, p. 27.

5 Education: Sex-Role Socialization

Increasingly, research in the field of education points to the crucial role that schools play in the development of a child's personality. From earliest experiences at home, in day care centers, and in nursery schools, children learn about themselves and about those around them. In this process, teachers and classmates develop, reinforce, or challenge attitudes about sex roles and sex differences. Unfortunately, young girls and boys often learn early in their lives that girls should limit their goals and pursue lesser aspirations than their male playmates. Within the education system itself, they learn through experience that girls grow up to be elementary-school teachers while boys become college professors, that women are assistants and men executives. In later years, the roles often become more rigidly defined as young adolescents are encouraged to take such courses as home economics if they are female, and industrial arts if they are male. By the time these students enter college, information that challenges well-learned traditional sex-role values often causes ambivalence and confusion about one's identity.

The more education a woman has, the more likely she is to work. However, the nature of her education influences the kind of work she is likely to seek, as well as the kind of work to which she has access. Because employment practices themselves serve as a form of education, some of the types of discrimination that students, teachers, and other employees meet within all levels of educational institutions are discussed in this chapter. After a brief historical overview, the status of women in elementary, secondary, and higher education is examined.

Equal educational opportunity for women is a prerequisite for equal opportunity in the labor force. In the United States, however, women have traditionally not had equal educational opportunity. While, more often than not, women now have access to the same classroom as men, this has not always been the case. The colonial belief that women were intellectually inferior to men, and that a woman's place was in the home, left no room for institutional female education. Women learned the skills they needed to run a home by working as apprentices to their mothers.

In the "dame schools" of New England and the Middle Colonies in the seventeenth and eighteenth centuries, boys and girls were trained to fill different roles: girls learned the social graces while boys learned arithmetic.[1] These dame schools were replaced by infant schools at the beginning of the nineteenth century and kindergartens at the end of the nineteenth century.[2]

In the middle of the seventeenth century, Massachusetts and Connecticut enacted laws requiring towns of fifty families to establish elementary schools and towns twice that size to open Latin grammar schools. However, the exact status of girls in these early New England town schools is unclear. Although the value of admitting women was seriously discussed while these schools were being formed, women were almost invariably excluded from them until after the Revolutionary War.[3] Girls in the middle and southern states did not even fare this well. Only a few parochial and charity schools were available to educate the poorer girls, and well-to-do families often had to hire tutors or send their daughters to England to "finish" a dubious education.[4]

Indeed, it was often difficult for even a brilliant woman to receive a good education. The private day and boarding schools of the eighteenth century generally emphasized "womanly" accomplishments (such as needlework, drawing, dancing) at the expense of rigorous academic training.[5] After the American Revolution, however, the situation began to improve. Some schools began to allow girls to attend classes early in the morning and late in the afternoon, when the boys were not in school.[6] In addition, many more female academies were opened. Although they were often poorly staffed, meagerly financed, inadequately equipped, expensive, inconvenient, and academically inferior, these seminaries were the most common provider of girls' education until 1865.[7] By the 1800s, most New England towns offered some sort of free elementary education to girls as well as boys. However, the first public high school for girls was not opened until 1824.[8]

It is not surprising, then, that at the end of the eighteenth century only a few women and men felt that a woman's education should extend beyond the home. These early advocates of female education, including Emma Willard, believed that education would enable women to be better assistants to their husbands and better educators of their children. In her careful proposal to New York Governor Clinton for a female seminary, Willard explained that "housewifery might be greatly improved by being taught, not only in practice, but in theory."[9]

Educational opportunities for women changed significantly after common schools were established in the 1820s. These schools (which were designed to prepare white male children to participate in the democratic government of the country) needed teachers, and the taxpayers wanted to pay these teachers as little as possible. Women had already been teaching their own children at home. Thus, the step to being a teacher at school was relatively easy and in keeping with the traditional nurturing female role. To train these elementary-school teachers normal schools were established in the East and middle West.[10]

The job of teaching rapidly became identified as intrinsically female, and a pattern that has since become all too familiar developed. When a job that required some of the qualities associated with homemaker and mother was designed, and men were either unavailable or unwilling to fill these positions, women were employed. The job subsequently became defined as a low-status, low-paying job—a job only for women.

Until the middle of the nineteenth century, women were virtually excluded from institutions of higher education in the United States. Most people assumed that women were intellectually inferior to men and that an educated wife or daughter was a "luxury" that most men neither wanted nor could afford. As late as 1872, a Harvard Medical School professor wrote that if women studied too hard, they could become infertile.[11]

In light of these arguments, the colleges that did admit women in the nineteenth century had the task of proving that women could learn as well as men. Although the female and male schools provided roughly equivalent institutional frameworks and academic degrees, the products of female and male institutions were not identical, nor were the opportunities offered the graduates of the institutions. While teachers' training colleges (normal schools) had clearly prepared women for a profession, the imitative colleges were less explicit in their goals. Their graduates had wider interests than those of the teachers' training colleges, yet no other professional opportunities existed.

The new problems and rewards of higher education were not confined to the East. While "separate but equal" education was struggling for acceptance in New England, the question of coeducation was being confronted in the West. In 1837, Oberlin in Ohio became the first college in the United States to admit women and to grant them the regular arts degree.[12] Oberlin was, however, an exception in many respects. It was largely state institutions—Iowa, Wisconsin, and Michigan, in particular—which were responsible for the growing acceptance of coeducation.[13] Social structure in the West was less rigid, and the cost of building separate institutions seemed unnecessary to the practical western educators. Still, women were routinely discouraged from enrolling in certain programs, and in many coeducational institutions they were viewed, by themselves as well as by others, as second-class citizens. Though more subtle today, many prejudices and traditions still linger, making it difficult for women to acquire equal skills and educational credentials.

Recently women have begun to ask for an end to all forms of discrimination, and changes, particularly at colleges and universities, are beginning to take place. Women's efforts to eliminate discrimination in education are supported by a number of federal, state, and local laws that prohibit sex discrimination in schools and colleges. The legislation prohibiting sex discrimination in employment was discussed earlier. Since one federal law, Title IX of the Education Amendments of 1972, applies only to sex discrimination in educational institutions, it is discussed here.

Title IX of the Education Amendments of 1972

Unlike Title VII of the Civil Rights Act of 1964 and other legislation discussed previously, Title IX applies only to federally assisted education programs, including educational institutions that receive federal assistance. It applies to educational institutions at all levels, and it prohibits discrimination against *students*, as well as employees.[14] This is the first comprehensive legislation prohibiting sex discrimination against students.[15] The key section of Title IX reads: "No person in the United States shall, on the basis of sex, be excluded from participation in, be denied the benefits of, or be subjected to discrimination under any educational program or activity receiving Federal financial assistance."[16]

All educational institutions—preschools, elementary and secondary schools, and colleges and universities—that receive federal monies by way of a grant, loan, or contract (other than a contract of insurance or guaranty) are subject to the provisions of Title IX. There are only three exemptions to this coverage. Religious institutions are exempt if the application of the antidiscrimination provision is not consistent with the religious tenets of the organization. Military schools are exempt if their primary purpose is to train individuals for the military services of the United States or the merchant marine. Discrimination in admissions is prohibited in vocational institutions (including vocational high schools), graduate and professional institutions, and public undergraduate coeducational institutions.[17] Private undergraduate institutions are exempt from the admissions provision only, but are still subject to all other antidiscrimination provisions of the act.[18]

Unequal treatment of students on the basis of sex is currently widespread. For example, athletic opportunities and facilities for women at all levels are generally considerably less than those for men: there are usually far more team opportunities for men than women, and the athletic facilities for men are almost always far superior to those for women. Schools often have different hours or social rules for women and men. Courses such as shop or home economics are often required of one sex, while the other sex is flatly denied admission to them. often required of one sex, while the other sex has been denied admission to them. appearing to prescribe curriculum, the implications of Title IX for sex stereotyping in textbooks and curriculum are clear. In fact, many textbook publishers are already beginning to revise their materials with an eye to eliminating discriminatory references.

Like most of the other laws that prohibit discrimination on the basis of sex, a complaint under Title IX may be made on an individual basis or on the basis of a pattern of discrimination. The Office for Civil Rights (Division of Higher Education) of the Department of Health, Education and Welfare has primary enforcement powers to conduct reviews and investigations. Under Title IX, this office has the power to delay new awards, to revoke current awards, and to debar an educational institution from eligibility for future awards. In addition, the Department of Justice may bring suit at HEW's request.

Already, individual students as well as women's groups have begun to file charges of sex discrimination against elementary and secondary schools, colleges, and universities. In April of 1973, the Texas division of the Women's Equity

Action League (WEAL) filed charges against the Waco public school system for sex discrimination in athletic programs and student course assignments, as well as in its employment practices.[19] A number of institutions, including the University of Michigan, the University of Minnesota, and the University of Wisconsin, have been charged with violating Title IX for providing unequal opportunity in athletics and sports programs.[20] At the University of Wisconsin, a group of women medical students filed charges of sex discrimination under Title IX, claiming that a professor's remarks showed disrespect for women medical students. They substantiated their claims with tape recordings.[21] After WEAL filed charges against twenty-five institutions for sponsoring Phi Delta Kappa (the national men's education honorary society), a policy change was voted and women were admitted.[22]

The Educational Amendments Act was signed by the president on June 23 and became effective July 1, 1972. Two years later, in June 1974, proposed regulations for Title IX were issued for comment.[23] Drafting of these regulations caused considerable controversy both within the government and outside. The provisions regarding equal opportunity in athletic programs were challenged by the National Collegiate Athletic Association (NCAA), which oversees inter-collegiate athletics for men. Before the proposed regulations take effect, they will have to be approved by the president, a requirement that concerns many women on campus and many women's organizations. Although Title IX is a potentially powerful piece of legislation, its ultimate effectiveness will be determined by the manner in which the government implements its provisions and the degree to which the government uses the sanctions available.

Legislation alone cannot change patterns of discrimination that have been part of the country's educational system for generations. The discussion that follows of the ways in which the educational system at all levels places women at a disadvantage identifies some areas of primary concern not necessarily covered by the legislation.

Primary and Secondary Education

Women as Students[a]

While some generally consistent differences between women and men have been identified, there is disagreement about the extent to which these differences are due to genetics or to environment.[24] But there is no doubt that there are indeed tremendous differences in the social and environmental pressures placed on boys and girls, and that the environment profoundly influences the development of values.

[a]The discussion of children's television and literature is from Lenore J. Weitzman, "Sociological Perspectives on Discrimination Against Working Women," prepared for the Twentieth Century Fund Task Force, January 1971.

The importance of schooling as a major socializing factor should not be underestimated. Since education is mandatory in virtually every state until a person reaches sixteen, young people spend many of their waking hours in school. Because of the enormous potential influence of this environment on children, public schools have a particularly strong responsibility to provide all students with equal educational opportunity. Many schools have failed to meet this responsibility.

Even *Sesame Street*, the much praised and innovative television classroom which millions of preschool age children watch, has contributed to sex-role stereotypes. In 1970, Jo Ann Gardner studied the program and reported the following example to illustrate Sesame Street's bias:

On one program, Big Bird (having said that he would like to be a member of a family and having been told that Gordon and Susan would be his family) is told that he will have to help with the work and that since he is a boy bird, he will have to do men's work—the heavy work, the "important" work, and also that he should get a girl (bird) to help Susan with *her* work arranging flowers, redecorating, etc. There was more and virtually all of it emphasized that there is men's work and then there is women's work—that men's work is outside the home and women's work is in the home.[25]

Since that time, *Sesame Street* programmers have become more sensitive to such sex typing and now screen prospective programs for sexism.

From the day children first enter school, they learn about traditional sex roles. Sometimes the ways in which schools condition boys and girls to fit into rigid sex-stereotyped behavior are obvious—often they are not.

In elementary school, although the actual curriculum is usually the same for girls and boys, the experience is often quite different. Most parents and teachers encourage boys, but not girls, to adopt the personality characteristics related to occupational success. While girls are encouraged to be sweet and passive, boys are told to be active and aggressive. Girls receive more affection and more protection. They are subject to more control and more restrictions. In contrast, higher standards are set for boys, more achievement is demanded of them, and they are punished more often if they do not succeed.[26]

The subtle differences in sex-role expectations are usually part of children's academic training as well as social conditioning. For example, in a study of children's books, Elizabeth Fisher found that there were five times as many males as females in titles, and four times as many male animals as female animals pictured. She noted:

It is in the earliest years that children form images of their worth, their future roles, the conscious and unconscious expectations placed upon them. Investigating books for young children in book stores and libraries I found an almost incredible conspiracy of conditioning. Boys are brought up to express themselves; girls to please. The general image of the female ranges from frail to degrading to invisible.[27]

Two of Fisher's findings are of special interest to our examination of women workers. First, Fisher noted that most of the girls and women in the stories "sit and watch" while boys and men do things. Moreover, she found that few of the women in the children's books had jobs or careers. Although about 40 percent of the women in this country are in the labor force, only one of the books was about working women.

Similarly, another study of the roles of adult women in children's books that had received the Caldecott or Newberry award concluded that children's books do not present girls with varied role models of working women:

Thus, there are few role models available to the little girl who thinks it might be interesting to work. In the great majority of the books there are simply no working women: all of the females are found with that ubiquitous apron. However, even in the rare book, where there were some working women, all of these were shown in a limited number of stereotyped feminine occupations: they are the nurse, not the doctor; the stewardess, not the pilot; the secretary, not the executive. All of these women's jobs involved pleasing the men . . . who always had the better paying, more prestigious job of the pair.[28]

However, in 1973, the Children's Book Council reported that many new children's books with feminist themes were being published. The growing influence of the women's movement has pressured publishers into an acceptance of many themes that were regarded as taboo just a few years ago.

Children are also subjected to sex stereotyping through the textbooks they receive in school. In 1972 one analysis of popular textbooks found that 147 role possibilities were suggested for boys, while only 26 were suggested for girls—and two of these were the roles of "queen" and "witch." However, due to vigorous lobbying from feminist groups, new legal remedies, and the emergence of feminist publishing companies, many traditional publishing companies are now attempting to eliminate or minimize such stereotypes.[29]

Like most textbooks, most courses taught in the schools are male oriented and put little emphasis on the accomplishments or problems of women. Virtually all courses—from history to English to French—emphasize the leadership and productivity of men and virtually ignore the contributions of women. Some courses designed to make up for this deficiency are beginning to appear, especially at the high-school level. In some ways, these courses about the contributions and history of women are analogous to black studies programs; both attempt to cover important topics not discussed in traditional textbooks or classes. Ultimately, the topics covered in these "women's courses" should be incorporated into the regular curricula. Until that time, however, schools at all levels should offer courses that emphasize women—their history, their literature, their roles in the economic and political life of the country, and their psychological and sociological characteristics.

By the time students reach junior high school, they are usually well conditioned to accept traditional female and male roles. It is at this level where different courses for females and males have often been required, and until recently, these requirements were not questioned. In 1968, 55 percent of junior high schools and 35 percent of junior-senior high schools required home economics and/or industrial arts courses of seventh and eighth graders; 20 percent of junior high schools and 25 percent of junior-senior high schools required these courses for ninth-graders. Only 2 percent of all seventh-grade boys took home economics, and only 2 percent of the nearly four million students enrolled in industrial arts courses were girls in 1968.[30] It is clear that many students have been routinely channeled, either formally or informally, into courses on the basis of sex. Now, however, this type of sex-based tracking is being challenged on legal, as well as moral and educational, grounds. Title IX of the Education Amendments of 1972 prohibits institutions receiving federal financial assistance from, among other things, offering students different courses on the basis of sex.

Tracking on the basis of sex occurs in other areas as well. A look at all vocational education programs shows that women are channeled into the least desirable jobs and men into the most desirable. In 1968 over three-fourths of the students receiving training in such areas as home economics and office work were women. On the other hand, over 90 percent of the students enrolled in the traditionally male and better-paying areas (technical, trades and industry, and agriculture) were men. For example, men outnumbered women eleven to one in technical courses.[31]

Single-sex schools are another way of perpetuating traditional roles. Not all public elementary and secondary schools are coeducational, and even at coeducational schools, there is often overt discrimination.[32] Alice de Rivera, a former student in the New York City school system, found: "At the seven co-ed vocational schools, boys can learn clerical work, food preparation, and beauty care along with the girls. But the courses that would normally be found in a boys' school are not open to girls."[33]

Diverse and superior facilities and courses are often available to men but not to women. Stuyvesant High School in New York City, a public school for men, admitted women on these grounds. Boston Latin High School, previously an all-male public school, has been ordered by the courts to admit women. In 1969 a female student was admitted into a ninth-grade metal-working class in a New York junior high school only after a threat of court action had been given.[34]

An examination of the courses and programs offered to girls and boys points up only some areas in which men and women are treated differently. The type of guidance students receive is as important as the formal curriculum. One study showed that girls who had serious career plans when they were in twelfth grade had had counseling about college in the ninth grade.[35]

Guidance counselors, like most teachers, pass on their own beliefs about women's and men's roles and careers. Unfortunately, these beliefs often cause them to encourage students to fit into sex-stereotyped roles, regardless of the students' individual interests and abilities. Girls are encouraged to take home economics and boys to take shop. Girls gifted in the sciences are encouraged to become nurses or medical technicians and boys to become doctors. Girls are urged to take secretarial courses, while boys are urged to take courses in automotive engineering.

Higher education and specialized training are viewed by many school counselors and parents as less important for females than for males, on the theory that all women marry and that all wives are financially dependent on their husbands. This ignores the fact that 11 percent of American families are headed by females and perpetuates discriminatory practices that cause a disproportionate percentage of families headed by women to fall below the poverty line.[36] Existing patterns of employment do not justify encouraging a female student to limit her aspirations or to consider only training that will lead to a traditionally female job.

Women and men are also treated differently outside the classroom and the guidance counselor's office. This is perhaps most obvious in the area of athletics. Beginning in elementary school, boys are encouraged to be more active and physically fit than girls. By the time students are in high school this pattern is so well established that most people do not even consider it strange or discriminatory for schools to spend thousands of dollars on boys' varsity and junior varsity sports and to provide no athletic programs at all for girls. Several cases are currently pending which attack unequal athletic facilities on the basis of sex in public-school programs. The earlier cases brought by women seeking to participate on "male" teams did not yield favorable court decisions.[37] In 1971 in *Hollander v. the Connecticut Interscholastic Athletic Conference, Inc.*, the courts wrote a particularly unfortunate decision. A high-school sophomore sued to be allowed to participate in the school's cross-country track team, which was limited by the state athletic association rules to boys only. The court *denied* a permanent injunction against the athletic association. Although the judge cited several chivalrous and protective reasons for denying the female student the right to participate on the cross-country team, much of his reasoning was based on stereotyped ideas about females and males:

The present generation of our younger male population has not become so decadent that boys will experience a thrill in defeating girls in running contests, whether the girls be members of their own team or an adversary team.... Athletic competition builds character in our boys. We do not need that kind of character in our girls, the women of tomorrow.[38]

In more recent decisions, however, the courts in Nebraska and Minnesota have ordered that women be admitted to previously all-male golf, tennis, cross-country track, and cross-country skiing teams.[39] And in June 1974, the Little League officially changed its policy so that it no longer prohibits females from playing on Little League teams.[40] With increasing regularity, schools are finding themselves charged with sex discrimination in athletics under Title IX of the Education Amendments of 1972, as well as under the Fourteenth Amendment.

Until a few years ago, female students who were pregnant were routinely expelled from school, while boys who fathered children were not similarly expelled. For the most part, these policies no longer exist. However, pregnant students often have to contend with hostile attitudes and unofficial practices that make it difficult for them to continue their education, which they may desperately need in order to support themselves and their children. Some schools offer these students alternatives to remaining in the classroom—either separate classes or tutoring. If schools are to meet the needs of all students, they must be supportive of students who are pregnant or who have children, and encourage them to continue their normal studies.

Women as Teachers and Administrators

During the nineteenth century, teaching was one of the few acceptable professions for a woman. Even today many people consider teaching, especially teaching young children, a "woman's" job and invariable use the pronoun "she" when writing about an elementary-school teacher. Because so many women are employed by the primary and secondary schools in the United States, it is important to understand how equitably these women are treated as employees.

This treatment affects others beside female employees. Students learn how to regard themselves and their roles from watching the adult women and men around them. Since each child is in a position to observe how school employees are treated, it is especially important for women teachers to have equal opportunity in their jobs.

While close to two-thirds (64 percent) of all public school professional employees in 1970-71 were women, they were not equally distributed among the various job categories: two-thirds of all teachers were women, but less than a sixth of all principals were women. Even in elementary schools, where over 80 percent of the teachers are female, only one-fifth of the principals were women; and, in junior and senior high schools, only 3 to 4 percent of the principals were women. The number of female assistant principals was nearly as small as the number of principals.[41]

The distribution of women and men in other instructional staff positions followed a similar pattern. The more prestigious and highly paid positions were generally held by men, while women held less prestigious, traditionally female, and lower-paying jobs. For example, the overwhelming majority of people in such jobs as school nurse, librarian, and social worker were women. At the same time, seven out of ten department heads were men.

The distribution of central office administrators was even more noticeably divided along sex lines. Overall, about one-fourth of the central office administrators were women. However, less than 1 percent of the 14,379 superintendents studied by the National Education Association in 1970 were women. The female professionals in the central office were concentrated in middle-level administration jobs.[42]

Despite the high educational and intellectual requirements for the job, teachers earn considerably less than workers in predominantly male occupations with equivalent training and ability. In 1970, the National Education Association reported that the average teacher had eleven years of teaching experience, almost all teachers had bachelor's degrees, and well over a third held advanced degrees. Although pay scales vary among different parts of the country, the mean annual income was only $8700 for elementary-school teachers and $9000 for secondary-school teachers.[43]

Because teaching has been considered women's work, all teachers are paid relatively poorly. Because it pays poorly, it has attracted few men. And because men have not been employed as teachers in large numbers and women teachers have not organized effectively, school administrators, legislators, and the general public have allowed salaries to remain low. If one looks at the distribution of the salaries of female and male teachers, it becomes evident that women teachers make less on the average than male teachers. A study by the National Education Association of the 1971-72 salaries of teachers found that the average salary for male teachers was $10,013, compared to $9216 for women—a difference of $800.[44]

All teachers should be more adequately paid. However, it is important that as teachers' salaries become more competitive and desirable, teaching not be redefined as a "male only" job. Nor should the influx of more men into the teaching profession make it even more difficult for competent women to become administrators. *The goal is to eliminate discrimination, not to replace one pattern of sex discrimination with another.*

Until fairly recently, teachers have often had to rely on the insight and benevolence of school administrators to rectify discriminatory policies. However, the alternatives of union organizations and collective bargaining are being used increasingly. Although teachers' unions have done much to advance the position of teachers in general, they have been somewhat slow to address themselves to the special problems of women. The position of the American Federation of Teachers (AFT) is somewhat inconsistent. Although the union now supports equal rights for women in principle and has a women's rights committee (which has made statements on benefit and leave policies), in 1971 only 17 percent of the presidents of their 900 union locals were women.[45]

The National Education Association (NEA), both older and more conservative than the AFT, is making some progress in the area of equal rights and protection for women. The association has formed a professional rights and responsibilities committee which, along with their DuShane Emergency Fund, has supported a major reform of existing maternity policies.[46] In addition, the teacher rights division of the NEA has been active on issues of special relevance to female teachers. The Resource Center on Sex Roles in Education, which is funded by the Ford Foundation and sponsored by the National Foundation for Improvement in Education, is largely a result of the concern and activities of the NEA.

Teachers' professional organizations and unions are increasingly playing roles similar to other, more conventional types of labor unions—negotiating contracts through collective bargaining to achieve improved working conditions and competitive salaries. In the future, these organizations will undoubtedly assume an even more important role. But the policies these unions accept will depend in a large part on the kind of people in leadership positions in the unions.

Women and Higher Education

College-educated women have an impact far out of proportion to their numbers; compared to other women, these women have greater access to positions of power or importance. Yet for many women the college experience is as difficult as it is significant. During their college years, women are faced with pressures that encourage them to take a secondary role and to focus on men and marriage, rather than to make serious plans for a career. The choices that women make during their college years may seriously limit their options later in life.

College women often experience what psychologist and Radcliffe College president Matina Horner calls a woman's "desire to avoid success," a factor that makes it especially difficult for women to excel, either in college or in the world of work. Horner explains the dilemma almost every college woman faces:

Consciously or unconsciously the girl equates intellectual achievement with a loss of femininity. A bright woman is caught in a double bind. In testing and other achievement-oriented situations, she worries not only about failure, but also about success. If she fails, she is not living up to her own standards of performance; if she succeeds she is not living up to societal expectations about the female role. Men in our society do not have this kind of ambivalence, because they are not only permitted but actively encouraged to do well.[47]

The number of women and men who attend high school is approximately equal, but fewer women than men go to college, and fewer still obtain graduate degrees. In 1973 only 45 percent of the college entrants were female.[48] In 1970 women earned 40 percent of all masters degrees and only 13.3 percent of all doctorates.[49] Although this was a significant increase from the 1967 figures of 34 percent and 11 percent,[50] the figures in 1930 were 40 percent and 15 percent.[51] Similarly, although the number of women in medical and law school has increased markedly in the past fifteen years, in 1971 only 12 percent of the students in law school and 13 percent of the students in medical school were women.[52] In the same year, 16 percent of entering law school students and 17 percent of entering medical school students were women.[53]

The percentage of women on faculties is consistently lower than the percentage of female students. Although the percentage of female students has changed in the past decade, the overall proportion of women in the various ranks has changed little in the past ten years; women were 19 percent of the faculty in four-year institutions in 1963 and 20.6 percent in 1973.[54]

Undergraduate Students

Presently there are fewer places for women at the best quality institutions than there are for men. The response to efforts to increase the percentage of women at these institutions varies according to the "best interests" of those at these institutions. For example, some formerly all-male institutions have begun to accept female students because of financial problems or because they felt that the presence of women on campus was necessary to attract the best male students. Even when they admit women, many institutions have a quota on the number of women they admit or require women to be more highly qualified in order to be admitted.

Female and male undergraduates on most campuses have access to the same classes, professors, and facilities. But equal educational opportunity is by no means defined solely by apparent access to resources; other types of opportunity are equally important. In many instances, women do not receive the same respect and support for their academic endeavors as men. Often they are actively discouraged by professors or advisors from pursuing demanding studies or entering traditionally male fields.[55] In addition, women often have greater difficulty than men in obtaining financial aid: one manifestation of this is that, at every socioeconomic status and ability level, females are much less likely than males to continue their education.[56] Women rarely have the same opportunity in sports programs or other extracurricular activities as men.

Similarly, women's psychological concerns receive little attention. Ellen and Kenneth Keniston note that women need strong support during their college years if they are to succeed.

During her late teens and early twenties, many a girl who might otherwise be capable of more confirms her surrender to the pressures of popularity. Adequate modes of adult identification can sustain one against strong internal and social pressure; when they are absent, one surrenders at the first push.[57]

David Riesman and Christopher Jencks put it another way: "Women need more guidance than men in making their way in the somewhat alien, if often indulgent, academic and postacademic world."[58]

It is clear from studies that, in most universities and colleges, strong female role and career models, be they faculty members, historical figures or authors, are seriously lacking for the undergraduate. Often the few women who do hold prominent positions are viewed as so exceptional that most women undergraduates find it hard to identify with them. A study of a number of institutions by M. Elizabeth Tidball of George Washington University confirms on a statistical basis the importance of female faculty to women students. She found that the number of "career successful women" students was directly proportional to the number of women faculty present in the achievers' undergraduate institutions at the time they were students.[59] In fact, the correlation was a practically perfect +0.953. Clearly, the visibility of women successfully performing highly professional jobs positively influences the career aspirations of female students.[60]

Nearly every aspect of the undergraduate experience either opens or closes options for young women. The curriculum is as important in college as it is at elementary and secondary schools. The history of the women's rights movement, the influence of female authors in literature, and the impact of women in politics, as well as psychological and sociological analyses of women should be integrated into the regular curriculum. Such courses are needed to enhance the self-image of female students, while providing them with a chance to examine different careers and life styles carefully and to learn how to deal with discrimination. All too often, women students are unaware of the extent of sex discrimination that they will meet when they join the paid labor force. Nor are they prepared to deal with discriminatory practices once they meet them.

Courses on women are increasingly appearing in college catalogs, but they often have "fringe" status and are rarely recognized as permanent, legitimate parts of the academic program. At Yale University, for example, most of the courses on women have been taught by women who do not have regular faculty appointments. Graduate students, visiting faculty members supported by outside foundations, and faculty wives most often teach these courses.[61] At many universities, courses on women are taught by concerned female faculty members in addition to their regular course load.

Continuing education programs for adult women are also important. They can provide women with a chance to finish a degree, to learn the latest techniques in their field so that they can reenter the work force or to pursue an area of study in which they may have developed an interest only after leaving school. A recent study confirms that participation in a continuing education program gives women who have not worked since college, the self-esteem required to develop a career. But merely opening doors to adult students is not enough. These students often need special guidance and support in making the difficult transition back to student life. They often encounter many unique problems adjusting academically and socially to a system that is largely designed for postadolescents. In many instances, continuing education is a self-supporting or profit-making wing of the university, which operates independently from the regular degree programs and is isolated from the mainstream of the university. The courses offered often lack the quality of the university's "regular" program. Consequently, the benefits of having older and younger students work and learn together are lost, and the older students may receive a second-rate education.

A university's advising and counseling system can have a profound effect upon women undergraduates. When one woman senior at a prominent Ivy League College told a senior administrator she wanted to go to law school, his response was hardly designed to be encouraging: "What a waste. When you are thirty-five, you'll be home with your children." This same student had read in her student newspaper only a month before an interview with another administrator whose work brought him into daily contact with students. The administrator said,

Quite simply, I do not see highly educated women making startling strides in contributing to our society in the forseeable future. They are not, in my opinion, going to stop getting married and/or having children. They will fail in their present role as women if they do.[62]

From these examples, it is clear that women have not been encouraged to take themselves and their career aspirations seriously or to pursue rigorous academic programs that require long-range commitments. Those who have seem to have done so in spite of, rather than because of, the counseling they received.

Many women are encouraged to pursue such "feminine" fields as child study, education, or the humanities. The disproportionately high number of women in these areas is to some extent a response to the advice and encouragement they receive. Studies show, for example, that women science students who are not supported either by their family, their boyfriend, or their faculty advisor tend to switch into a more "feminine" field. It is not surprising, then, that 36 percent of the women who graduated from college in 1970 received bachelor's degrees in education, that 26 percent received degrees in the arts and humanities, and 17 percent in the social sciences, while only 3.2 percent of the B.A. degrees in the biological sciences and 0.9 percent in the physical sciences were awarded to women.[63]

Placement offices at the college level also influence what happens to women students. The attitude of the placement office staff can either support women students in their career choice or channel them into other, more feminine fields. Generally, however, both women and men counselors show an unconscious bias by encouraging women, no matter what their abilities and interests, to choose traditionally feminine fields.[64] Placement offices should provide women with realistic advice about the demands of different career patterns so that they can make career decisions with a full understanding of the options as well as the implications of different choices. Finally, placement officers who permit interviewers to come to a campus and speak only with male students are breaking the law as well as denying women a chance to pursue all job possibilities.

Sex discrimination at the undergraduate level remains a subtle matter. It is still possible for students and observers alike to believe that the women undergraduate students are receiving a truly equal educational experience. Often, however, the female students are simply being allowed to participate in programs that were specifically designed to meet the needs of white male undergraduates—not women or minorities of either sex.

Graduate Students

Those women who choose graduate school and professional training after college face a different kind of bias than undergraduates. Women are treated differently in graduate school from the moment they fill out their admissions application. A medical school in Texas, for example, until recently required female, but not male, applicants to have a psychiatric interview. Until recently, many graduate and professional schools had either formal or informal quotas to limit the number of women or required that women be more qualified than men in order to be admitted. These policies and practices have been illegal since the admissions provisions of Title IX of the Education Amendments of 1972 became effective in July 1973.

The reasons most often heard for limiting the number of women in graduate school are that women will perhaps never complete graduate school, and that if they do, they will not pursue a career. A study of students admitted to Ph.D. programs at the Graduate Center of the City University of New York between 1962 and 1970, however, found that women formed nearly as large a percentage of those who received the Ph.D. by 1972 as they did of students admitted.[65] Similarly, prior to the time when the women's movement heightened the awareness of sex discrimination, Helen Astin analyzed the career development and work patterns of professional women. Her large-scale survey of women who received doctorates showed a high level of career commitment. Astin found that 91 percent of the women still were working in their field years after they had completed their education. The few career interruptions they had taken were of short duration.[66]

In spite of such data, many graduate schools persist in discouraging female applicants and students. Sometimes the attitude that women do not really belong in graduate school is openly conveyed; women are asked by professors, other students, and friends what they plan to do with their graduate degree, if they are really serious in their pursuit of a degree, and if they would not be happier in a less ambitious program. More often, however, these attitudes are more subtly conveyed; women students are ignored in class, their professors will not have serious discussions with them and seldom develop the mentor-apprentice relationship that often leads to a sharing of research and other opportunities. Professors and peers alike have lower expectations for female students. These attitudes alone could account for the higher attrition rates of women where they exist.

The policies and structures of colleges and universities also often discourage women from pursuing a degree. Regulations prohibiting part-time study, for example, prevent many women with small children from completing their academic training. Admissions and financial aid offices often view these students as "poor risks," even though experience suggests that many of them are unusually highly motivated and committed to completing their degrees. Some universities are now beginning to review and change these restrictive practices.

Once women gain admission to graduate school, they must compete with men for financial aid. Many of the best graduate scholarships are limited to men.[67] Part-time students, many of whom are married women, are not eligible for federal scholarship and loan aid.[68] And even women who can carry a full-time course load can be denied access to programs of financial aid by a "Catch 22." For example, it was the policy of Northwestern University in 1970 not to grant full-time status "where a student's outside activities represent a substantial commitment of time or are deemed incompatible with the demands of a full-time graduate program."[69] At that time they considered children to be a "substantial commitment." Married women who did enroll as full-time students found still more financial barriers. Fully half of the married women graduate students received no financial aid from Northwestern in 1970, compared to one in three for single women and one in four for male students.[70] To compensate for the lack of financial aid, 30 percent of married full-time female students at Northwestern University worked between twenty and forty hours a week in addition to fulfilling home responsibilities.[71]

In 1969 the University of Chicago Committee on the Status of Women found that some departments intentionally favored men in the distribution of financial aid, because they felt men would make better use than women of their training.[72] As Astin's data suggest, this assumption is not valid. Still, it remains a prevalent belief and is extremely detrimental to the careers of female graduate students.

An even more permanent form of discrimination takes place in job opportunities at school. In graduate schools, women tend to earn their scholarship money by working as research assistants and research associates, while men are put immediately on the teaching ladder as teaching assistants. This makes it much easier for men to move to a regular position on a teaching faculty once they have their degrees. This is not an insignificant cause for complaint. People who work as graduate teaching assistants during the period of doctoral training are more likely than others to work full time successfully some years later.[73]

Increasingly, women graduate students are taking action aimed at eliminating discrimination against them. Women are forming graduate women's groups and filing charges of sex discrimination aimed at identifying and rectifying discrimination.

Women as Faculty Members

Much of the difficulty encountered by female undergraduates and graduate students stems from the lack of female faculty. Alice Rossi has found that at least in sociology departments, there is a significant correlation between the number of women on a faculty and the number of female students who seek graduate degrees:

In the departments with at least ten percent women on the faculty, 57 percent have a high proportion of women among the Ph.D. students (31 percent or more women); for departments in which women represent less than ten percent of the faculty, only 28 percent have this high proportion of women among the doctoral students.[74]

These findings are consistent with those of Tidball cited earlier.

Federal law now requires that all colleges and universities eliminate employment discrimination against women as well as racial minorities. In addition, institutions with federal contracts must develop official, written affirmative action plans to overcome in a systematic fashion the effects of previous discrimination. Despite this governmental prod, progress has been slow. By the fall of 1973, women had filed about five hundred charges of sex discrimination against colleges under Executive Order 11246. Also, at that time around five hundred charges of sex discrimination in higher education were pending under Title VII of the 1964 Civil Rights Act.

To what extent are women represented among faculties in higher education? In 1973 women made up only 19 percent of the faculty in four-year institutions. One finds the fewest women in the higher and tenured ranks and in the prestigious research universities. Astin reported in 1968 that 70 percent of all women doctorates were employed in academic institutions. However, most of these women were employed in small colleges and universities.[75] In 1973 women made up 32.3 percent of the faculty at public, and 45.4 percent of the faculty at private, junior colleges, but only 17.1 percent of the faculty at public universities and 14.4 percent of the faculty at private universities.[76]

Overall, women do not teach at elite schools but rather in the smaller, poorer, and less prestigious institutions, where they often have heavy teaching schedules and little time for writing and research in their fields. In addition, women faculty tend to be concentrated at the lower levels, and, like women students, are found in the "less prestigious" fields of education, social work, and home economics—disciplines that are "suitable" for women. This trend can be seen rather significantly in those universities classified by the Carnegie Commission as public research universities, where women comprised 41.7 percent of the undergraduate population and 12.9 percent of the faculty. In the biological sciences 12 percent of the assistant professors, 9 percent of the associate professors, and 2 percent of the full professors were women, while 19 percent of assistant professors, 19 percent of associate professors, and 15 percent of full professors were women in the field of education.[77]

Despit affirmative action, some institutions now have *fewer* women faculty than they did several years ago. The prospect is not encouraging. If 100 percent of the new faculty hired were women, the total percentage of women faculty would not reach 50 percent until the 1980s. In order to reach an average of 30 percent women in 1990, universities as a whole would have to maintain a constant proportion of women among the new hires of 50 percent. That they will do so is highly unlikely.[78]

There is evidence that the situation will become more, rather than less, severe for female academics. Astin reports that women experience the tightening job market more severely than men. She notes that the proportion of men with signed contracts for the year following their graduation in 1970 dropped four percentage points from what it was in 1960; for women, however, the drop was eight percentage points.[79]

While women faculty members are more likely than men to have masters degrees rather than doctorates, this alone does not explain the concentration of women in the lower ranks of the teaching faculty. In sociology, Rossi found:

A sharp difference persists in the distribution of men and women by rank: a full 42 percent of the men with a doctoral degree are full professors, compared with only 16 percent of women with a doctoral degree. Few such women are pegged at the instructorship level. . . , but the Ph.D. seems merely to facilitate their appointment as assistant professors where 54 percent of the women are located.[80]

Helen Astin and Alan Bayer have surveyed sex differentials in rank and salary, correcting for the length of time since the Ph.D. degree was received, interruptions in career, productivity, and other relevant factors. They have found that women tended to be promoted less regularly than men, and that "academic income" and salaries were lower for women than for men—even within the same work setting, field, and rank. Specifically, "their mean salaries are as low as 83.8 percent of the mean salary reported by men and as high as 98.9 percent of the male mean salary."[81] Most other studies confirm these data, but efforts to isolate the cause of this differential are less successful. For example, a report on women in the field of political science warns:

before one labels all of this discrimination by sex, it should be noted that the "withdrawal" of the '40s and '50s meant almost a couple of generations of women lost to research and teaching in political science. Then too the greater proportion of jobs in the small colleges means that women have heavier teaching schedules and less time as well as facilities for research.[82]

The Carnegie Commission found that, after controlling for all the predictor variables included in their equations, the actual average salary of male faculty members exceeded the average that would have been predicted on the basis of the female equation by nearly $2300. Two components were identified as apparently underlying the differences between male and female salaries:

(1) a general shift ... of the entire distribution of male salary residuals, amounting to about $2,000 so that a man of specified qualifications tends to earn about $2,000 more than a woman of the same qualifications; and (2) an excess of men with exceptionally high salary deviations.[83]

Many universities do not give their women faculty full academic rank or appropriate rewards for their work. Jessie Bernard has pointed out the advantage to universities of having women in "fringe benefit status," allowing them to work part-time but denying them tenure or high rank:

The term fringe benefit implies a status which is on the fringe of the profession; it implies also, however, that the person occupying this status is of great benefit to the institution where the work is done. There may be occasional men in this status, but by far the majority are women. For the most part, they are the wives of deans, professors, instructors, graduate students, or often, even of townsmen. They constitute an elastic labor pool, hired and furloughed as needed. They carry a large share of the backbreaking load of introductory work in English composition, modern languages, history, mathematics, natural sciences and the like.[84]

Members of the "fringe benefit" group who are satisfied with their roles apparently identify with other women employees rather than with other faculty members. Interestingly, the women who are the *least* willing to accept fringe status and lower salaries are the most productive. These women tend to compare their positions with those of male colleagues rather than with those of other women.[85]

As on the graduate and undergraduate level, the attitudes of peers are important. Male faculty members often do not take the work of their female colleagues as seriously as they take the work of their male colleagues. Writing and research are lonely occupations, and support and encouragement from colleagues can be important factors in the completion of this work.

Some universities have had rules that prevent women from exercising a free choice about whether or not they will have professional careers in college teaching. For example, formal and informal anti-nepotism rules have kept two members of the same family from being employed in the same institution or department. Because these policies have a disproportionate impact on the careers of women, they are now prohibited by federal legislation prohibiting sex discrimination. Until recently, however, these policies were common. A 1966 study of nepotism of 363 institutions showed that 45 percent of the institutions that responded had either formal anti-nepotism rules or restrictive policies. These policies took different forms—witholding full faculty status from one member of the family, restricting the two people to one vote in matters of policy, limiting sabbaticals and pension plans, and/or simply viewing the woman as a stopgap temporary employee.[86]

Perhaps the most devastating example of anti-nepotism practices is that described of Maria Goeppert Mayer:

Mayer, the only woman since Dr. Marie Curie to win the Nobel Prize in Physics, once worked as a "volunteer associate" at Johns Hopkins in order to keep on doing physics. She could not be paid, because her husband was on the faculty, but the University didn't object to getting her free. "I sensed the resentment of the role of women in American academic life," she says, "so I learned to be inconspicuous."[87]

University attitudes towards part-time work also tend to make it difficult for women faculty members to achieve higher-ranking positions. While most universities permit faculty members to teach part time and consult for the government or business part time, or to teach part time in one department and part time in another, they do not make it easy for faculty members to divide their time between the university and their family. Nor do part-time faculty members receive benefits. This policy should be changed; part-time employees should receive benefits on a pro-rata basis.

Several universities, including Princeton, Stanford, and Harvard, now have tenure policies that allow part-time faculty members to be eligible for promotion on a regular basis.[88] Considerations for part-time faculty appointments must be made on the expectation of part-time and not full-time scholarship. For example, at a university where a professor is expected to teach half-time and do research half-time, a half-time appointment should involve quarter-time teaching and quarter-time research, to enable the individual to keep up in the field.

Discriminatory hiring practices also keep women out of professional positions in academe. Hiring is usually done through the "old boy" network: the chairman of a department calls a colleague at another university. Rarely do these male professors think of placing their female graduate students as they do their male graduate students. When women are interviewed for faculty appointments, they find that they are taken less seriously. A woman has to be exceptional to become a part of these networks that are open to mediocre, as well as exceptional, men.

The general lack of child care facilities and maternity and parental leaves only aggravates the problems of a woman seeking an academic career. In 1971 only about one campus in four provided any sort of child care.[89] Very few colleges have clear and fair policies governing pregnancy and maternity leave. The problem of childbearing leaves is somewhat different for women in higher education than for women who teach at the elementary or secondary level. Women in higher education often cannot take *any* leave for childbirth without seriously injuring their careers, while the problem for many public-school teachers is that they have been *required* to take a leave of absence. Both policies, however, are rigid and arbitrary, denying women equal opportunity. Both policies are also equally in violation of federal antidiscrimination guidelines, which require that, for all job-related purposes, employers treat disabilities related to pregnancy and childbirth like any other physical disability.

In addition, federal policy now requires that federal contractors allow both women and men to take leave for child *rearing*, if leave is available for other personal reasons.[90]

A combination of genuine concern for fairness towards women and a fear of being charged with sex discrimination has caused many colleges to take the first easy steps in eliminating discrimination; a few token women are being hired and the most obvious forms of discrimination have been dropped. The next steps, however, promise to be more difficult. There was already considerable backlash to affirmative action by 1973, in large part because of modest, but much advertised hiring progress and a severely tightening academic job market.

The university's employment practices have implications that extend beyond the institution. As the Assembly on University Goals and Governances pointed out:

Universities and colleges in their own employment policies ought to become model employers, demonstrating their readiness to engage women at every teaching, research, administrative and staff level. They ought to work through their placement and other offices to educate employers to pursue the same policy, thereby securing for women many more positions at salaries equal to those of men.[91]

The practices of educational institutions and the attitudes of people in these institutions are as important as any formal learning provided in the classroom. All too often they reinforce traditional images of women and men. In addition, without concerned counseling at all levels of education and without successful women to work with and to emulate, few women will be able to overcome current stereotyped beliefs regarding their capabilities, motivations, and commitments.

Notes

1. Willystine Goodsell, ed., *Pioneers of Women's Education in the United States* (New York: McGraw-Hill Book Co., Inc., 1931), pp. 2-5.

2. Thomas Woody, *A History of Women's Education in the United States*, (New York: Octagon Books, Inc., 1966), vol. 1, pp. 137-38.

3. Goodsell, *Pioneers of Women's Education*, pp. 2-5.

4. Ibid., p. 6.

5. Ibid., p. 7.

6. Woody, *History of Women's Education*, vol. 1, p. 92.

7. Ibid., p. 108.

8. Ibid., p. 519.

9. Ibid., p. 310.

10. Ibid., p. 460.

11. Edward Clarke, *Sex in Education: Or a Fair Chance for the Girls* (Boston: J.R. Osgood and Company, 1873).

12. Woody, *A History of Women's Education*, vol. 2, p. 231.

13. Ibid., pp. 238-248.

14. The sex discrimination provisions of Title IX are patterned after Title VI of the Civil Rights Act of 1964, which forbids discrimination on the basis of race, color, and national origin in all federally assisted programs. By specific exemption, the prohibitions of Title VI do not cover employment practices (except where the primary objective of the Federal aid is to provide employment). However, there is no similar exemption for employment for Title IX.

15. In November of 1971, Titles VII (Section 799A) and VIII (Section 845) of the Public Health Service Act were amended by the Comprehensive Health Manpower Training Act and the Nurse Training Amendments Act to prohibit discrimination in admissions on the basis of sex to programs training people in the health professions.

16. Education Amendments of 1972, Title IX, Sec. 901(a).

17. Single-sex professional graduate and vocational schools at all levels have until no later than July 1979 to achieve nondiscriminatory admissions, provided they present plans that are approved by the Commissioner of Education.

18. If *public* single-sex undergraduate institutions decide to admit both sexes, they will have up to seven years to admit female and male students on a nondiscriminatory basis, provided their plans are approved by the Commissioner of Education.

19. Dr. Paula Latimer (President of Texas Division of the Women's Equity Action League). (Letter to Ms. Dorothy Stuck [Director of HEW's Office for Civil Rights], April 11, 1973.)

20. "Issue of Women in Sports Heating Up," Project on the Status and Education of Women, *Newsletter*, December 1973.

21. "Students Fight Sexist Comments in the Classroom," Project on the Status and Education of Women, *Newsletter*, December 1973, p. 9.
Women, December 1973, p. 9.

22. "Institutions Sponsoring Phi Delta Kappa Charged with Sex Discrimination," Project on the Status and Education of Women, *Newsletter*, May 1973, p. 13.

23. 45 CFR Part 86, 39 *Federal Register*, June 20, 1974, pp. 22, 228-40.

24. For a more complete discussion of sex-role differences, see Eleanor E. Maccoby, *The Development of Sex Differences* (Stanford: Stanford University Press, 1966).

25. Jo Ann Gardner, "Sesame Street and Sex Role Stereotypes," *Women*, Spring, 1970.

26. R.R. Sears, E.E. Maccoby, and H. Levin, *Patterns of Child Rearing* (Evanston, Ill.: Rowe, Peterson, 1957).

27. Elizabeth Fisher, "The Second Sex, Junior Division," *The New York Times Book Review*, May 4, 1970, p. 6.

28. Lenore J. Weitzman, "Sex Role Socialization in Children's Books" (Paper prepared for meetings of the American Sociological Association, August 1971.)

29. Women on Words and Images, *Dick and Jane as Victims* (Princeton, New Jersey: Women on Words and Images, 1972).

30. U.S., Department of Health, Education and Welfare, *Office of Education,* Vocational and Technical Education: Annual Report, Fiscal Year 1968 (1970).

31. Ibid.

32. Title IX of the Education Amendments of 1972 requires that all vocational elementary and secondary schools that receive federal financial assistance have nondiscriminatory admissions.

33. Alice de Rivera, "On Desegregating Stuyvesant High," in *Sisterhood is Powerful* (New York: Vintage Books, 1970), p. 370.

34. Board of Education v. Sanchez (New York, December 1969). From information obtained from Bruce J. Ennis and Alan H. Levine, Civil Liberties Union, New York, 1969.

35. Anne Anastasi and Charles E. Schaefer, "Biographical Correlates of Artistic and Literary Creativity in Adolescent Girls," *Journal of Applied Psychology*, 1969, p. 267-68.

36. U.S., Women's Bureau, *1969 Handbook on Women Workers*, pp. 28-32. *Workers: Bulletin 294* (1969), p. 28-32.

37. Bucha v. Illinois High School Association, 41 L.W. 2277 (N.D.Ill., 1972) and Hollander, *infra.*

38. Hollander v. The Connecticut Interscholastic Athletic Conference, Inc., no. 12 4927, March 29, 1971. On appeal to Connecticut Supreme Court.

39. Brenden v. Independent School District 742, 342 F. Supp. 1224 (D. Minn. 1972) and Reed. v. Nebraska School Activities Association, 341 F. Supp. 258 (D.Neb. 1972).

40. "Little League Admits Girls, Effective Now." *The Washington Post*, June 13, 1974.

41. National Education Association, Research Division, *NEA Research Bulletin* (Washington, D.C.: NEA, October 1971), p. 68.

42. Ibid.

43. Letty Cottin Pogrebin, "The Working Woman," *Ladies Home Journal*, October 1971, p. 54.

44. Resource Center on Sex Roles in Education, National Foundation for Improvement of Education, "Salary Differentials of Elementary Secondary Teachers," *Research Action Notes*, June 20, 1973, p. 3.

45. Pogrebin, "The Working Woman," p. 64.

46. Ibid.

47. Matina Horner, "Fail: Bright Women," *Psychology Today*, vol. 2 (1969): 37. Reprinted from *Psychology Today* Magazine, November 1969. Copyright © Ziff Davis Publishing Company.

48. Carnegie Commission on Higher Education, *Opportunities for Women in Higher Education* (New York: McGraw-Hill 1973), p. 35.

49. Carnegie Commission on Higher Education, *Opportunities for Women*, pp. 82-83.

50. Pamela Roby, *Structural and Internalized Barriers to Women in Higher Education* (Baltimore: Department of Sociology and Center for Manpower Policy Studies, George Washington University, March, 1971).

51. Carnegie Commission on Higher Education, *Opportunities for Women*, p. 83.

52. Ibid., pp. 100, 103. In 1961 only 3.6 percent of the students enrolled in law school were women; in 1957 only 9.3 percent of all medical students were women.

53. John Parrish, "Women in Professional Training," *Monthly Labor Review*, May 1974, p. 42.

54. Robert L. Jacobson, "Faculty Women Earning 17 Percent Less than Men," *The Chronicle of Higher Education*, March 12, 1973, pp. 1, 6.

55. Carnegie Commission on Higher Education, *Opportunities for Women*, p. 68.

56. Ibid., pp. 38-39.

57. E. and K. Keniston, "An American Anachronism: The Image of Women and Work," *American Scholar*, vol. 33 (1964): 370.

58. David Reisman and Christopher Jencks, *Academic Revolution* (Garden City, N.Y.: Doubleday, 1968), p. 309.

59. For investigative purposes, "career successful women" were defined as those listed in *Who's Who of American Women*.

60. M. Elizabeth Tidball, "Perspectives on Academic Women and Affirmative Action," *Educational Record*, May 1973, pp. 130-135.

61. Subcommittee for the Health, Education and Welfare Review, Yale Faculty and Professional Women's Forum, Lenore Weitzman, Frances Pitlick, Margie Ferguson, *Women on the Yale Faculty* (Unpublished report, New Haven, March 2, 1971), pp. 5-9.

62. *The Harvard Crimson*, November 6, 1970, p. 1.

63. Carnegie Commission on Higher Education, *Opportunities for Women*, pp. 188-89.

64. Lorraine Eyde, "Eliminating Barriers to Career Development of Women," *Personnel and Guidance Journal*, September 1970, pp. 25-26.

65. Carnegie Commission on Higher Education, *Opportunities for Women*, pp. 91-93.

66. Helen Astin, *The Woman Doctorate in America* (New York: Russell Sage Foundation, 1969), p. 57.

67. Roby, *Structural and Internalized Barriers to Women*, p. 19.

68. Ibid., p. 7.

69. Janet Abu-Lughod, "A Proposal Concerning Women and Higher Education at Northwestern University," (Report prepared January 1970), Appendix A, pp. A1-A2.

70. Ibid., p. 6.

71. Ibid., Appendix B., p. B5.

72. *University of Chicago Report on the Status of Women* (Chicago: University of Chicago Press, 1969), p. 42.

73. Astin, *The Woman Doctorate in America*, p. 70.

74. Alice Rossi reported this to a meeting of the American Sociological Association on September 3, 1969. For excerpts, see Alice Rossi, "Women and Professional Advancement," *Science*, vol. 166 (1969): 356.

75. Astin, *The Woman Doctorate in America*, p. 70.

76. Jacobson, "Faculty Women Earning Less," p. 1.

77. Carnegie Commission on Higher Education, *Opportunities for Women*, p. 200.

78. Ibid., p. 124.

79. Helen S. Astin, "Career Profiles of Academic Women," *Academic Women on the Move* (New York: Russell Sage Foundation, 1973), p. 158.

80. Rossi, p. 356.

81. Alan Bayer and Helen Astin, "Sex Discrimination in Academe," *Educational Record*, Spring 1972, pp. 101-18.

82. Victoria Schuck, "Women in Political Science," *Political Science*, Fall 1969, p. 642.

83. Carnegie Commission on Higher Education, *Opportunities for Women*, pp. 116, 226.

84. Jessie Bernard, *Academic Women* (New York: The World Publishing Co., 1964), p. 100.

85. Ibid., p. 101.

86. Rita J. Simon, Shirley M. Clark and Larry L. Tifft, "Of Nepotism, Marriage and the Pursuit of an Academic Career," *Sociology of Education*, vol. 39 (1966): 357.

87. Caroline Bird, *Born Female* (New York: The World Publishing Co., 1964), p. 100.

88. "Tenured Part-Time Appointments," Project on the Status and Education of Women, *Newsletter*, November 1971, p. 1.

89. Carnegie Commission on Higher Education, *Opportunities for Women*, p. 159.

90. Project on the Status and Education of Women, Association of American Colleges, *Summary of Federal Policy Concerning Twenty-Five Affirmative Action Issues in Employment*, November 1972, p. 2.

91. Assembly on University Goals and Governance, *A First Report* (Cambridge, Mass., 1971).

6 Child Care

The lack of good, reasonably priced, and convenient child care is a major barrier to equal rights for women. In part because of the lack of child care, employers are reluctant to hire mothers, place them in positions of responsibility, or provide them with training opportunities. Some mothers have been unable to enter the work force at all because they were unable to make satisfactory arrangements for the care of their children.

Informal alternative arrangements for child care have always been available in the form of relatives or neighbors caring for children, but such arrangements rarely meet the needs of the children or of their families. The effectiveness and impact of more formal alternate methods of child care are examined in this chapter. To comprehend the scope of the problem, and to understand how negative attitudes toward formal child care facilities developed, it is important to review the history of child care in the United States.

Historical Perspective

Child care includes two types of services not usually thought of together, day care centers and nursery schools. Day care centers have been considered custodial and are associated with poor parents who have to work, while nursery schools have been seen as "educational" and are associated with middle- or upper-class parents who want their children to have as many experiences as possible. These two types of care have developed independently; they are only now beginning to merge.

The movement for free preschool education or kindergarten began in the United States in the 1860s. By 1893 there were over three thousand kindergartens, a sixth of which were connected with public school systems.[1] Still, these kindergartens were separate from custodial care centers, which specifically provided care for children whose mothers were working. Such custodial day care has been both more acceptable and more prevalent in times of crisis, particularly war and economic stress. During the Civil War, many centers were founded, and were expanded after the war when many widows had to work to provide for themselves and their children.[2] Similarly, during World War I, child care facilities were established so that women could work in factories. Moreover, at that time, the problem of child care became one of national concern as a result of studies that showed that the illnesses that made men unfit for military service had their beginnings in early childhood, between birth and six years of age.[3]

In the early 1920s, nursery schools patterned after English nurseries were started in the United States and began to attract the attention of specialists interested in child psychology, health, education, and other fields. These nurseries were designed to educate rather than merely to oversee. In 1920, when schools such as the Ruggles Street Nursery School transformed their schools from custodial to educative nurseries, parents and professionals were enthusiastic. It became clear that working parents desired day care facilities whose programs could satisfy multiple needs; while supervising children, they also provided a variety of learning activities.

In 1928 the Office of Education published a report on nursery schools in operation during the decade 1920 to 1930. The report attributed the rapid growth of nurseries during this period to a growing concern about the strain that increased urbanization and mobility might have placed on the emotional and social adjustment of individuals and families.[4] The sudden increase in nursery schools was a response to the feeling that the psychological and educative needs of the children were not being met. This same report still described institutional day care as a supplementary, corrective, noneducational facility.

In 1930, when President Hoover's White House Conference on Child Health and Protection studied provisions for preschool child care, the published report stated, "Day nurseries and relief nursery schools exist primarily for the relief of unsatisfactory or unwholesome conditions in the home,"[5] while nursery schools and kindergartens existed for the "education and training of young children."[6] The shift toward educational group care was only briefly cited.

Concern for the welfare of children increased as the Depression became more severe. In 1933 the Federal Emergency Relief Administration (later known as the Works Projects Administration), in cooperation with the Office of Education, included nursery schools as an integral part of a federally sponsored program to relieve unemployment and assist existing educational programs. By 1936 there were approximately 1650 federally sponsored nursery schools.

World War II further increased the need for child care centers. During the spring of 1942, a "Policy on Young Children and the War" was adopted which focused on extending school facilities and providing necessary day care. A special day care section was set up in the Office of Defense Health and Welfare Services, and in August of 1942, President Roosevelt allocated $400,000 to set up planned day care programs for children whose mothers worked in war industries.[7]

The most extensive funding for custodial day care facilities was provided for under the Lanham Act of 1941. At the time, some 1100 low-income day nurseries were already being maintained under the Works Projects Administration, which was about to expire as an agency. By means of grants under the Lanham Act, these nurseries were converted to meet wartime needs and continued under the Federal Works Agency. Although the Lanham Act did not specifically call for subsidizing day care, 95 percent of all of the grants under the Lanham Act were made to programs run by educational authorities.[8]

The Lanham Act was clearly an emergency measure. Subsequently, bills were introduced in Congress to provide for more permanent day care facilities, but they were defeated. Wartime child care centers were predictably temporary facilities designed primarily to maintain our industrial production by enabling women to participate in the labor force. The legislation never intended to give women the freedom to work on a permanent basis. Furthermore, it never attempted to provide an educational setting for children.

Funds for day care under the Lanham Act were discontinued early in 1946, and day care did not become a major political issue again until 1962, when the Public Welfare Amendments of the Social Security Act authorized the first appropriation of federal funds specifically for the day care of children in peacetime. Although the Headstart program was specifically concerned with the care of poor children, it has had a significant impact on legislators and on attitudes toward other child care programs.[9]

Child care again became a national issue during the Nixon administration. Prompted by changing views on the status of women, civil-rights groups, women's organizations and some unions joined forces to draft the Comprehensive Child Development Bill of 1971.[10] Although the bill passed both the House and the Senate, it was vetoed by the president. In his veto message, Nixon claimed that the need for child care had not been established, that group child care would weaken the family structure in the country, that the bill duplicated the proposed Family Assistance Plan, and that it was too expensive. In brief, the president was not persuaded of the urgency of the need for child care. In vetoing the bill he spoke for many Americans who have been traditionally hostile to child care.[11]

Attitudes Toward Child Care

Before considering ways of improving child care facilities in the United States, it is important to understand the deep hostility in this country toward group child care, a negative attitude that President Nixon's veto of the 1971 Child Development Bill both exploited and reinforced.

Opponents of group child care view it as a necessity for families that are somehow inadequate: children of women who are poor, divorced, or deserted, and who are usually black. Those in a position to facilitate educative group child care only reinforce these misconceptions either through overtly hostile action or by simply failing to provide active support. Good child care programs have consistently been defeated or made ineffective by legislatures, courts, and social service agencies. The reason often given is that child care undermines the family.

Elinor Guggenheimer of the New York City Planning Commission was not being altogether facetious when she stated to a Labor Department consultation group in 1967: "My conclusion is that the average legislator is a man, and the average man simply cannot bear to think that there was ever a time when his mother did not want to be with him twenty-four hours a day."[1][2]

Legislators are not alone in this belief. One study of professionals and board members in public and private child and family agencies, local businessmen, and labor leaders indicated widespread opposition to child care and disapproval of the growing number of working mothers. It should not be surprising that only ten years ago, an organization like the Child Welfare League believed, "The purpose of day care is to protect children by providing part-time care, supervision and guidance when their families are unable to meet their needs without assistance from the community."[1][3]

The Children's Bureau of the Department of Health, Education and Welfare, another giant in the child care industry, took a similar position. A 1968 brochure posed the question: "Who needs day care?" and responded:

Robin does. Her mother is divorced and works as a clerk in a downtown store. At noon, Robin comes home to their small apartment from her split-session third grade class. Then eight-year old Robin is on her own until her mother arrives home at 6 P.M.

Giorgi does. When his father deserted the family, his mother found work as a domestic.

Alice does. Her father is a salesman who was seriously disabled in an automobile accident.

Esther does. She is four and mentally retarded.

Paul does. Paul is the youngest in a family of nine. His father is unemployed, mother hospitalized.[1][4]

Those who believe that children over three are better off at home are even more outspoken when talking about younger children. The years before three are generally agreed to be crucial in development. Most state legislatures have concluded, therefore, that maternal employment and day care for small children are harmful to children. Consequently, they have made any form of group care or care not in a private home, for children under three, illegal or prohibitively expensive.

Proponents of day care and women's rights cite the considerable evidence that suggests that maternal employment is not harmful to children. Studies of working mothers have made several points: delinquency is not caused by maternal employment uncomplicated by other factors; maternal employment does not significantly change family interactions or relations; and a child's social adjustment may be easier if separation from the mother is begun at infancy. Thus, the physical presence of a parent in the home does not, in itself, ensure the health or emotional development of the child; the type and quality of the care are more important.[15] The typical working mother neither rejects her children nor neglects their needs; instead, she can serve as a positive model for them. Moreover, the whole family may benefit when the mother works. Housewives separated from the occupational world often feel boredom, frustration, and isolation, and may become hostile and anxious mothers.[16] Some sociologists observe that if there is continuous subservience of the mother to the needs of the child, the relationship can be frustrating to the mother and can result in an unhealthy environment for the entire family. In fact, there seems to be no difference in the anxiety scores between children of employed mothers and mothers at home. School achievement levels of children of employed and nonemployed mothers do not differ.[17] A 1972 study of welfare mothers confirmed both that working mothers' self-esteem was greater than that of nonworking mothers and that this positive self-perception had some impact on the children.[18]

The Need for Child Care[a]

Since the period immediately before World War II, the number of working mothers has more than doubled. As of March 1973, 12.8 million mothers of children under eighteen years of age were either in the labor force or seeking to enter it. Six million of their children were under six. Nearly 3 million of these women with children under six are heads of households; 59 percent of the women who are heads of households and who have children between three and five years old work full time. Some work because their families need the income; other women work because they want to; yet licensed day care is available for only one million children.[19]

The need for adequate child care is not limited to poor or single-parent families. But low-income women are in a double bind: they must work to clothe and feed their children, yet they cannot make enough money to pay for good child care. Many poor mothers, given a choice between a low-paying, unrewarding job and staying home to care for young children, would prefer to stay home. But they have no choice under present welfare legislation. Middle-class mothers who have managed to overcome social pressures to stay home and who have found jobs they like have not had adequate institutional alternatives either. Yet, until recently, they have neither put pressure on existing preschools to serve their needs nor created new institutions.

Employers consider young working women and mothers high-risk employees, since a mother or a potential mother may have to leave her job at any time for

---

[a]The sections on the Need for Child Care, Attitudes Towards Child Care, and Parent Participation are based on Antonia Chayes's and Adele Simmons's "Child Care, What Next," unpublished, Cambridge, 1972.

her children. While some mothers of young children choose not to work for pay, many stop work because of inadequate child care facilities. Because there is so little good child care in the country, we cannot know how many women would work if quality child care were available.

Child care arrangements available to working mothers are haphazard according to the most recent study, published in 1968.[20] The type of care varies with the income of the family, the age of the children, the type of work the mother does, and the availability of day care opportunities. Middle-class mothers have resorted to the ever shrinking supply of domestic help and au pair girls. Poor children and older children look after themselves more than young or middle-class children. In 1965 only 10 percent of the children between three and five whose mothers work were cared for in groups—nursery or child care programs or "play-groups"—while 5 percent of the children under three were cared for in groups. Although care by a relative other than the father was more frequent among poor families than middle-class families, it is still the most widely used form of child care.[21]

Parents are not happy with these arrangements. The 1965 survey of working mothers asked whether they were satisfied with the quality of care their children received. This is a hard and complicated question, for a negative answer stimulates guilt among most mothers and requires them either to find another form of child care or to consider giving up a job. The group of women who were not in a position to give up their jobs and stay home with children—single heads of households and the very poor—expressed the greatest dissatisfaction with existing arrangements, and most of them complained about the quality of care the children received when they stayed home with an older relative.[22]

Quality Child Care

Child care can and must be an educational experience. A carefully planned program will serve the needs of both parents and children. The Child Development Act made this clear partly through avoiding the words *day care*, which carry so many negative images and imply custodial care, in favor of the more comprehensive term *child development*. The bill was addressed "as a matter of right" to all children regardless of economic, social, or family background.[23] It emphasized comprehensive, high-quality educational programs with a full range of social, health, and supportive services. However, the bill itself made no attempt to define quality child care.

Although some determinants of effective child care projects are identifiable, debate begins in trying to evaluate the unique quality of the educational experience for children, given an inevitable variety of environments and personalities. Few generalizations are possible. However, a number of specific components are seen as basic to any well-integrated educational program. The controversy is in deciding to what degree each aspect should be stressed.

Parents and professionals define quality differently. Some place greater emphasis on cognitive development, others on social and emotional development. Because it is easier to measure, most evaluations have focused on cognitive development. Yet, such a focus implies a relationship between performance and competence that may not be appropriate, particularly for children from different cultural backgrounds. The current controversy about IQ measurements is evidence of general concern and skepticism about methods of measuring competence. It is clear that today's theories about what constitutes good education should not be forced to fit the mold of rigid curriculum requirements, and that even broad standards need review in light of new findings.

A second determinant of a quality program, the emotional and social development of a child, is much harder to measure. The methods of evaluating such growth are rudimentary; longitudinal data is virtually nonexistent. Yet, affective rather than cognitive growth was the primary goal of most Headstart officials, in accordance with many educational theories that stress the importance of the socialization experience in preschool rather than the learning of specific "academic" content.

Most recently, the federal government has tried to regulate standards for child care by a rigid set of regulations about the physical facilities. While such requirements are necessary to ensure that children are not endangered by simply being in the building, these requirements have, in many cases, been so stringent that they have discouraged people from establishing centers. Before physical regulations are too rigidly defined by a national body, the implications of these regulations should be fully understood.

A central determinant of quality is the staff, both in the establishment of low student-teacher ratios and in choosing certain types of personnel. Centers with a low student-teacher ratio usually provide more individual attention for children. They offer children greater choice and respond more readily to their needs. In addition to maintaining student-teacher ratios on the scale of approximately eight to one, future legislation must contain adequate provision for the training of child care personnel. Because so little is known about the kind of intervention that encourages child development: the prospect of spending money to train people to work in a still unexplored area is awesome. In 1970 there were approximately 78,000 people working in child development centers. Five hundred thousand people would be required to maintain an eight-to-one ratio, if four million children are to be cared for.[24] Traditional methods of training are not appropriate; the traditional degree route is not adequate. New techniques of training child care workers are required so that larger numbers can be given good training. The experience and success with New Careers paraprofessional personnel indicate the results of such an approach, which permits much of the training to be done in the centers themselves. Paraprofessionals should not be dead-ended in supportive roles, however. Colleges and universities will need financial support to develop career advancement programs to permit the paraprofessionals to gain the theoretical knowledge and broad educational background to attain professional status and salary. A great deal of careful attention must be given to financing methods of flexible personnel training and education in any future legislation. The specter of a new army of traditional, authoritarian school bureaucrats spawning fixed and uncreative programs is not pleasant to contemplate. Child development departments that now train nursery-school teachers will have to adapt their curriculum to include the special problems of all-day centers.

An important component for quality child care is its provision for parental and community participation. The Child Development Act formally stated three specific levels at which parental involvement could take place.[25] The particular form of parent participation is not crucial. But no child care legislation should now pass Congress without providing for extensive parent involvement at the local project level, at broader policy levels situated in prime areas, and at the level of federal standard-setting. Parent education is an important corollary of parent involvement.

Experience with federally funded Headstart has shown that parent participation in child care provides an important contact point and focus for the family on issues of education, health, jobs, social services, and politics. An HEW study found that as a result of the impact of Headstart, there was increased involvement of the parents with institutions, particularly at decision-making levels and in decision-making capacities; greater employment of local persons in paraprofessional occupations; greater educational emphasis on the particular needs of the poor and minorities; and a modification of health services and practices to serve the poor better and more sensitively.[26] The report covers a wide range of issues from hot school breakfasts to fundamental reorganization of local health and mental health clinics, and the findings are contrasted with the lesser community change in non-Headstart areas.

If parental responsibility is important, it is universally important. No distinction should be permitted because of a child's race or social and economic position. The undercurrent of hostility and derision for all poor parents, especially those with illegitimate children, should be ended before new welfare legislation becomes entrenched policy.

A final determinant of quality is the socioeconomic mix of the children in the center. Despite the controversy about the significance of the Coleman Report, it is widely accepted that the mixing of children from lower social and economic backgrounds with those from wealthier and more educated groups is significantly beneficial in achievement terms.[27] While Headstart was confined by law to the poor and was obliged to reinforce economic and social isolation, the Child Development Act proposed a mixture of children of different social and economic classes, and ethnic and racial groups, within a single program. Socioeconomic mix will be an important aspect of legislation to be proposed to Congress in the future. However, suggesting that the majority of centers be neighborhood-based implies that child care centers inevitably reflect patterns of residential segregation. Although this dilemma cannot be solved easily, legislation can provide that most centers include children from a variety of backgrounds. Child care centers at universities, at places of employment, and located on the edge of residential communities can provide the mix that many experts feel is valuable.

"Effectiveness" presumably refers to some proven result, an evaluation of the integration of both affective and cognitive development within the child. How to measure this will probably provoke continued debate between scholars and bureaucrats. New methods for measuring the impact of social programs are required before we will have definitive answers about what kind of child care is best in what circumstances.

Until we know more about a child's development in a variety of environments, and until we have longitudinal data, most attempts to apply the economists' methods of cost-benefit analysis to measure the "effectiveness" of child care will be futile. Child care is expensive, but what are the social and economic costs of failing to provide it for both the child and the mother? Does child care help to prevent future welfare dependence and encourage productivity of the children themselves? What is the extent of the human resources in women who are presently engaged in child rearing and who would prefer to work? Can child care centers give both men and women greater choice about how to spend their time? The answers will evolve as programs develop. It is essential that ongoing evaluation accompany any child care program. In addition, every effort must be made to continue experimenting with existing programs and to avoid becoming rigid or self-satisfied, for we need much more information before we can say what constitutes quality child care.

Types of Child Care

Extensive elaboration on the various types of child care is not possible. However, it is important to begin to break away from some of the more traditional images of institutional child care to more flexible programs with more flexible hours.

It is ironic that, while child care is sharply criticized, nursery school is generally recognized as beneficial for children. Many of the same people who think child care programs are only for children whose families fail to provide adequate home lives often pay large sums to educate and socialize their children three hours a day. Once the time period of preschool is extended past lunchtime into the late afternoon, the institution is called a day care center.

Traditionally, nursery schools have been middle- or upper-class and white; day care centers have been for the poor and the black. While many middle-class white nursery schools, especially in or near urban areas, have actively recruited both black and poor children, the short day and distance from home make it difficult for working parents to enroll their children. These nursery schools have lacked the flexibility to extend their hours or vary their programs to meet present day needs of differing family groups.

The distinction between child care centers and nursery schools is based more on theoretical issues than on the quality of care actually provided. While nursery schools are seen as a service to children and regard the needs of family members, especially mothers, as irrelevant, intrusive, or a diversion from the main purpose of the school, day care centers are seen as a service to parents. Clearly the distinction is artificial. All facilities should benefit both parents and children. There is, however, a need for a variety of child care arrangements, for the standard nine-to-five center simply does not meet the needs of all working women. On the whole, these other types of care provide greater family flexibility, allowing parents to be alone while their child is well taken care of, thus alleviating much family pressure.

Experience with *twenty-four-hour child care facilities* is limited. However, to serve parents who work at night or parents who have evening meetings, some kinds of facilities are required. To prevent these centers from becoming a substitute for the home, maximum numbers of hours during which a child can remain in a twenty-four hour center may need to be defined. But the danger of abuse of such a center should not prevent its establishment under carefully controlled guidelines.

Similarly, this country has little experience with a service already available in Scandinavia—*homemaker services.* Sick children and family crises are often a concern of working parents. While, on the one hand, employer practices can change to permit greater flexibility in these circumstances, on the other, homemaker services should be available so that in emergencies children will not be left totally alone. Rather, someone will be available to come to the home for a limited period to look after the children.

All-day child care centers often cannot accommodate the numbers of children who seek an alternative to returning to an empty house after school. While some children emerge from school to a range of activities from piano lessons to supervised play at a club, most do not have these alternatives. *After-school care* is an area that has been given little thought by the experts. Utilizing older children's help in day care centers in the afternoons, making extensive use of school and church facilities as well as public playgrounds in the afternoons are possibilities that require further exploration.

Most of the discussion of group child care brings to mind places outside the home, where groups of ten to twenty children are cared for by professionals. However, family care, essentially an outgrowth of the "play group" concept that many nonworking mothers have used, provides for child care in the home of one parent, rather than in a center.

Family care is a particularly desirable way of caring for children under three, who often are not toilet-trained, who do not need large amounts of space to play in, and who cannot yet talk. More widespread use of family care has been explored by Abt Associates.[28] In 1973 the Office of Child Development funded a demonstration family day care program in six cities. The Office of Child Development is hoping that providing training, technical assistance, and resource centers which might have toys, large play areas, health facilities, and testing will mean that family day care can be better coordinated, and the quality of the programs can improve. If the demonstration project is successful, it is possible that family day care opportunities can increase considerably without the costly overhead that more formal day care centers require. A 1972 study of working welfare mothers reported that many women preferred family care to formal day care arrangements, primarily because it was more convenient.[29]

Sources of Child Care

Once there is general acceptance of the need for quality child care the question becomes how to provide it. Between 1965 and 1973 the number of spaces in licensed centers increased from 475,000 to one million.[30] However, the task of supplying day care is enormously complicated by the high cost of early childhood education. A 1965 study by the Department of Health, Education and Welfare found that group care, on the average, cost over ten dollars per week per child. The cost has risen considerably since then, and educative group care by qualified professionals is still more expensive. In 1972 the operating cost ranged from thirteen dollars per child per week in an industry program in North Carolina to more than fifty dollars in a model budget compiled by a nonprofit agency which runs sixteen centers in the District of Columbia.[31] By 1974 welfare was paying $60 per week per child in some states. Programs such as Headstart with strong educative and enrichment components, which must comply with high government standards, are particularly costly.[32] Supportive services such as transportation and health programs further add to the cost. Even if measures to cut costs and efforts to pool resources or hire paraprofessionals are taken, the cost of good child care is still extremely high. Because costs vary greatly in different parts of the country and because money alone cannot ensure good care, cost is not necessarily a true measure of the quality of a program.

Although many people argue that the education of young children should not become an extension of the public school system, the responsibility of the government to provide funds for educative child care cannot be overlooked. At the same time, other sources that now provide or could undertake child care—industry, labor unions, and profit-making franchise organizations—need to be examined.

Industry

Industry's involvement in child care is fairly recent. During World War II, a labor shortage led businessmen to consider ways to expand their labor pool, keep employees they had trained, and reduce absenteeism. As a result, some businesses with large numbers of female employees began to provide child care facilities.

Some southern textile companies have traditionally provided day care centers for the children of their employees. While the care offered by many of the textile companies is simply custodial, some of these centers have educative programs. Recently, more industries have shown an increased interest in child care. In March 1970, fifty companies paid $300 each to send representatives to a conference on Industry and Day Care organized by the Urban Research Corporation.[33] Companies are beginning to realize that it is good business to provide child care facilities, and that it is often cheaper to offer day care than to train new women for work. Specifically, they hope to reduce turnover and absenteeism and to improve company, employee, and community relations.

Industry can play a number of roles in promoting good child care facilities. First, some companies operate, either singly or jointly, child care centers for the children of all their employees. Furthermore, industries such as Whirlpool Corporation have assumed a "leadership-catalyst" role in the Twin Cities area, promoting and facilitating the idea of a community child care center by making their own business training and administration resources publicly available.[34] Banks, too, can serve child care in this capacity through extending low-interest loans to cover some of the initial costs of establishing child care centers. A related role of industry is the provision of financial donations to child care facilities. Rather than actually operating a day care center, some industries help employees find suitable alternatives. Some companies, including the Illinois Bell Telephone Company, act as clearinghouses and assist employees in finding the day care facilities that best meet their needs.

In this program, as in many industry-sponsored programs, there is little quality control. Most often the programs benefit the industry by providing custodial care that allows mothers to work. This does not assure quality care or offer the educative emphasis that parents would prefer.

Unions

By providing financial support and pressure on legislators, unions can be an important force in promoting the expansion and acceptance of child care. The Amalgamated Clothing Workers of America, 80 percent of whose members are women, have pressed for an amendment of the Taft-Hartley Act which permits employers and unions to discuss day care at the bargaining table, if the employers are willing to do so.[35] In addition, employers are now permitted to make contributions to trust funds to establish child care centers for preschool and school-age dependents of employees.

Amalgamated has both raised funds and made substantial contributions to begin five day care centers in the Baltimore region. To supplement the union's efforts, seventy employers and manufacturers contributed 2 percent of their gross payrolls to the day care programs.[36]

Franchise Centers

Nearly half of the licensed day care centers are operated on a profit-making basis. The sudden increase in the number of profit-making centers has been a source of alarm. Many people assume that anyone making a profit from the education and care of small children is exploitative. Although information about cost for many of these centers is hard to find, most of them hope to make money on a maximum fee of $25 per child per week.[37] Joseph Featherstone, writing in *The New Republic*, says he believes that "for-profit centers can never offer good programs, because good programs cost too much." He concluded "People operating licensed for-profit centers are in the day care business to make a living, not because they are interested in children."[38]

In fact, however, the quality of profit-making centers varies greatly. While some profit-making centers are purely custodial, others do have educational programs. American Child Care Centers in Nashville, Tennessee, which according to the present budget should gross a 20 percent profit, has been considered by several organizations to be the best of the profit-making group. They opened a model center in 1969 after a year of construction and a year of careful curriculum planning. Using a team-teaching concept and maintaining a student-teacher ratio of ten to one, the centers were staffed with well-trained and experienced professionals. Education experts claim that the model is a good one and that the low costs simply reflect careful planning and organization.

Universities

Prodded by students and faculty, within the last several years some universities have begun to provide day care centers on campuses. Their reluctance is almost paradoxical, for the university has accessibility to its own laboratory centers, making experimenting with new curricula, new staffing patterns, and new equipment a relatively uncomplicated process. In addition, a heterogeneous student and employee population usually already exists within the university, easily facilitating a broad socioeconomic mix among children. University day care centers should become models, possibly providing a place for trying experimental programs, which could then be implemented in the community at large.

Federal Programs

Though most of the federal money available for child care is for families below the poverty line, these programs do not begin to meet the needs of the poor.

Furthermore, they reinforce the belief that child care is needed only for children of parents who are somehow inadequate. Federal programs are often limited by an inadequate appropriation of funds or an unwillingness on the state level to take advantage of federal funds when they are available. Moreover, most federal day care programs do not provide money for construction of much needed facilities.[39]

The largest federal program is Headstart. As of July 1974, nearly 5 million children had participated in Headstart programs across the country. In 1973-74, 379,000 children were enrolled in 1545 programs (see Table 6-1). Headstart was originally administered by the Office of Economic Opportunity, but President Nixon has transferred the program to the Office of Education in the Department of Health, Education and Welfare.

Present guidelines limit Headstart participation to children of the poor. Thus, the educational advantages believed to result from classrooms that include children with a variety of backgrounds are rarely available to Headstart children. Appropriations for Headstart have leveled off at $400 million dollars. The cost per child is high, but the educational component of Headstart is considerable.

The Work Incentive Program (WIN) stipulates that welfare mothers who receive training must be provided with child care services. On paper, therefore, the WIN program allocates funds for child care for all children of enrollees. The problems arise in the actual transference of these funds, for the federal government contributes only a certain percentage of the cost. As of fiscal year 1970, the federal government was authorized to pay only 75 percent of the program's cost, while the state shouldered the remainder of the burden,[41] and in 1971 the government share increased to 90 percent. In March 1974, 67,357 mothers enrolled 139,850 children in child care programs under WIN.[42]

In 1969, when $22.6 million was appropriated by the federal government for

Table 6-1
Headstart Day Care Appropriations[40]

Year	Children	Budget
1965	561,000	96.4 million dollars
1966	733,000	198.9
1967	681,400	349.2
1968	693,900	316.2
1969	663,600	333.9
1970	434,000	326.0
1971	415,800	360.0
1972	379,000	376.3
1973	379,000	400.7
1974	379,000	400.7

day care under the WIN program, it was predicted that "only about 11 to 12 million dollars of the 22.6 million dollars originally earmarked for day care . . . will actually be used."[43] The report was overly optimistic. Of the 22.6 million dollars appropriated in 1969, only four million were used. In 1970, of the $52 million available for day care in the WIN program, only $18 million was actually used. While only $38 million of the $97 million available was used in 1973, the government believes that improved, computerized reporting systems will mean that all of the $110 million appropriated in 1974 will be used.[44]

The issues surrounding child care are closely related to the potential success of WIN, yet they also present one of the basic paradoxes of WIN and AFDC:

It costs more to provide "quality" day care to children than most states are willing to pay mothers to take care of their own children. Therefore, the commitment to WIN on a large scale may result more in a transference of funds from the mothers to child care vendors with little reduction in actual costs, except for mothers with small families who can earn enough to offset the costs of the child care, or who can find care which will be less expensive to themselves and the state.[45]

Legal barriers in the states are responsible for blocking the flow of funds. The WIN funds that are available cannot be used for any construction or major renovation, a restriction that places additional strain on the already insufficient institutional and group facilities. In addition, the implementation of the WIN program is often inefficient and unfair. Some WIN policies encourage women to join the work force, while others encourage them to stay at home, as it is "cheaper" to keep them on welfare than to pay for child care services. Those in the program find that payments are often delayed, or they may be withheld if a woman does not send her child to a specific center. Sometimes child care is just not available and women are forced to make their own arrangements. In 1973, the federal government issued new Social Service Regulations that may limit the number of children eligible for care under federal programs. The new regulations moved the government further away from a position that would offer welfare parents a real choice between working and looking after their children. To receive federal child care funds, parents must be willing to work or to enter job-training programs. They cannot take college-level courses.[46]

At the same time, standards for child care were relaxed, and parental involvement in the control of facilities is no longer required. Even so, the government estimates that the number of children receiving day care under the WIN program will continue to increase, in part because of the improved reporting systems mentioned earlier.

Remaining federal assistance to day care is scattered under the umbrella of a number of laws and programs: the Social Security Act, the Community Mental Health Centers Construction Act of 1963, Title I and Title III of the Elementary and Secondary Education Act, Title II of the Economic Opportunity Act, and

Title VII of the 1965 Housing and Urban Development Act, and the Parent and Child Center program, which provides funds for children under three. In total, nine departments in Washington have had some involvement in day care: Health, Education and Welfare; Labor; Agriculture; Commerce; Interior; Defense; Housing and Urban Development; the Office of Economic Opportunity; and the Bureau of the Budget. A federal panel on early childhood education, established in 1968, includes members of each of these departments and agencies, and has developed a plan to coordinate all programs for child care and drawn up Federal interagency day care requirements, stringent standards that must be met by all day care centers receiving any federal funds.

However, to enable day care programs to begin on a large scale, new sources of funding are required. The 1971 legislation permitting parents earning up to $18,000 a year to deduct as a personal expense up to $400 per month for child care and household services (for children under fourteen and dependent parents or spouses) is a first step. But this legislation is of no real assistance to the poor or lower-middle-income families who pay low taxes anyway, and it makes no provision for day care facilities.

Legislation such as the Family Assistance Plan (H.R.1) proposed in 1969 by President Nixon is not of significant help either. The Family Assistance Plan was written for poor parents only, by those who feel that welfare mothers should be working. It ensured that day care would continue to be custodial and that it would be available to the poor only. The proposed legislation perpetuated the belief that a mother who works because she wishes to is inadequate.

The 1971 Child Development Act was written for parents and children. Revised versions of this act will be considered by Congress in 1975. Whether the proposed legislation will be simply an expanded Headstart program or will contain the proposals for comprehensive child care described in the 1971 legislation depends on the prevailing mood in Congress. The Child Development Act explicitly acknowledged the right of mothers of small children to work, developed models of community participation which reached beyond those described in earlier legislation, and accepted the fact that the federal government has responsibility for the care and education of preschool children. It included numerous provisions to ensure that children would receive quality care.

Many people who participated in the drafting of the bill now agree that the delivery system described in the bill was unwieldy and unworkable, that it would have required scores of bureaucrats to administer the program, in addition to the teachers. A new delivery system needs to be devised which ensures that those who need and want child care have access to federal funds. Channeling funds through states alone will not do this; some kind of voucher system might, however, be effective. While only the poor should receive child care free, child care centers should serve parents and children of all backgrounds; they should provide comprehensive services, including an educational program and health care; and there should be standards to ensure quality. Rigid standards are not always helpful. Yet few pieces of federal legislation provide the flexibility that would be important in good day care legislation. Finally, the legislation should provide funds to train professionals and paraprofessionals to staff the child care facilities and to continue research so that we can move to a better definition of quality care.

Child care is a complex issue, but without child care, the right of women to work will not be a reality. The availability of child care does not mean that all women will work, but it does mean that all women will have an *opportunity* to work if they wish. Until child care is available to all families, women will feel obliged to stop working during a crucial period of career development. They will continue to take refuge in regarding their paid work as a job rather than a career, and they will continue to find employers who, given a choice, will employ men or women past child-bearing age.

It should be clear, however, that custodial child care is not what parents and children want. Child care should, by now, be synonymous with an educational experience. However, as long as the president of the United States can veto legislation for educative child care and support legislation that provides custodial care for the poor, much remains to be done to change attitudes towards child care and working women.

Notes

1. Lydia Hoyt Farmer, *The National Exposition Souvenir: What America Owes to Women* (New York: Charles Wells Moulton, 1893), p. 220.

2. Florence A. Ruderman, *Child Care and Working Mothers: A Study of Arrangements Made for Daytime Care of Children* (New York: Child Welfare League of America, Inc., 1968), p. 12.

3. National Commission for Young Children, *Children's Centers: A Guide for Those Who Care For and About Young Children, ed. Rose H. Alschuler* (New York: William Morrow and Co., 1942), p. 6.

4. Ibid., pp. 7-8.

5. White House Conference on Child Health and Protection, *White House Conference, 1930: Addresses and Abstracts of Committee Reports, White House Conference on Child Health and Protection, called by President Hoover* (New York: The Century Co., 1931), p. 155.

6. Ibid.

7. "All-Day School Programs for Children of Working Mothers," *Education for Victory*, official biweekly of the U.S. Office of Education, Federal Security Agency, October 15, 1942, p. 1.

8. President's Commission on the Status of Women, *American Women; the Report of the President's Commission on the Status of Women and Other Publications of the Commission*, ed. Margaret Mead and Frances Kaplan (New York: Charles Scribner's Sons, 1965), p. 113.

9. Ibid.

10. U.S., Congress, Senate, Committee on Labor and Public Welfare, *Comprehensive Child Development Act of 1971 S. 1512*, 92nd Congress, 1st Sess., April 5, 1971.

11. *New York Times*, December 12, 1971.

12. Consultation on Working Women and Day Care Needs, Washington, D.C., 1967, *Report* (Washington, D.C.: U.S. Department of Labor, Women's Bureau, 1968), p. 71.

13. Child Welfare League of America, *Child Welfare League of America's Standards for Day Care Services* (New York: Child Welfare League of America, 1960).

14. U.S., Children's Bureau, *What Is Day Care?* (1968), p. 3. p. 3.

15. F. Ivan Nye and Lois Wladis Hoffman, *The Employed Mother in America* (Chicago: Rand McNally, 1963), pp. 102-5.

16. For a fuller discussion of the problems of middle-class housewives, see Betty Friedan, *The Feminine Mystique* (New York: Dell Publishing Co., Inc., 1963).

17. Nye and Hoffman, *The Employed Mother*, p. 120.

18. Harold and Margaret Feldman, *A Study of the Effects on the Family Due to Employment of the Welfare Mother* (Washington, D.C.: Manpower Administration, 1972), vol. I, p. 171.

19. U.S., Women's Bureau, *Women Working Today* (1971), p. 2.

20. Elizabeth Waldman and Robert Whitmore, "Children of Working Mothers, March 1973," *Monthly Labor Review*, May 1974, pp. 50-58.

21. U.S., Department of Health, Education and Welfare and U.S., Department of Labor, Seth Low, Children's Bureau, and Pearl S. Spindler, Women's Bureau, *Child Care Arrangements of Working Mothers in the U.S.* (Washington, D.C.: U.S. Government Printing Office, 1968), pp. 15-16. See also U.S., Department of Health, Education and Welfare, "Child Care Arrangements Under the Incentive Program as of June 30, 1973."

22. *Child Care Arrangements*, pp. 25-26.

23. *Comprehensive Child Development Act, 1971*, pp. 1-2.

24. Lynn C. Thompson, *A Study in Child Care 1970-71*, volume 3: *Cost and Quality Issues for Operators* (Cambridge: Abt Associates, 1971).

25. *Comprehensive Child Development Act, 1971*.

26. Mary P. Rowe et al., *A Study in Child Care 1970-71*, volume 1: *Findings* (Cambridge: Abt Associates, 1971), pp. 35-36.

27. James S. Coleman, *Equality of Educational Opportunity* (Washington, D.C.: U.S. Government Printing Office, 1966), pp. 469-88.

28. Richard Roupp et al., *A Study in Child Care 1970-71* volume 2B, *Systems Case Studies* (Cambridge: Abt Associates, 1971).

29. Harold and Margaret Feldman, *Effects on the Family Due to Employment of the Welfare Mother*, p. 250.

30. Elizabeth Waldman and Robert Whitmore, "Children of Working Mothers," *Monthly Labor Review*, May 1974, p. 57.

31. Roupp et al., *A Study in Child Care 1970-71*, vol. 11B *System Case Studies* (Cambridge, Mass.: Abt Associates, 1971).

32. U.S., Department of Health, Education and Welfare, Education and Public Welfare Division, *Federal Involvement in Day Care*, ed. Margaret Malone, March 3, 1969, p. 13.

33. Urban Research Corporation, *Industry and Day Care* (Chicago: Urban Research Corporation, 1971).

34. U.S., Women's Bureau, "Day Care Services," *Industry's Involvement Bulletin 296* (1971), 19-20.

35. Baltimore Regional Joint Board, Health and Welfare Fund, Amalgamated Clothing Workers of America, AFL-CIO, *The Facts; The Problem; The Solution* (Baltimore: Ashton-Worthington, Inc., 1971).

36. Ibid., pp. 1-2.

37. Edward Breathitt, president, American Child Care Centers, Inc., (Speech given at the Industry and Day Care Conference, March 19, 1970).

38. Joseph Feathertone, "The Day Care Problem: Kentucky Fried Children," *The New Republic*, Sept. 12, 1970, p. 14.

39. U.S., Department of Health, Education and Welfare, *Federal Involvement in Day Care*, pp. 33-35.

40. Ibid., p. 13.

41. Ibid., p. 6.

42. Office of the Work Incentive Program, Operational and Fiscal Information.

43. Ibid.

44. Ibid.

45. U.S., Congress, Senate, Committee on Finance, Excerpts from the Report of the Auerback Corporation, *An Appraisal of the Work Incentive Program*, March 15, 1970, as cited in *Child Care, Data and Materials* (Washington, D.C.: U.S. Government Printing Office, June 16, 1971), p. 108.

46. *Dollars and Sense*, May 1974, p. 12.

7 Conclusion

Men and women, employers and employees, legislators and union leaders, must all participate in bringing about the changes required to ensure that women and men have equal opportunity in the labor market. These changes cannot be confined to the work place, but must extend to schools and to the home. Making the changes will not be easy, particularly for the group that must assume major responsibility for their implementation: men. Some men are likely to claim that the women's movement has limited their own opportunities for promotion or for admission to desirable occupations. In a few cases, this may be true. It is not as easy now to include women in the labor force and pay them equally as it was when the economy was expanding, without restricting opportunities for male workers. But the policies and practices that reenforce and perpetuate injustices are no less wrong in a time of economic crisis than in a time of economic prosperity.

The women's movement gained national recognition in 1968; we began to write this book in 1970. Since then there has been some progress. Some men have articulated the importance of hiring women in jobs from which they have been excluded; and some women have moved into positions of responsibility. Women in the media now cover political events, and men shop in supermarkets and note the rising price of meat. An Ivy League university has a woman provost; the telephone company now advertises that women climb telephone poles to make repairs; the AFL-CIO supports the Equal Rights Amendment. Today 30 percent of the nation's bartenders are women, while in 1940 only 2½ percent were women.

Developments such as these have been widely publicized, but they do not, as yet, signify enough of a shift in the opportunities, jobs, and rewards available to most women in America to alter national statistics significantly. The injustices generally persist. The gap between the median income of men and women remains substantial. Women on welfare still do not have a real choice between working and staying at home, or between menial jobs and receiving quality training and education to prepare for more satisfying and remunerative work. Many firms now regularly interview women for traditionally male positions, but they rarely hire them, particularly if they have young children.

Continuing progress requires a continuing commitment on the part of those who have already been involved in improving the status of women and a new commitment from those who have watched with skepticism. This commitment is all the more important at this particular time. As the novelty of the women's

189

movement wears off and the first woman to enter a "male" occupation is no longer headline news, employers may lose interest in providing equal opportunity. The very real prospect of a general recession makes the possibility of neglect or resistance all the more likely. Old questions about the legitimacy and validity of equal opportunity may be raised, and sex discriminatory practices, perhaps more subtle in form than those of the past, may become generally accepted.

In adjusting to the new concerns of women, employers have generally responded, but they have often responded in the easiest ways: employing some women on their staffs, changing benefits policies, and in some cases reviewing salary levels to ensure that equal pay is given for equal work. These changes are not insignificant, but by themselves they do not represent equal opportunity. Even so, there seems to be a tendency for some employers to be satisfied with token efforts, to feel that they have made their contribution to the women's movement, and to return to "business as usual."

Will the new women vice-presidents ever be seriously considered for the next promotion? Will traditionally male businesses employ and promote women in significant numbers? Will employers, unions, and male employees make the kinds of adjustments necessary to make women feel truly welcome? The women who have recently made the headlines have all been determined and had the self-confidence to deal with existing discrimination. But not all women (or all men, for that matter) are this self-confident. Discrimination, however, can only be considered as ended when the average woman has access to the same jobs as the average man. This is not the case now.

The role of federal legislation in ending discrimination is now being widely debated. Which actions of the federal government have had the greatest impact on the practices of employers? Have the considerable regional differences in enforcement meant greater progress in some regions than others? Recent out-of-court settlements have resulted in some employers making significant back-pay awards to employees, but have these settlements had an impact on employer practices of companies other than those taken to court? There is now considerable discussion about the impact of the required affirmative action programs, but to date there seems to be little known about the actual effect of these plans on women.

If sex discrimination is eliminated without other changes in the economic and political structure of the country, the burdens of unemployment, low pay, and unsatisfying work, which have traditionally fallen more heavily on women than on men, will merely be redistributed among all workers. The social conflict generated by this shift would be considerable. But it could lead workers of both sexes to question the system that deprives a large proportion of the population of satisfying work and a decent standard of living for the benefit of a few.

In developing strategies to bring about substantial change in women's economic and social status, it is crucial that good data be available, so that priorities can be established and the progress of women can be monitored. We need to know whether there has been real change or just an appearance of change. To what extent have the stereotypes been dispelled? In the past, sociologists, psychologists, and economists have focused their research on men. The gaps in available knowledge about women are considerable and, to some extent, make it easier to perpetuate stereotypes. New research needs to be done, and current research designs need to be altered to enable us to learn more about the general problems of working women and the particular problems of specific groups of working women.

The persistence of occupational segregation by sex in the labor market is the major obstacle to the attainment of economic equality for women. Yet we know little about the historical evolution of this employment pattern, and even less about the social and economic forces that might encourage a diffusion of the female labor force over a broader range of occupations and industries. Why do some occupational categories remain predominantly female or predominantly male over long periods of time, while sex labels change in others? Why does the movement of women into previously male job categories lead to a radical shift in the sex composition of the occupation from predominantly male to predominantly female in some cases and to sex integration in others? Only the most general knowledge about the relationship of occupational segregation to such factors as female labor force participation and pay and status differentials between men and women workers is now available.

The existing studies of turnover rates and absenteeism are inadequate and out of date, yet it would seem relatively easy for employers to collect this data and analyze it to determine the extent of sex differences in separation and absenteeism rates, and the reasons for such differences should they exist.

Available data suggest that part-time workers who are committed to their jobs work proportionately harder and are more productive than full-time workers. But again, specific information about a broad sample of part-time workers is required before a large number of employers can be persuaded of the value of flexible work schedules.

Georgina Smith has described the attitudes of male supervisors and co-workers towards women workers in New Jersey in the early 1960s. How have these attitudes changed with new practices? A Harvard Business School study of executives has suggested that the attitudes of men toward women change when men have an opportunity to work with women. Is this true at all levels? How do men feel about working for women supervisors? If it is correct that some men can work more effectively for and with women than others, what are the reasons for these differences? The attitudes of women about working for and with other women are also important. In the past some women have accepted stereotypes about men and women and felt that they had greater prestige if their co-workers and bosses were men. Have the more traditional attitudes about women held by women changed in the past few years?

More information about specific occupations—for example, those of household worker and secretary—would help us further understand the attitudes of female workers in these occupations. Can these jobs be restructured so that they are more rewarding? How can they become part of a career ladder? Do employers expect the same of men and women who perform these services?

Much of the sociological and psychological research about women excludes poor and working-class women. For example, we know something about the pressures college students feel when making choices about careers and marriage. But we know very little about the attitudes towards work of those women who are not college educated. Would they choose to work in assembly lines if they did not have to provide economic support for themselves and their families? What alternatives do they have?

Recent data on women in labor unions show that when women in white-collar jobs join unions, they are likely to experience wage increases nearly as much as men in similar jobs. The same is not true of women in blue-collar jobs. What are the factors that keep these women at a disadvantage in unions? To what extent are they related to the economic situation of a given point in time? Have recent activities of women in unions actually improved the position of women at the bargaining table? Are "women's issues," such as child care and maternity benefits and child-rearing leaves being considered by a significant number of unions?

Probably more research has been done on the problems of women in higher education than any other area, in part because the people who do research are usually associated with universities, and they have a primary interest in their own situations. On the one hand, this trend is disturbing, because women in higher education represent such a small proportion of women in the country. On the other hand, most women at one point or another do have contact with the educational system at some level, and it is important to know as much as possible about sex roles and education. It has been suggested that women who attend single-sex schools are more likely to have a long-standing interest in a profession. Is this true? If so, at what level and why? At what point do boys and men develop their attitudes and expectations of women? What kind of intervention is most effective at each state of the process? What impact does the sex of the teacher have on the student? While we talk about the importance of having "role models" available for students, what in fact is important about having women teachers? Are they more likely to take an active interest in women students? Or do women students respond positively simply because the teachers are women?

Perhaps the subject that has caused greatest controversy and the highest level of emotion is that of child care. We know that many mothers are unhappy with their current child care arrangements and that some women are not working because they cannot find adequate child care. But the most recent large-scale survey of child care was made in 1964, and there is reason to believe that attitudes towards child care and practices of many mothers have changed considerably in the past decade. A national study of current child care arrangements and the attitudes of both parents and children towards them is long overdue.

There are a variety of ways of providing child care, but we know very little about their impact on children. Attempts to define quality child care and its components should reflect careful study of a number of diverse programs. As child care becomes a focus for federal legislation, evaluations of current programs become more and more important. While legislation should be as flexible as possible, clearly some choices will have to be made, and careful studies of current child care options and opportunities will help legislators and parents to make wise choices.

More generally, we need to understand better the relationship of women's roles in the home to women's roles in the labor force. What would happen if women and men who stayed home to do housework and look after children were paid salaries? Would women be discouraged from taking jobs outside the home? Would men be encouraged to become housespouses? Should we move toward full-time jobs for the majority of adults of both sexes, or part-time work with parents sharing child care and household responsibilities? Should we endeavor to eliminate domestic work by developing commercial services and social structures to make housework more efficient, or should domestic work be encouraged, but on a professional basis? Does the entrance of women into the labor force in increasing numbers reflect an increase in individual freedom or merely a decrease in the ability of the family unit to attain its desired standard of living on one salary?

Some of our efforts to study sex discrimination were hampered by methods of data collection. For example, detailed analysis of some federal programs was difficult because data were not consistently available on the basis of sex. In addition, there seems to be little concerted effort to ensure that data that are collected is comparable, and when such an effort is made, for example by the Department of Health, Education and Welfare in the area of higher education, institutions resist such efforts.

While many questions remain about employers, unions, women and sex discrimination, there is no doubt that sex discrimination is a basic reality of our present society. This report is one of many recent efforts to document the problems, ask questions about causes, and identify possible solutions. We can only hope that it will help stimulate employers, legislators, union leaders, educators, and workers of both sexes to make the changes that will end sex discrimination in the work place and ensure that all people regardless of sex receive the opportunities that are rightfully theirs.

Bibliography

Bibliography

This Bibliography includes those books and articles the authors found of most general use in writing the background paper. In addition, the Women's Bureau of the Labor Department produces regular pamphlets and fact sheets on the status of women, and the *Monthly Labor Review* periodically devotes part of an issue to women workers. *The Spokeswoman* and *Women Today* newsletters have chronicled the impact of the women's movement on a monthly and biweekly basis. The Project on the Status and Education of Women of the Association of American Colleges publishes a variety of materials concerning women employees and students in colleges and universities. Legal cases are described in the quarterly *Women's Rights Law Reporter*. Ms Magazine is a more popular source of fact and opinion relating to the women's movement, while the new magazine *womenSports* covers women's athletics. All of these regular publications are invaluable to people interested in the status of working women in the United States.

Astin, Helen S., et al. *Women: A Bibliography on Their Education and Careers.* Washington, D.C.: Human Service Press, 1971.

Astin, Helen S. *The Woman Doctorate in America.* New York: The Russell Sage Foundation, 1969.

Astin, Helen S. and Bayer, Alan. "Sex Differences in Academic Rank and Salary Among Science Doctorates in Teaching." *The Journal of Human Resources* 3:2 (1968): 191-99.

Babcock, Freedman, Norton and Ross, *Sex Discrimination and the Law: Causes and Remedies.* Boston: Little, Brown and Co., 1974.

Baker, Elizabeth F. *Technology and Woman's Work.* New York and London: Columbia University Press, 1964.

Benet, Mary Kathleen. *The Secretary.* London: Sidgwick & Jackson, 1972.

Bergmann, Barbara and Adelman, Irma. "The 1973 Report of the Council of Economic Advisors: The Economic Role of Women." *American Economic Review* 63:4 (1973).

Bernard, Jessie. *Academic Women.* University Park, Pa.: Pennsylvania State University Press, 1964.

Blau, Francine (Weisskoff). "Women's Place in the Labor Market." *American Economic Review* 62:2 (1972).

Bowman, G.W.; Worthy, N.B.; and Greyser, S.A. "Problems in Review: Are Women Executives People?" Reprinted from *Harvard Business Review*. (July/August 1965): 14-16.

Bird, Caroline. *Born Female.* New York: Pocket Books, 1969.

Brown, Emerson, Falk, and Freedman. *The Equal Rights Amendment: A Constitutional Basis for Equal Rights for Women,* 80 Yale L.J. 871 (1971).

Bynum, Caroline Walker and Martin, Janet M. "The Sad Status of Women Teaching at Harvard or 'From What You Said I Would Never Have Known You Were A Woman.' "*Radcliffe Quarterly* 54:2 (1970): 12-15.

Caplow, Theodore. *The Sociology of Work.* Minneapolis, Minnesota: University of Minnesota Press, 1970.

Carnegie Commission on Higher Education, *The Opportunities for Women in Higher Education, Their Current Participation, Prospects for the Future and Recommendations for Action.* New York: McGraw-Hill, 1973.

Chafe, William H. *The American Woman, Her Changing Social, Economic and Political Roles, 1920-1970.* New York: Oxford University Press, 1972.

Coleman, James S. *Equality of Educational Opportunity.* Washington, D.C.: U.S. Dept. of Health, Education and Welfare, Office of Education, 1966.

Consultation on Working Women and Day Care Needs, Washington, D.C., 1967. *Report.* Washington, D.C.: U.S. Dept. of Labor, Women's Bureau, 1968.

Dunkle, Margaret. *What Constitutes Equality for Women in Sport?*, Washington, D.C.: Association of American Colleges, 1974.

Epstein, Cynthia Fuchs. *Woman's Place: Options and Limits on Professional Careers.* Berkeley: University of California Press, 1970.

Eyde, Lorraine D. "Eliminating Barriers to Career Development of Women." *Personnel and Guidance Journal* 49:1 (1970): 24-27.

Farber, Seymour M. and Wilson, Roger M.L., eds. *The Potential of Women.* San Francisco: McGraw-Hill, 1963.

Featherstone, Joseph. "The Day Care Problem: Kentucky Fried Children." *The New Republic* (September 12, 1970): 12-16.

Finkelman, Jack. "Maternal Employment, Family Relationships, and Parental Role Perception." Unpublished Ph.D. dissertation, Yeshiva University, 1966.

"For Nixon, It's An Idea Whose Time's Not Yet." *New York Times*, 12 December, 1971.

Fuchs, Victor. "Differences in Hourly Earnings Between Men and Women." *Monthly Labor Review* (May 1971): 9-15.

Galenson, Majorie. *Women and Work: An International Campaign.* Ithaca: Cornell University, 1973.

Ginzberg, Eli and Yohalem, Alice M., eds. *Corporate Lib. Women's Challenge to Man's Management.* Baltimore: Johns Hopkins University Press, 1973.

Goldberg, Philip. "Are Women Prejudiced Against Women?" *Trans-Action* (April 1968): 28-30.

Graham, Patricia A. "Women in Academe." *Science* 169:3952 (1970): 1284-90.

Grubb, Erica. "Love's Labors Lost: New Conception of Maternity Leaves." *Harvard Civil Rights—Civil Liberties Law Review* (1972).

Harris, Ann Sutherland. "The Second Sex in Academe." *American Association of University Professors Bulletin* (Fall 1970): 283-95.

Hedges, Janet Neipert. "Women Workers and Manpower Demands in the 1970s." *Monthly Labor Review* (June 1970): 19-29.

Horner, Matina S. "Fail: Bright Women." *Psychology Today* 3:6 (1969): 36-41.

Kanowitz, Leo. *Women and the Law: The Unfinished Revolution.* Albuquerque: University of New Mexico Press, 1969.

Kreps, Juanita. *Sex in the Market Place.* Baltimore: Johns Hopkins University Press, 1971.

Lifton, Robert J., ed. *The Woman in America.* Boston: Houghton Mifflin, 1965.

Low, Seth and Spindler, Pearl S. *Child Care Arrangements for Working Mothers in the U.S.* Washington, 1968.

Maccoby, Eleanor E. *The Development of Sex Differences.* Stanford, Calif.: Stanford University Press, 1966.

Mattfeld, Jacquelyn A. and Van Aken, Carol G., eds. *Women and the Scientific Professions: The M.I.T. Symposium on American Women in Science and Engineering.* Cambridge, Mass.: M.I.T. Press, 1965.

McNally, Gertrude Bancroft. "Patterns of Female Labor Force Activity." *Industrial Relations* (May 1968).

Morgan, Robin, ed. *Sisterhood Is Powerful.* New York: Vintage Books, 1970.

Ms. Magazine, 370 Lexington Ave., New York, N.Y. 10017.

Nye, F. Ivan and Hoffman, Lois Wladis. *The Employed Mother in America.* Chicago: Rand McNally, 1963.

Oppenheimer, Valerie. "The Sex-Labeling of Jobs." *Industrial Relations* (March 1968): 219-34.

Parella, Vera C. "Women and the Labor Force." *Special Labor Force Report No. 93* (February 1968).

Presidential Task Force on Women's Rights and Responsibilities. *A Matter of Simple Justice: The Report of the President's Task Force on Women's Rights and Responsibilities* (April 1970).

President's Commission on the Status of Women. *American Women; The Report of the President's Commission on the Status of Women and Other Publications of the Commission*, ed. Margaret Mead and Frances Kaplan. New York: Charles Scribners' Sons, 1965.

Project on the Status and Education of Women, Association of American Colleges, 1818 R St., N.W., Washington, D.C. 20009.

Riesman, David and Jencks, Christopher. *Academic Revolution.* Garden City, N.Y.: Doubleday, 1968.

Roby, Pamela. *Child Care, Who Cares?* New York: Basic Books, 1973.

Roby, Pamela. *Structural and Internalized Barriers to Women in Higher Education.* Baltimore: George Washington University, 1971.

Ross, Susan C. *The Rights of Women.* New York: Avon Books, 1973.

Rossi, Alice S. and Calderwood, Ann, eds. *Academic Women on the Move.* New York: Russell Sage Foundation, 1973.

Rossi, Alice S. "Status of Women in Graduate Department of Sociology, 1968-1969." *The American Sociologist* 5:1 (1970): 1-12.

Ruderman, Florence A. *Child Care and Working Mothers: A Study of Arrangements Made for Daytime Care of Children.* New York: Child Welfare League of America, Inc., 1968.

Sears, R.R.; Maccoby, E.E.; and Levin, H. *Patterns of Child Rearing.* Evanston, Ill.: Row, Peterson, 1957.

Silverberg, Majorie and Eyde, Lorraine B. *Career Part-Time Employment: Personnel Implications of the Health, Education, and Welfare Professional and Executive Corps.* Washington, D.C.: 1970.

Simon, Rita; Clark, James; Merrit, Shirley; and Tifft, Larry L. "Of Nepotism, Marriage, and the Pursuit of an Academic Career." *Sociology of Education* 39:4 (1966): 344-58.

Smith, Georgina M. *Help Wanted-Female: A Study of Demand and Supply in a Local Job Market for Women.* New Brunswick, N.J.: Institute of Management and Labor Relations, Rutgers University.

Spokeswoman, 5464 South Shore Drive, Chicago, Ill. 60615.

Steinfels, Margaret O'Brien. *Who's Minding the Children?* New York: Simon and Schuster, 1973.

Suter, Larry E. and Miller, Herman P. "Income Differences Between Men and Career Women." In Huber, Joan, ed. *Changing Women in a Changing Society.* Chicago: University of Chicago Press, 1973.

Travis, Sophia. "The U.S. Labor Force: Projections to 1985." *Monthly Labor Review* (May 1970): 3-12.

Urban Research Corporation. *Industry and Day Care.* Chicago: Urban Research Corporation, 1971.

U.S., Bureau of Labor Statistics. *Facts on Absenteeism and Labor Turnover Among Women Workers* (August 1969).

U.S., Civil Service Commission, Manpower Statistics Division. *Study of Employment of Women in the Federal Government* (1969).

U.S., Department of Health, Education and Welfare. *Report of the Women's Action Program* (January 1972).

U.S., Department of Health, Education and Welfare, Education and Public Welfare Division. *Federal Involvement in Day Care*, ed. Margaret Malone (1969).

U.S., Department of Labor. *Economic Report of the President*, Chapter 4 (January 1973).

U.S., Department of Labor. *The Manpower Report of the President* (March 1972).

U.S., Department of Labor. *Monthly Labor Review*, (May 1970 and May 1974).

U.S., Women's Bureau. *1969 Handbook on Women Workers* (Bulletin 294, 1969).

Weitzman, Lenore. "Sociological Perspectives on Discrimination against Working Women," prepared for the Twentieth Century Fund Task Force, January 1971.

Women's Rights Law Reporter, 180 University Avenue, Newark, N.J.

womenSports, 1660 South Amphlett Blvd., San Mateo, Calif.

Women Today, Today Publications and News Service, National Press Building, Washington, D.C. 20004.

About the Authors

Adele Simmons, a graduate of Radcliffe College, received the doctorate at Oxford University. Her involvement in women's issues, particularly those relating to education, began in 1969 when she became assistant dean—and later dean—of Jackson College, Tufts University. She is Dean of Student Affairs at Princeton University, where she has helped sponsor programs to make undergraduates of both sexes more aware of the opportunities and the implications of the women's movement. Dr. Simmons is on the Advisory Committee of the Association of American Colleges project on the status of women, and of the mid-Atlantic Office of Higher Education Resource Services for Women—a recently-funded program to improve the environment for women in higher education in the mid-Atlantic region.

Ann E. Freedman is a graduate of Radcliffe College and Yale University Law School. She has been active in the women's movement and helped found the Woman's Law Project, a nonprofit, feminist legal research, litigation, and education organization in Philadelphia, where she is a staff attorney. She is the coauthor of *Sex Discrimination and the Law: Causes and Remedies*, (Little, Brown, 1975), and has taught courses in sex discrimination and the law at Georgetown University Law Center and Villanova Law School.

Margaret C. Dunkle is Project Associate with the Project on the Status and Education of Women of the Association of American Colleges, developing topical and in-depth materials on issues of concern to educators and women, and working with educational associations and government agencies. Ms. Dunkle has written a number of articles on equal opportunity (among them "What Constitutes Equality for Women in Sport?") and is a frequent speaker at college campuses and meetings of professional education associations on women in education.

Francine Blau is a research associate at the Center for Human Resource Research, The Ohio State University, where she is engaged in the study of the labor market behavior of women. She received the B.S. from Cornell University and the M.A. from Harvard University. Ms. Blau has taught women's studies at Trinity College and Yale University and has published several articles on women in the economy. She is a member of the American Economic Association Committee on the Status of Women in the Economics Profession.